THAD STEM'S
FIRST READER

Thad Stem, Jr.

MOORE PUBLISHING COMPANY
Durham, North Carolina 27705

Library of Congress Catalog Card Number: 76-1456
ISBN 0-87716-061-9

Also by Thad Stem, Jr.

Picture Poems
The Jackknife Horse
The Perennial Almanac
The Animal Fair
Penny Whistles and Wild Plums
Spur Line
Light and Rest
Impact: History 1919-1969
A Flagstone Walk
Journey Proud
Entries From Oxford
The Tar Heel Press
Senator Sam Ervin's Best Stories
(with Alan Butler)
Colonial History of Johnston County

FOREWORD

Johnathan Daniels

From his encyclopedic knowledge of all things great and small, Thad Stem likes to quote Heine as saying that the Romans would never have found time to conquer the world if they had been obliged to learn Latin first. My own Latin is strictly limited. Yet I know that almost the only phrase for Thad Stem is *sui generis*. There is nothing or nobody like him. So he is as precious as he is rare. Yet, in a world which rejoices in labels, he is catalogued in the coterie of the poets. And, of course, he is one — and one who in rhythmical turn and whirl is cathedral singer and carnival barker, a nightingale on a rose bush or Chanticleer on a Granville County dung hill.

Actually, he has invented his own art form though he gives me credit for naming it. In his capacity as politician, which must never be minimized, he called at my office at my request when, in 1956, he was in Raleigh attending and possibly helping rig the Democratic State Convention. Before that time I had been aware of his light — and some surprisingly tough — touch in the language, whether chopped up into lines of poetry or running straight along in supposed prose. Also, I was aware that the editorial page of *The News and Observer* of Raleigh, over which I presided, was sometimes heavy handed in pointing with pride and viewing with alarm. So I asked him if he would write some "rock wall editorials" for the paper.

The term may seem obscure. By it I meant and he understood the phrase as label for those brief charming essays about walls and lanes and streams and people of which he is the master. Without the background orchestration of great news events, they provided a music sweet and sometimes shrill which gave a lyrical lift to a heavy page. An expectant readership responded daily to his prose. Compounded of nostalgia, irony, and lively concern, they have appealed, also, to the readers of his fourteen books.

This salty selection is certainly among the best he has written. They prove that at Stem's hand poetry never lapses in his prose. Wise man and smirking boy by turns, and always the maker of the secretly sophisticated country music he brings, Stem clings to his small town residence as tenaciously as Diogenese did to his barrel. No great Alexanders awe him. But the light of his lantern, held high in broad daylight, will help honest men to find the true America and hold it closer in their hearts.

Johnathan Daniels

INTRODUCTION AND ACKNOWLEDGMENT

When Edward Gibbon kneeled dutifully in 1781 to present volume two of his *Decline and Fall of the Roman Empire* to the Duke of Gloucester, His Royal Highness snorted: "Another damned thick book. Always scribble, scribble, scribble. Eh, Mr. Gibbon?" Perhaps, that anecdote leavens some of the chagrin of some of my old friends who prefer as a token of affectionate esteem something more than a book.

The fortunate majority are not excited, or damned, by "scribendi cacoethes," or as Juvenile put it in one of his *Satires:* "An incurable itch for scribbling takes possession of many and grows inveterate in their insane hearts." Jonathan Swift, in his classic, *A Tale of a Tub*, told how many books are written, especially by those rarefied, self-winding aesthetes who deny it so passionately: "If it were not for a rainy day, a drunken vigil, a fit of the spleen, a course of psychic, a sleepy Sunday, an evil run at dice, a long tailor's bill, a beggar's purse, a factious head, a hot sun, a costive diet, want of books, and a just contempt for learning — but for these the number of authors and of writing would dwindle away to a degree most woeful to behold."

And serious, honest writers are indebted to Samuel Johnson for two declarations: "No man but a blockhead ever wrote except for money," and "Nothing excites a man to write but necessity." And there are as many diverse, elusive kinds of necessity as there are weathers upon a March day.

Trying sincerely to express affectionate gratitude may be as anomolous as it is shockingly incomplete. My late father probably had the right answer. Another Oxford lawyer, an intelligent, irascible man, obtained a government job. He said to my father: "When I leave Oxford I am turning all of my law practice over to you."

"No, don't do that, John. Just turn it loose in front of the courthouse and give all the lawyers a whack at it."

If one is likely to wear out quicker than his oldest wrinkle, many men are beautiful and heroic even in what youngsters construe as physical delapidation. Everything ages but the heart, and in the spirit of the old World War II song that "blessed" (but only for the benefit of civilian euphemy) "the long and the short and the tall," I give loving thanks to a host of friends, and I believe, again with Samuel Johnson, that a man's best portion is contained in his book.

In my immediate family there are, world without end, Dety, Bill, Lide, my mother, Grace and Obie, and Irene and Jack. Within the same fellowship there are, always, Johnathan D., Sam R., Mike Questell, Cheryl, Tom W., Jean McCamy, Jean and Walter S., Dave Taylor, Betsy Brent, and old Shi. No man was ever inspired by such fetching girlfriends as Lu Long, Margie, Lucy I., Linda W., Elizabeth Green, Julia S., Mary, Maria, Kathryn, Gene S., Margaret R., Aileene, Mae, Miss May, Bess C., Lovelace, Esther B., Dorothy T., Sarah J., Peyton, and Lil Dworsky. A special nosegay goes to Faye Apple, for many acts of kindness, and I bequeath my blessing to my godchildren, Charlotte and Lewis Thaddeus.

Much better than money from home are friends such as Gene G., Ed and Betty Hodges, Rod C., Paul Green, Kit and Sallie, Tom Lassiter, Tom Ellis, Hig, Maurice P., Ben Powell, Shack Martin, Bob Howard, Legette B., Glenn T., Bill Mitchell, Bob Ray, Three Wilson, Ed Taylor, Charlie Wade, Charles Blackburn, Jr., and A.C. Jordan, my old English teacher. And the top of the morning to Dick Walser and Guy Owen for suggesting this book, even if they have forgotten the suggestion.

My *Reader* begins with some informal, personal history,

followed with a few short stories, poems, essays, and longer pieces of fiction and prose. I hope the reader can turn to any page and find entertainment, but the reading is likely to go better if the material is read in consecutive order. For I have an underlying unit, a loose chronology in mind as I attempt to capture the essence of a man's time of life and the fascinating ways of life he encountered.

FIRST READER

A SMATTERING OF TRUTH

A sycophant declared airily to James McNeill Whistler, "Ah, master, you were born in Lowell, Massachusetts, and in 1834." Whistler adjusted his monacle as if it were a lazer beam: "I was never guilty of any transgression so vulgar as being born in Lowell, Massachusetts. Sometimes I was born in St. Petersburg (he did live there a while when his father was a civil engineer for the Czar). I have been born in Paris several times, but I refuse, absolutely, to be born in 1834."

I don't want to deny that I was born in Oxford, North Carolina, that I still live on the street on which I was born. But without arrogating to myself the grandiose ways that came to Whistler so naturally, I have, in recent years, been guilty of sporadic sins of omission relative to my age. And, frankly, I doubt that Browning was doing more than writing memorable lines when he exulted, in "Rabbi Ben Ezra:"

> "Grow old along with me!
> The best is yet to be,
> The last of life, for which the first was made."

And I am afraid that I find Lord Tennyson's ringing affirmation, from *Ulysses* more doleful than inspirational:

"Tho' much is taken, much abides; and tho'
We are not that strength which in the old days
Moved earth and heaven; that which we are, we are —
One equal temper of heroic hearts,
Made weak by time and fate, but strong in will
To strive, to seek, to find, and not to yield."

Albeit, having been an original settler, a permanent dweller in Oxford, hasn't yet brought to me the left-handed accolade "Mr. Dooley" mentioned: "Many a man that cudden't direct ye to th' drug store on th' corner whin he is thirty will get a respectful hearin' when age has further impaired his mind."

But advancing age carries two excellent consolations or expediencies. One does not have to stay in a tizzy and to expend tons of labor and sweat fretting about what is in and what is out. If I ever succumbed to the virus, I am, by now, free from the slug-nutty compulsion to be able to rattle off last week's imposing list of deathless authors, painters, pop singers, movies, and athletes. It's salutary to be able to say, of this morning's effervescent morning-glory, "No, I never heard of him, and what's more, I don't give a damn."

One misses out on reading many best-sellers, but in the long haul it is resilient to be spared infinite drudgery. And there is the pristine wisdom accorded to the late Maurice Chevalier, who must know the option by now: "Old age isn't so bad when you consider the alternative." The thought of death is almost as morbid as the fact of death. Depending upon my mood, I take a sort of glum consolation from Shakespeare's sardonic, or democratic, lines from *Hamlet:* "Imperious Caesar, dead and turn'd to clay,/Might stop a hole to keep the wind away." But despite all the cruel ruses of the flesh, the spirit can be a stainless rapier lashing out, just as poor Keats wrote Fanny Brawnex: "There is a great difference between going off in warm blood like Romeo, and making one's exit like a frog in a frost." But, and not just incidentally, I disagree, powerfully, with the late Alduous Huxley's contention that death is the only thing we haven't succeeded in vulgarizing. For all of Huxley's brilliance and erudition, I think he dropped his bait guord with that observation.

If old age doesn't bring happiness in a rippling, positive flood the way a downhill creek brings water, perhaps, old age absorbs many of the unhappinesses that fester and pester the virile years of yeasty exhilarations. Anyway, it shall be interesting to learn. And Robert Burns did more than to immortalize the patently obvious when he wrote: "Nae man can tether time or tide." So be it.

My years have been almost as destitute of specific plans and programs as my hours have been bereft of affirmative declarations. I could have been one of the Three Princes of Serendip, never seeking a specific destination, never making any travelling plans, but always finding excitement accidentally. Like the Princes, I have dropped the reins, pretty much, to let the horse take me where he will, and this has turned up incessant excitements and diversions, or things that excite me, anyway. Most of what I know I stumbled on accidentally while I was looking up something else in a dictionary, encyclopedia, or reference book. There are continents of adventures between "H" and "J", and my most pleasant journeys have been taken without adhering to road-maps, or even to the contours of bridal-paths.*

William Howard Taft said he left the Presidency in 1913 with the full approval of the American people, after his miserable bid for reelection in 1912, and I left Duke

*I imagine footnotes are atrocious in a book of this type, but the great Gerald Johnson, whom I am proud to call my friend, says, in *Incredible Era*, one of his many memorable books, that Ceylon was Serendip, originally. This is the sort of thing I liked to pull on my son who has a way of telling me wild, remote things such as the alleged fact that Saint Ambrose is supposed to be the first man in history to read silently without moving his lips.

University in the late spring of 1938 endowed by the administration and faculty with much the same spirit of acquiescence. Then in the fallow fall of 1938, a serious illness forced me to quit my first job, one I had on a weekly newspaper in Burnsville, N.C., then high in the unsullied mountains of Yancey County. My doctor told me I should try a hot, dry climate. I knew damned well he meant some place like Arizona, but I caught a ride, entirely by accident, to Florida. That state seemed hot and dry enough for me. Two or three days later I was in West Palm Beach, holding less than ten dollars in folding money.

I made a fast, furtive pilgrimage around swanky Palm Beach. It was an incredibly opulent neo-Disneyland, and I doubt that my harrowing sense of utter unreality has ever been so acute, so damnable. For a petrified fact, when I had quit my informal excursion of this corporate Big Rock Candy Mountain I was ready to sign up with the Bolsheviks. (Whether or not it was a nuance of my own semantical limitations, "Bolshevik" had much more relevance for me than "Communist.")

Then, like Mark Twain's Sir Boss, in reverse, I walked from Camelot to the tag-end of the 20th century depression. In a park, on the outer limits of West Palm Beach, I saw men painting coconuts. They were handed sacks of coconuts, and different ones were painted red, green, orange, even blue, and some other colors. I remember, precisely, my sardonic, "sophisticated" chortle as I recalled Hoss Hines, the undertaker in *Look Homeward, Angel*, who embalmed poor Ben Gant, and "improved on nature."

I needed a job desperately, and I circumvented the Renoirs in white caps for a man whom I took to be the dispatcher, the yard master. I offered him a cigarette, the ultimate largess, and as we blew some North Carolina blue magic in Florida, I made some oblique allusion to Claude Pepper, who had just been nominated to the U.S. Senate by the Democrats.

4

He, the W.P.A. panjandrum of the coconuts' painting crew, asked where I was from. "Dade County," I replied casually, adding, "It's hot," which wasn't a lie. Across the highway, or street, was a spacious place with a huge sign:

"Flaminco Bar"

"Home of Ruby Collins, Tom Collins' Famous Sister."

My acquaintanceship with Tom Collins was infinitesimal, and I was appallingly ignorant of any siblings, in skirts or glasses, but I sprang for two beers. After a few sips of his beer, and after a few drags on the second cigarette from me, the W.P.A. straw boss made some loose reference to Dade County, took me back to his headquarters shack, filled out a card, and put me to painting coconuts.

As I splashed all the colors of Joseph's coat, and then some, on coconuts, it occurred to me that it must have been for this exalted moment that my parents sacrificed willingly to send me to Darlington School (prep) and to Duke University. But if Epicetus was correct, and only the educated are free, I felt as free as a possum with the only keys to the henhouse as I splattered paint on coconuts.

After two days the foreman elevated my position, but not my pay, to supervising a road crew that made decorative mounds of the painted coconuts and posted these piles of genre art at certain intervals along the highway. (I told the foreman I was a high school graduate, not a Duke alumnus, but it was my being a man, or boy, of "edicashion" that resulted in my temporary appointment as a sort of strolling, architectural, artistic supervisor.)

When my fellow craftsmen and I had raked brightly-painted coconuts into a sort of inverted V cone, I hit upon the device of painting the top-knot nut, the apex nut, three colors. These resembled some of the modern basketballs, or, perhaps, as if it were the offspring of a monkey or a zebra.

But if art is long, event may be capricious. After several days and many, many inverted V's, a station-wagon disgourged a woman in jodphurs and a man in putees, big dogs in the W.P.A.'s artistic meathouse. The foreman, assuming I had some in with Claude Pepper, whom I had never seen save at a distance, tipped me off to the coming of these two members of the public works' Sanhedrin. Before the station wagon screeched to a halt I was off fifteen yards from the mound of coconuts just built holding my open hands in front of my eyes the way photographers used to frame imaginary pictures. As I pretended to be artistically unaware of the visitors, I walked to the pile of nuts a couple of times to rearrange the top coconut, prefacing each trip with one of the aforementioned frames.

The supervisors were entranced, and I was told, forthwith, there was a job waiting for me in the artistic echelon more commensurate with my considerable talents. Alas, the preliminary talk about my richly deserved promotion necessitated allusions to "home county" and "voting precinct." Prudence, simple expediency, won, not innate honesty, and art, or certainly painted coconuts, lost. I failed to show for the big, full appointment.

Back in the heart of West Palm Beach I applied for a job at the city's principal newspaper. It didn't need any help, but as I was leaving I was told there was another newspaper, and I might apply there. This intelligence was relayed the same way one might have told a homeless Hebrew to check out the sleeping quarters in the lions' den currently occupied by Daniel.

Had the *Florida Liberator*, to which my short pilgrimage brought me, had an indoor shuffleboard court, it would have seemed more nearly a mission for elderly indigents than a newspaper office. One septuagenerian was asleep with his head on a typewriter, but since he wore a sunshade, I knew he was a newspaperman.

Another, even older, struck up several hefty kitchen matches trying to light a corncob pipe with quivering fingers.

Failing, and burning his finger a little, he asked if I was from a local undertaking firm. When I said "no", he replied, with obvious distemper, "Then you didn't bring no ad?" When I apologized for the omission, he kicked a round of his chair, lightly, and I noticed he was wearing Congress gaiters.

Without prelude he said, rather than asked: "You ain't never read *Tristram Shandy*. Well, 'en," and he proceeded to tell me how Uncle Toby catches a fly, and when Uncle Toby threw the fly out the window and his nephew asks an explanation, Uncle Toby says the world is big enough for him and the fly.

He poked me in the ribs with his elbow and chortled: "You git hit, heh?" I smiled my yes-and-no smile, and he snorted: "Well, and Jesus Christ on a mountaintop, if that feller Rooze-velt knowed the country is big ernuff for him and Doc Townsend both, you wouldn't have your ass in sich a crack, heh, heh."

Then he genuflected toward the wall, and I saw a large photo of an emaciated looking man whom I took to be Dr. Townsend, the California health officer who was going to pension everyone of sixty-five, as I recall, at $200 a month.

I was in the newsroom, and there must have been five or six different pictures of Dr. Townsend on various walls. My acquaintance, having debilitated himself from striking matches and kicking the chair and telling me about Uncle Toby and the fly, sank into his chair much as I imagined old Sarah Bernhardt did a stage faint. With a wobbly backhand flourish, he motioned me on to the next man.

A sign on his desk said, "Mr. Brown," and Mr. Brown looked like "Terrible Tempered Mr. Bangs" of the old comic strip. He was going over some copy with a pencil, whistling "Jesus Loves Me", and punctuating each fourth bar with "Armenian crap," a brand new form of excrement to me.

I stood there silently about five minutes. He switched to whistling "The Little Brown Church in the Wildwood," but instead of whistling or humming all those "come, comes" he said "seven syphilitic saints," a social condition that would not occur to me ordinarily.

He flipped to his last galley and whistled "The Glowworm" much as if a cricket had laryngitis, but in lieu of whistling "glimmer, glimmer" Mr. Brown rasped "St. Peter's constipated peafowl," bringing me graduate education in Bible and animal husbandry and making me wonder, despite my home-training, if St. Peter was one of the seven contaminated saints?

Then he held out his hand and said, "Gimme a smoke." I had three cigarettes left. He took two. He lighted one and he stuck one behind his left ear.

I asked if the paper needed anyone, and he started laughing, only his laughter sounded to me as if Hitler had just learned he and Battling Levinsky were close kin. Without saying yeah or nay he pointed to, stabbed at, as if he were killing a lethal pest, a glassed-in enclosure, and I walked there, almost keeping cadence to Mr. Brown's guttural gales of bitter, sardonic laughter.

Printed on the glass door was:

"L. Garland Biggers, Editor and Publisher
The Florida Liberator"

I was christened "Thaddeus Garland Stem, Jr.", although neither given name has ever been more than nebulously elliptical. If Washington Irving had ever seen L. Garland Biggers he shouldn't have troubled to have invented Icabod Crane. There wasn't enough blood in Mr. Biggers to sustain a fishing worm, and his Adam's apple was so disportionate to the remainder of his cadaverous body, his shoulders, arms, torso, and legs looked as if they had been pasted onto his Adam's apple, with spittle, and as an afterthought.

His dentures seemed abnormally large to me, and they clicked and clacked loudly, as if thirty-two shod hooves were striking cobblestones. Then, as during my months of employment on the *Liberator*, it was, precisely, as if he made three speeches to my one: He said whatever it was he wanted to say, as his dentures, or Roebuckers, to be exact, furnished strident accompaniment, as if a telegraph instrument were prancing as background music to spoken English. Then, he removed his false teeth and said again what he had just said.

I went in that morning as Thad Stem, Jr., but I was at least three persons when I emerged. For, I introduced myself as "T. Garland Stem," and that was the sole basis for my employment. Henceforth, Mr. Biggers called me "Garland," and, shortly, I was writing items for the women's section of the paper under the name "Effie Barksdale Ravenal." We derived Effie Barksdale from Mrs. Biggers' maiden name, Effie Barksdale, and I appended "Ravenal", probably from the gambler in *Show Boat*, as I had always thought that names such as Edna St. Vincent Millay, William Rose Benet et al, carried more authority and pizzaz than truncated Thad Stem, Jr.

Our paper's be-all was the Townsend Plan. At first, from the supercilious brashness of embolded youth, I assumed my associates saw through Doc Townsend's sincere quack-salvery, but, not everyone believed this was an unvarnished full-blown panacea. (Everyone with the exception of me and the irascible Mr. Brown, who was the sort of fellow who would send his mother a congratulatory message on his own birthday.)

In almost every issue, Mr. Biggers ran an editorial, often on the front page, in which he said there would be no more jails, poor houses, welfare, none of that, when all the old folks started getting two hundred bucks a month. One day I asked Mr. Biggers why FDR didn't go ahead and do it? He snarled as if I had suggested that former New York Mayor, Jimmy Walker, be given the chair of humanities at Sweetwater Seminary, Mrs. Biggers' alma mater. "Those folks can make their own blunders. I told Teddy not to fool with that imbecilic Panama Canal. Look what happened, and this Roosevelt can go to hell in his very own hack." (He always whipped out a tattered clipping, from an old newspaper, in Eufala, Alabama, I think, in which he had admonished Theodore Roosevelt against building the Panama Canal.) Anyway, making the Townsend Plan the law of the land was our battle-cry, our holy oriflame, our sole idea, even if it was a wrong idea as Samuel Johnson said about the fellow with one idea. Albeit, Mr. Biggers, Mr. Rutherford, and Mr. Derryberry were positive Congress would enact the Townsend Plan. In fact, Mr. Biggers liked to say that he had such and such a number of Congressmen in his pocket. While the figure changed several times a day — it was larger just before dinner, — all I ever saw in his pocket was a sack of Mary Jane mints, which he and Mrs. Biggers sucked on two or three times a day, and a huge, red bandana with which he swobbed his face and forehead every few seconds.

Once there was a tremendous rally of Townsend adherents at Miami's Bay Front Park. It seemed to me that those who didn't carry canes and didn't have dentures were in almost as much of a minority as Noah was in on a celebrated occasion, but the fervor generated was sufficient to tilt the Atlantic seaboard. With the arrogance and misinformation of cock-sure youth I saw this garrulous, passionate assemblage in terms of Pettigru's crack about South Carolina when the state was inflamed with secession: "Too big to be a lunatic asylum and not big enough to be a feudal monarchy."

Then I walked around among the crowd and talked to many of the old people, and they were remarkably like my relatives and older friends back in Oxford. The Townsendites had dreams and backaches, and if you cut them they bled. Pettigru's brilliant but smart-assed analogy faded. I swallowed hard on my acerbities, and I saw all of these elderly folks almost as heroic spirits paying the piper cheerfully for their last, convoluted dance, for their final tune this side the river. For a stark minute I had the same terrifying depression I have had ever since when I have visited a nursing home for the elderly: "Abandon hope all who enter here," or whatever it was Dante said about those who enter the inferno.

But there was a small band composed of Townsend delegates, about fifteen or twenty instruments, mostly brass, and the average age must have been beyond seventy. It was a tin-horn literally and figuratively, but as they blared and jingled out a medley of "Onward Christian Soldiers" and "At a Georgia Camp Meeting" the three or four thousand old folks staged an impromptu cake-walk around the park, singing and shouting "Doctor Townsend will shine tonight" to the chorus of "At a Georgia Camp Meeting."

Three or four members of the band were elderly women, and as the music, the singing, and the walk-around mounted in exuberance I thought of two lines from Vachel Lindsay's "General Booth Enters Heaven":

> "The banjos rattled and the tambourines
> Jing-jing-jingled in the hands of Queens."

Mr. Biggers made a big damn speech about the *Liberator's* being the Townsend movement's impeccable cloud by day and pillar of fire by night, and many, perhaps, most, of the old people subscribed to the paper, or made small, outright contributions for the "cause," just as if the *Liberator* were the last ferry boat across the Jordan. The paper ended up with slightly more than three thousand dollars in cash. There was so much loose change, including nickels and pennies, Mr. Brown and I got several paper sacks to hold what I was beginning to think of as the widow's mite but what he called "A damn certain sign of insanity or senility or both."

Mr. Biggers stuffed all of the folding money into his pockets, and on our way back to West Palm Beach he made Mr. Brown park the car alongside a pretty stretch of the ocean. He pulled off his seersucker britches and went for a swim. In lieu of underwear, he wore swimming trunks, and Mr. Brown said Mr. Biggers did this everyday on the theory that if he got a chance to swim he'd be ready.

Half-naked he resembled a two-legged scarecrow. His chest went in, not out, and his legs were those of a superannuated mockingbird's, flecked with a few gray hairs. I thought if Sally Rand every saw Mr. Biggers half-naked she would renounce strip-teasing and start shaking the tambourine for the Salvation Army.

Mr. Brown held his trousers, stuffed with the three thousand bucks. He pulled out a couple of Mary Janes and we sucked and slurped while the old man took on the breakers head first. For such an old, pursy human mockingbird, Mr. Biggers swam amazingly well. He rode a series of waves, and everytime he bobbed up I got the impression of an under-nourished Triton, with store-bought teeth in lieu of wreathed horn. Once, when a tremendously heavy swell knocked Mr. Biggers halfway to Jacksonville, Mr. Brown whistled a few snatches of "Jesus Saviour, Pilot Me," and observed: "If the old bastard drowns we can buy us a lot of booze with this three thousand smacks."

I mentioned my becoming at least three personalities. Just about everyone on our scanty staff did an extra chore that involved a pseudonym. Mr. Biggers wrote a regular column on international affairs under the name of "Lorenzo d' Garlande," his full name being Lawrence Garland Biggers. Mr. Derryberry wrote a feature on books called "In the Study With St. John Berryman Bloomsdale."

Somewhere, Mr. Biggers had learned that the British pronounce "St. John" "Sinjin," and he loved to say it. "Good show, Sinjin" was his way of bestowing the accolade on Mr. Derryberry. In virtually every column Mr. Derryberry got around to Henry George's *Progress and Poverty*, whether he was reviewing a current book, such as Jonathan Daniels' admirable *A Southerner Discovers the South*, or a collection of Robert Frost's poems. It was, he said many times each day, "the greatest, best, most important book every written."

He had, he told me one day in excessive confidence, spent most of the 20th century writing an addendum to *Progress and Poverty*.

Each day he lugged to the office a small mountain of pages, typed and handwritten, and he was terrified lest someone should steal his magnum opus. He toted this incredible array of pages in a blue haversack, the kind kids used to use for school books. If he left the office, even to go to the men's room, he put the haversack on his shoulder. Betimes his life's work rested between his feet at his desk, but if he tottered to the water cooler, he looked back over his shoulder, two or three times, at the blue haversack.

Mr. Rutherford wrote a column on games, chess, chiefly, and how to crack various ciphers, under the name of John Minor Allan. I always imagined this was inspired by Edgar Allan Poe. He called Dr. Townsend "the new Moses," but, even so, America was doomed because John C. Calhoun was Abraham Lincoln's father. That made Lincoln some kind of social, political schizophrenic, and the results "are obvious to anyone with the brains of a misbegotten amoebia."

Mr. Rutherford came from Illinois, originally. (I can't recall ever talking to anyone in Florida who was born in the state.) His fellow Illinoisian, Carl Sandburg, was anathema to him, principally, I thought because Sandburg was famous and Mr. Rutherford wasn't. I asked him, once, with a straight face if Sandburg knew Calhoun was Lincoln's father.

He answered, "Aside from being shot by John Wilkes Booth, the worst thing that ever happened to Lincoln was falling into Sandburg's hands." I'm sure the late Edmund Wilson never heard of poor old Mr. Rutherford, but Wilson wrote the same libels, substantially. Mr. Rutherford called Sandburg a "near-beer Socialist," and he said that Sandburg spent two hours a day combing his hair so that it would look as if it had never been combed.

Aside from some pretty slovenly reportorial work, of a

general nature, I wrote a column, "Running the Gamut With Thad Stem," and I did the society notes ascribed to "Effie Barksdale Ravenal." Women would call my desk, about some tea party, and ask to speak to Effie. I'd say she had just stepped out, but that I would pass the story along.

We had no women on our newspaper aside from Mrs. Biggers who came in twice a day to suck Mary Janes with Mr. Biggers. Once a week, as "The Constant Muse", she did a column on music. Actually, this was more a perpetual requiem for Edward MacDowell than essays about music. Nothing of importance had occurred in music since MacDowell's tragic demise in 1908. (At home she had a tremendous harp, one which must have been old in David's time. Occasionally, she brought invitations written in elaborate Spenserian script inviting us to a musicale at her home. She would sit at the huge harp for an hour pouring over MacDowell's "To a Wild Rose" with variations, she explained.

I don't believe MacDowell would have recognized his song, but she and Mr. Biggers always got an extra sack of Mary Janes for the musicale, and this saved me around a dime on supper.

Mr. Brown was impervious to pseudonyms, but he always called me "George Bernard" or "Young Shaw," amid savage derision. He was the only person on the paper, and one of a limited few in North America, who knew of my Walter Mitty existence. For, light years beyond reporting, writing my own column, and being Effie Barksdale Ravenal, I was a creative writer.

I had a short story published while I was working on the paper at Burnsville, N.C., and another I wrote in Burnsville was published while I was with the *Liberator*. This story was called "Girls In Summer Hats," and I showed Mr. Brown the magazine. He sniffed the pages, rather than looking at them, for a few seconds, whistled "Power In the Blood," rasping "Holy Hohenzollern horse turds" each time he was supposed to whistle all of those "there's power, power, power, wonder working power." He handed over the magazine with the relief which I imagined Atlas finally forked over the world. "Young Shaw, you better tell old 'Sinjin' to polish up a nice obituary column about Wilbur Daniel Steele. I imagine he'll cut his throat when he hears about your story."

Autres temps, autres moeurs! For a long time, Wilbur Daniel Steel was honored as one of creation's premier short story writers. He was assured of enduring literary life, along with James Branch Cabell and others whom one never hears of today from one year to the next.

I clutched the copy of the old *Southern Literary Messenger*, with my lodestone within its opulent covers, as if the magazine were the last coals of fire on earth and creation was in for an egregiously rough winter. I must have thought I was the only fried chicken at a revival on-the-grounds dinner. In fact, Doc Townsend's zeal to share the nation's wealth was a mere picayune to my desire to share my creative genius and self-effacing charms.

I hit the street below about the way that Christopher Columbus must have walked on the beach that day back in 1492. I must have glittered with the sparkle of a newly minted penny as I sashshayed up the street, using store windows and the tiny mirrors in every set of weighing scales to strike what I imagined were rakish, debonair poses. Sometimes the reflection seemed to be William Saroyan sailing along on his own magic flying trapeze, and again the image reflected what I imagined was the tremulous pain-ecstasy of the out-of-this-world artiste, but I probably really looked as if I needed to go the men's room, but couldn't find one, or didn't have a nickel.

I had projected such a gladsome, triumphant morning endlessly, when, as Thomas Wolfe put it, I should have cheated hunger and slain death. In my incessant reverie birds sang in rippling, exultant harmony with my spiritual buoyancy, but aside from a couple of sparrows snacking in the street, all the birds seemed to have returned to Capistrano.

I really expected West Palm Beach to be transfigured by my own magic, but no pilgrims came along to toss nosegays, and the sidewalks and streets were infinitely more a larger version of Gopher Prairie than Zanadu. But even if no one got out a measuring tape, I was at least fifteen feet tall. I was Somerset Maugham, Ring Lardner, and Hemingway in battered, slightly odiferous sneakers. God Almight's Sunday-go-to-meeting overcoat wasn't big enough to make me a pocket handerchief.

But, surely to God, or certainly to the ones on Parnassus, I ought to have a one-man celebration, at least, and I sauntered into a bar, but the proprietor obviously hadn't heard about "Girls in Summer Hats" because no hors d'oeuvres, much less free lunch, were on the bar, and no ragtime professor was knocking out contagious, low-down syncopations at the piano.

My budget really couldn't stand the ten-cent glass of beer, but, hell's bells, this was the sort of occasion on which meteors whizz by day and stars shoot at high noon. I, or the bartender, put the glass of beer, foaming over at the top, on the magazine, which I had placed on the bar, deftly and innocuously, I fancied.

The sudsy bottom of the glass stuck to the magazine, and while trying to remove the beer glass without additional defacement of the magazine, I sloshed beer on it and me. Now, I used to be able to say by heart all of A.E. Housman's once-famous "Epilogue" to *A Shropshire Lad*, and these lines came tumbling out:

"Then I saw the morning sky:
Heigho, the tale was all a lie;
The world, it was the old world yet,
I was I, my things were wet."

I put a pox on Philistine publicans, silently, and on the cusedness of matters in general, and as I sauntered down the

16

street my hindquarters were redolent with many invisible sprigs of mistletoe.

Cicero had said that we are all excited by the love of praise, and that it is the noblest spirits who feel it most. But I was the poor drudge who must get his praise off the rack, rather than tailor-made, and the damned suit wouldn't fit.

In my Walter Mitty realm I certainly wasn't inhibited by what I didn't know, and "Girls in Summer Hats" attempted to tell about a married woman, of the advanced age of thirty-odd, who dresses for a lawn party, a woman's soiree. Her husband is out of town, but amid meticulous zeal she puts on the outfit, accessories, perfume that turn him on. At the lawn party (I imagine they are obsolete now) she chats self-effacingly, disarmingly, but, actually, she replays in her throbbing mind spectacular making-out sessions she has had with her husband.

At this juncture American literature hadn't been liberated, and one couldn't employ graphic words and descriptions. So, I imagine I thought I was subtle as hell in conveying the sense of rapture via studied implications. But, for all that, and while I have no objection to the blatant mot juste, some of the brethren probably did an abler job at showing emotions back when subtle implications hadn't been routed by avalanches of terse words and descriptions. The very fact and force of today's lack of literary inhibitions causes many writers "to tell" rather than "to show." I have certainly been guilty of this myself, but I have been in choice company. For such oracles as Hemingway, Henry Miller, and John Updike, in the guise of free-wheeling metaphors and similes, really do infinitely more "telling," "saying," than "showing."

Anyway, "Girls in Summer Hats" caused a literary explosion. Lots of readers, maybe, as many as seven or eight, wrote the magazine to say I was crazy as hell, that a woman doesn't dress up to beguile an absent husband, that a woman doesn't go to a garden party to dwell on intimate, romantic history. Albeit, there was one lovely demurrer, from the late Marion Sims, of Charlotte, then one of the few novelists to write about the emergence of the urban South. She put down my traducers charmingly: "It should be obvious even to rule-of-thumb readers that Mr. Stem has created an extraordinary woman. One of the abiding virtues of fiction is that the ratio of extraordinary people to commonplace people is high; in daily living it may be the other way around."

It's probably just as well that Marion was married happily, and was seventeen years older than I. Otherwise, I should have thumbed straight to Charlotte armed with eloquent proposals of marriage. But when I returned to North Carolina a few months later, we became great friends, and our marvelous rapport lasted until Marion's death. (Somehow, it almost seems anachronistic that Marion's Charlotte novel, *City On the Hill*, was a critical and financial success several years before Harry Golden came along, Homer on a Greyhound bus, to discover the town.)

I was beginning to understand how Charles Evans Hughes felt when he awakened to find out he wasn't elected President. It was annoying and frustrating, to chase fire trucks and go to the sessions of police court and not only remain anonymous but, actually, "lonesomer than Crusoe's goat," as O. Henry put it. These calloused ingrates just didn't know I was a man of letters. They didn't seem to give the smallest part of a dried apple dam, either.

Now, there was "another writer" in West Palm Beach, Slammer Roe, a lawyer, a political aspirant, who sold fantastically lucrative sporting fiction to the big-paying slick magazines. From the consummate effrontery and vanity of being twenty-two years old, I thought Roe's stuff was trashy. And when I considered how Roe got reams of dough for writing tinsel and I almost starved serving the muse, I was about ready to admit with Housman that the world was made by a brute or blackguard.

18

A lady in the town library showed Roe the magazine with "Girls In Summer Hats." He came tearing into our sordid newsroom exuding all the lethal sulphur Stonewall Jackson must have discharged that May afternoon when he demolished Joe Hooker's left flank at Chancellorsville. A few tiny drops of saliva spilled from his quaking lips, and I was certain our wooden floor would catch afire. "Boy," he sizzled, "You didn't write this goddam story. I think a woman wrote it."

I beamed a smile sweet enough to make homemade ice cream: "You are exactly right, Mr. Roe. My sister wrote the story and let me sign my name to it." Completely mollified, he smiled: "That's more like it. I knew the whole goddam thing was a fraud." He wished me good luck and he marched, rather than walked, out of the office, whistling "Dipsy Doodle."

Mr. Brown knew I lied when I said "my sister wrote it." He knew I never had a sister, and for the only time in our acquaintanceship, he almost smiled, if one can imagine a tomcat with a sour stomach smiling: "Young Shaw, you just showed more sense than I'd ever have given you credit for having. I'm sure you see through this Townsend Plan hoax, and if you avoid preachers, civic clubs, drawing to inside straights, the clap, and soda pop chasers you may manage to elude the penitentiary."

That reminded me of Aunt Polly's saying that Tom Sawyer might grow up to be President, "If they don't hang him first."

Mr. Brown lambasted the unholy juxtaposition of booze and all chasers, save water. His left leg was a little shorter than his right, and he wore a lift in his left shoe. He said his left leg shrank up from drinking colas before he learned the danger.

This had happened when he was an orphan in South Carolina. Occasionally, he said he had been a youthful lay-brother in a Trappist Monastery in East Tennessee, and, every now and then, he said his folks were gypsies but he had been stolen by "big city folks from Macon." Anyway, he told me how he had been seduced by a drummer, an embodiment of Uriah Heep, who sold lamp chimneys. The sidewinder got the unsuspecting lad hooked on Coke, or Pepsi, some soft drink. The horrendous craving became so acute he squandered his Sunday School nickels on pop, and by the time he was twelve he had to use a cane. He didn't carry a cane when I knew him, but he surely sounded like Billy Graham, going in reverse, when he took out after pop and sodas as chasers. He got so worked up he reeled off countless statistics about the homes and bodies broken by soft drinks. He recounted a big revival at Vienna, Georgia (he pronounced it "Vi-anna") and how he had walked down to the pulpit, taken the soft drink pledge, and had given his young soul to Jesus.

I got a whitish-looking cartridge from a pawn shop. I told Mr. Brown my mother had given me this silver bullet, that I had promised her, on my oath, to wear it, eternally, next to my heart. Then one day I was passing a rowdy hotel. Someone threw a Gideon Bible out the window. The Bible hit me squarely in the heart. If it weren't for the silver bullet, why I'd be dead. Mr. Brown didn't laugh or smile. He spat, but I know he told Mr. Rutherford and Mr. Derryberry.

All the bartenders hated his guts because of the anti-soda pop harrangues he delivered. They didn't sell many soft drinks, but they said customers couldn't relax and enjoy booze, "with all his damn preaching going on," and would quit the joint after one drink.

I asked his wife, once, if he really meant all his screeds about pop. "Yes and no," she replied. "Not really, of course, but he's been ranting so long he's like the medicine show doc who starts taking his own magic elixir." She said his left leg was a bit shorter because he broke it when he was working for the *Miami Herald*. "He was drinking, but I don't remember what kind of chaser he used."

20

There were whole days when Mr. Brown wouldn't give you a single word if you were famishing for the sound of the human voice, and then, almost inexplicably, he'd launch an interminable tirade against soda pop, or lament all the intrepid investigative reporters he knew in Miami, Atlanta, Macon, and other metropolitan papers. I don't think it is original, but he said a good reporter went out and made news while a hack sat around and waited for news to happen.

Mr. Derryberry had an obsolete camera, which he called "Sweet Betsy," of the sort Matthew Brady used during the Civil War, and I decided to have pictures made of some of those mounds of coconuts I had painted and arranged, do a story, and make some news. I knew the photographs would be hazardous because half the time Mr. Derryberry took a photograph he would say, "Betsy ain't impressed," or "Betsy don't feel good today." Everytime he doubled as photographer he put on a long, white duster, the same as the blade wore when he took a Gibson Girl motoring in the early days of cars, and a baseball cap. When he focused, he put the baseball cap on bill-backwards, like a catcher, and I wish I had a photograph of Mr. Derryberry's making a photograph.

Mr. Derryberry looked at the coconuts and said, absently, "Betsy don't like coconuts. Set her teeth on edge." I didn't know whether he meant eating or looking, but he took several pictures of the mounds and several of the W.P.A.'ers painting coconuts. I pegged my story around, "New breed of artists at work." (John Faulkner, William's brother, wrote a current novel, *Men At Work*, about what his characters in the book called "the W.P. and A.," but I hadn't heard of it.)

I even used the outrageous phrase, "cocos nucifera," after I had looked up the fancy, technical name for the coconut palm tree. I got by with this brash idiocy because Mr. Biggers didn't know what it meant, but, surely as hell, would never admit it, and Mr. Brown dismissed it as a typical half-assed aberration.

Chiefly because of Mr. Derryberry's photographs, the coconuts' story did pretty well. One of the network radio newscasts had an item about it, and I understand there was a squib about it in the *Congressional Record*, if not inserted by one of the Congressmen Mr. Biggers had in his pocket, probably by one who waited, confidently, for William McKinley to rise from the graveyard.

I mean the popularity of the story wasn't predicated on what I had in mind. As my grandmother used to say, I shot at a rooster and killed a hen. My innocuous piece was perverted into a screed against governmental waste and frivolity. And in anticipation of Wrong-way Corrigan who started to California but soloed to Europe, I became a muckraker, a gadfly to sting F.D.R.'s nefarious social philosophies. As such I was invited to address the West Palm Beach Rotary Club.

The Rotarian who introduced me hadn't missed Sunday School for years and years, and he had metal insigne, annual awards for perfect attendance, from his lapel almost to his left knee. When he moved he sounded as if all the ghosts in Florida's history were rattling their chains simultaneously. I already knew that Father Coughlin, the "radio priest," was frothingly anti-F.D.R., but this man had found many implicit opprobriums in the Writ with which to castigate Roosevelt. And in presenting me he succumbed to his own fulminations and palmed me off as a youthful combination of Westbrook Pegler and John T. Flynn, neither of whom would give President and Mrs. Roosevelt half a biscuit if he owned the whole Pillsbury plant.

I was, am, a militant, if unsophisticated, New Dealer, but I was in no mood to relinquish the halo I was wearing so accidentally and precariously. Hence, I tried to talk around the coconuts, the same way my father used to orate about the weather, history, Shakespeare, or Will Rogers when he would rather not speak to a jury about a specific client. To try to be wittily disarming, I quoted Mencken, saying that the first Rotarian was the man who first called John the Baptist, Jack. The stunned silence that ensued was an ominous as the silence of a widow whose late husband had let his life insurance lapse.

As I recall, my talk contended that the east coast of Florida, and not the American west, was the nation's ultimate frontier. I told about the barefoot postman who walked the mail, and walking passengers, from Jacksonville to Miami, early in the century, and how the Audubon Society, organized to save the egret, furnished whatever law and order Miami had when the city was a village on stilts.

After my speech I was as alone as Benedict Arnold would have been at a reunion of George Washington's veterans. But the main thing that I remember is that not a one of those uptight, illiterate bastards even mentioned my short story, "Girls In Summer Hats." I wanted desperately to be hailed as a creative writer and not as some misbegotten political pundit.

But from then on I was hailed as "Coconuts" around the office and in the bars that had buffets. Mr. Brown alternated "Harpo" with "Young Shaw." Harpo Marx, was the mute, zany brother in the famous film, "Coconuts." Too, I walked out occasionally with a strikingly pretty girl named Ella Almayer whom I called, lovingly, jestingly, "Folly," after Joseph Conrad's once-celebrated novel, *Almayer's Folly*. She called me "Coconuts," and one night when I did something gauche, she spat, "Christ, dummy, you are Almayer's folly, doubled and in spades."

Almayer was pretty from the ground up, as sweet and succulent as a stick of peppermint to a starving boy, but I think I can put the erratic, unconsummated romance into proper historical perspective with this true vignette. One lambent-conjured night when the stars dipped low to anoint young lovers with magic wands, I told Almayer how the word "spooning" evolved from the time when poor Welch boys carved ornate, heavily-embossed wooden spoons for their lady-loves, in lieu of expensive engagement rings. When a Welch girl accepted a boy's spoon she had full parental permission to go walking in the moonlight with the boy, and sans chaperone.

I suppose I talked to this adorable girl as if she were a public meeting, as Queen Victoria said about William Gladstone. She faced me while moonbeams put yellow freckles to somersaulting on her nose and forehead. Her lips and tongue were quick with golden, tumbling elves when she said: "Karl Marx's mother said, 'If my boy, Karl, instead of all the time talking about capital, had made some capital, then everyone would be better off'." Q.E.D.

I backed into another good feature one day when a bartender asked: "How's the old Commodore?" He explained that he meant Mr. Derryberry, and I learned, almost as if I had been up on the mountain with Moses, that each Sunday of the year Mr. Derryberry sailed handsome toy boats on Jackson's Lake. He had five or six wonderful models of sailing ships, and each Sunday he took a different one to Jackson's Lake, a small, man-made pond in a public park.

Each Sunday he put on a white skipper's cap, with a lot of braid on it, the hard, leather visor glistening, a dilapidated but inordinately neat and clean blue blazer, white duck pants, and white Palm Beach shoes with heavy crape soles. Everybody at Jackson's Lake called him "Commodore," referred to him deferentially as "the Commodore."

Mr. Derryberry knew more about the history of ships, more about the technical minutiae, than Sir Thomas Lipton knew about boats, or about tea, for that matter. If you asked the Commodore about some little do-dad on one of his toy boats you'd get a charming, in-depth lecture on everything from the Ark, to quinquireme of Nineveh, to the stately Spanish galleon.

The Sunday races and lectures were the Commodore's reality, his poetry, religion, and his hope of heaven. The activities of the week days were fluff, meringue, vacuous time-markers important solely in that they led to Sunday.

My off-and-on girl, Almayer, was a camera buff and I got her to snap some photographs of the Commodore sailing a ship. Even in the ancient regality of his faded yachting outfit he resembled a gaunt, feeble Neptune, save for his eyes which radiated the blue sparkle of Mitchell's Falls when the sun crisps the water. And the story and pictures made another hit, probably because many people needed a refuge in 1938. The King of England had abdicated; Spain was ravaged by a savage Civil War; Hitler roared with the fury of a madman; money was tight at home, and I suppose a lot of people wanted to retreat to the relatively safe innocence of childhood by sailing princely little boats with old Commodore Derryberry.

Something fell from one of his coat pockets one Sunday. I picked it up. It was a tiny car, one that operated with a little battery, and on reaching any impediment would back up and change directions. He let me borrow this tiny marvel, but only after impressing me with the responsibility of steward-ship. I spent half of one morning running the car up and down the bar at the Flaminco, and at least a dozen different men, including the bartender, took turns playing with Mr. Derryberry's toy. Everytime it bumped against a glass, a beer mug, an ashtray, or a pretzel, everyone yelled as joyously as I imagine Archimedes did when he screamed "Eureka."

Oscar, the bartender, who had put me onto the sailing ships, exclaimed, about the tiny car: "Jesus, I'll bet he's got a dozen of them." I visited Mr. Derryberry's room and found out that he had at least a dozen toy cars, and on two or three card tables placed together, he had track, stations, water tanks, and tunnels for an old wind-up train.

He had no family. He lived alone in one dank room in a third-class rooming-house. His wife had been dead so long I was not sure that Mr. Derryberry even remembered her. He had an old tea pot, and his landlady let him boil water on her kitchen stove. Insofar as I know, he subsisted on tea and Graham crackers, almost exclusively. A couple of times I took him some of the cans of fruit that Mr. Brown and I got from merchants for the ads we ran in the *Liberator*, but he always smiled his thin, quivering smile and said: "Thanks, I ain't hungry." And, he'd get so excited about sailing a boat next Sunday, about running his cars and trains, and talking about automobiles and railroading, his tea would get cold.

Mrs. Brown had a box of Lipton's Tea, some of the stuff Mr. Brown and I conned at a supermarket, and one Saturday I took the tea to Mr. Derryberry's room. I was sure he could use the tea, and there was the added inducement of Sir Thomas Lipton, who spent several fortunes on sailing ships.

He was sitting in his chair by the card tables, his hand clutching a Baltimore and Ohio boxcar. And he was the deadest, whitest man I ever saw. No one claimed the body, and Mr. Biggers made arrangements for burial in the Potter's Field. No one came to the funeral home except the Browns, Mr. Biggers, and me.

He didn't hold with preachers. So, Mr. Biggers didn't get one, and a few of us from the paper stood around the grave just as if everyone was waiting for someone else to say something appropriate. When he was at the funeral home the undertaker saw me as I tried to slip a couple of Mr. Derryberry's toy cars into the coffin. The mortician was horrified by this "sacrilege." I told him what he could do, but he couldn't do that, not alone. But at the cemetery, amid a sort of quiet, subdued militance, I dropped a toy ship and a toy car into the grave. If the undertaker saw me, he didn't say anything.

Mr. Biggers let me write an obituary editorial. I got pretty fancy, but after all of these years, I don't take back a word of it. In my piece I took him straight from the Potter's Field to heaven, without detour or interrogation. I had St. Peter's giving him a special little lake on which the Commodore,

Noah, Sir Frances Drake, and Herman Melville sailed model ships throughout eternity. Betimes, he was playing train with Cayce Jones and running toy cars up and down the streets of gold with Barney Oldfield.

I assumed Mr. Brown would gag at this purple prose, but all he said was: "Young Shaw, if the chamber of commerce and the civic clubs read your description of heaven they'll pass resolutions saying, 'Congress ought to investigate the damned place'."

Today, I'm almost inexorably sedentary. I go from one year to the next and hardly leave sight of the smoke from my own chimney. Hence, it is amusing to recall the ease, or the effrontery, with which I sailed from Boca Raton to Tampico, on the east cost of Mexico, back when I was a boy-reporter in Florida.

On Thanksgiving I had somewhat less than fifty cents on which to subsist for several days. That $3,000 Mr. Biggers got from the big Townsend rally in Miami had gone to pay arrears to printers, chiefly. Since Mr. Bohannon and Mr. Gulley, our advertising solicitors, weren't bringing in enough cash to buy toothpicks for a rabbit, Mr. Brown enlisted me in a plan to sell ads for personal aggrandizement. His strategy was simple, and it was relatively free of moral tape.

In view of the anomolous character of the *Liberator* relative to local advertisers, we'd sell ads and instead of asking for cash, why, we would agree to eat, drink, or smoke them up. We got some free meals from cafes, a few free drinks from lounges, and some free groceries and cigarettes from a couple of supermarkets. Because I had one small room and no cooking equipment, I got canned goods and Mr. Brown took the fresh meats and vegetables.

The canned goods were a life-saver, temporarily, even if tuna fish and canned pineapple get a bit thick twice a day, especially for breakfast. A supermarket manager gave us a case of stuff without any labels. He swore it was "mixed stuff," but it turned out half tuna and half pineapple.

On Thanksgiving Day I went to the Flaminco because I knew there would be a buffet, some sort of free food, for all cash customers. I spent a dime for a draught beer much as an oil wild-cater spends a hunk of his small capital for another drilling rig. As I sipped meditatively I made a Dagwood sandwich that was much more compatible with my appetite than with my purchase. Then, eating bigger bites and swallowing faster than my mother allowed at home, I inched as unobtrusively as possible toward a gleaming bowl of hard-boiled eggs and a huge crock of dill pickles.

Enroute I was becalmed by a middle-aged drunk who was drinking whiskey sours from a beer mug. He wore a Brooks Brothers suit, a gray Homburg, a light gray vest, and pearl-gray spats. Rotating wildly and widely, just as if his feet were nailed to the floor, he tried to bet me five dollars he could say all of "Peter Piper picked a peck of pickled peppers" etc. without making a mistake.

I told him I was broke, and he said the old saw, letter-perfect, and he put a five dollar bill into the poor-box that rested on the bar. He drained his beer mug of its four or five inches of whiskey sour, sucking the last of it onto his Charlie Chaplin moustache, and then sucking on his moustache and smacking his lips, slightly, as if he were sampling Napoleon brandy. He was at least a yard from the bar, but he leaned, a human Tower of Pisa, and slid the beer mug to the bartender, without even shuffling his planted feet. The bartender made a hefty whiskey sour, wrote down the charge, and slid the glass back.

He nodded towards me, then towards the bartender. The bartender held up a beer mug and a glass, and I had a whiskey sour in the glass. We drank and the man offered to bet me another five bucks he could say every word of "As I was going to St. Ives" without a hitch or omission. He did, and once again he leaned like Harpo Marx and dropped a five dollar bill into the poor box. I made some disarming comment about his charity, or social awareness, and he mumbled, "Keeps me from having the jitters tomorrow."

He bought me several drinks, as he remained cemented to the same spot on the floor, and after a refill the bartender said: "Going for a record today?"

"No, just drinking," he replied.

After another refill I found out that the bartender meant a standing record, not a drinking record. "Four years ago, in March, he stood on the same spot from eleven in the morning till almost nine that night without once going to the head. But he was drinking martinis then and I think his kidneys were half olives anyway."

After an hour of almost steady drinking he told me his name was Captain N. Lewis, that he sold office equipment, up and down the east coast of Florida, and elsewhere. He spilled half of the last drink he took on his moustache and chin. He licked at his moustache as if he were sopping gravy with a piece of bread. He almost smiled: "Best damn drink I've had ever since me and Wilkes Booth Lincoln was born in the world."

I really beamed because I was sure this strange man, this gussied-up drunk of a drummer, was a devotee of *William Green Hill and Miss Minerva*, the exquisite, fascinating saga of William Green Hill, the little white boy, and his cherished companion, Wilkes Booth Lincoln, the little black boy. Eagerly, and smilingly enthusiastically, I said that Cap must like the old boys' novel as well as I. "What book?" he sort of drooled.

"Why, *William Green Hill and Miss Minerva*, the one you were just talking about."

"Never heard of it," he slurped.

"Then where did you hear about Wilkes Booth Lincoln?"

"From a medicine man in Yucatan. He told me when I sold him some filing cabinets for his office records."

His feet remained, a tree planted by the bar, and I almost whistled "I shall not be moved," but when his body finally dropped and drooped over to form a human croquet wicket, he asked, mumbling out one side of his mouth and then the other, if I'd accompany him to his hotel and type some notes to his customers in various towns telling them when Cap would be there.

Cap was a little swishy, and I suppose I suspected he was trying to pick me up, but Woodrow Wilson could have had my ticket when he said a man with an empty belly isn't concerned with morality, primarily. I went along with Cap to his hotel, if not with alacrity, certainly without much reluctance. It was a classy hotel — the Roosevelt or George Washington, named for some president — and he brought out a portable typewriter and some letterheads.

For God's sake, Cap wanted me for business, not for sex. Even though repugnance for homosexuality must have been puissant in my youthful intolerance, I had the distinct feeling that Cap was a consummate fraud.

As I made ready to leave, he asked me if I wanted to eat a deluxe Thanksgiving dinner. He gave me a card to hand to the person whom he called maitre d'hotel, "ma tr' d- tel'," at the Skylight Terrace, a swanky, expensive restaurant I knew only from the outside of the building. All the way to the restaurant I ran "ma' tr' de tel'" around my brain and tongue as if I were an Oxford hound and the phrase was European royalty posing as a red fox. I brushed two or three pedestrians saying the words not quite silently. I was so ensnared with the highfaluting resonance I crossed one street against the light, and once, I brushed against a mailbox.

I gave Cap's card to the major-domo. With a haughty gesture this worthy turned me over to a waiter much as one used to put an empty glass milk bottle on the porch. Waiters usually intimidate me, and the one at the Skylight, who resembled a British admiral in a C. Aubrey Smith movie, acted as if I had a smallpox quarantine sticker plastered on my forehead. I was parked at a small table in a remote corner, just the way poor relatives were parked at the back of the church at weddings in Oxford.

I never learned Cap's connection with this dazzling place nor any of the sacrosanct implications of the open sesame card he gave me. But being made to feel like a one-legged man at a public tail kicking certainly didn't impair my prodigious appetite. That was the first time I ever ran the gamut from cocktails, to wine, to brandy at a meal, and despite my seedy appearance, I imagined I was elegant, ultra-sophisticated Ronald Coleman. I was carrying on this charmingly brilliant Oxford, England conversation with lovely Greer Garson, and polishing my finger-bowl gestures, when I remembered I had less than forty cents, that even in those astringent times a tip of three or four bucks would be modest for such a sensational meal, for such impeccable, rarefied, if snot-nosed, service.

To avoid the embarrassment of not being able to pay the tip, I went to the men's room, deliberately leaving a cigarette burning in an ashtray. I opened a window, jumped down into the alley, and doubled as Leslie Howard's playing the Scarlet Pimpernel.

But, I must have detoured by Port Said to get to Tampico, like the insufferably loquacious fellow in Mark Twain's story who started out to tell about the bull that was ripping across the field straight at a man who was bended over. Mark's narrator got to talking about relatives of the fellow in the path of the bull, what dominations they belonged to, and never got around to telling what happened to the bull and the human target.

About two months after Thanksgiving, when Cap was almost an amusing but dim memory, I saw him again, planted to the floor of the Flaminco. Before I could say "glad to see you," he blurted, "You wanna a free trip to Tampico?" Now,

I didn't know what or where Tampico is, but it sounded romantic and mysterious and I said "yes," thinking, of course, that Cap meant next week or next month.

"Fine," I said, "When?" He looked at his wrist watch, reached for a whiskey sour, and said, "Well, we got almost an hour." I called Mr. Biggers. "Go ahead, Garland, my boy. Two, three days on the water and a few hours in Mexico will give the paper splendid leverage." He didn't elucidate, but Cap and I got to Boca Raton, the point of embarkation, with a minute or so to spare.

Cap had won the two free trips to Tampico for selling the most office supplies in some sort of sales' contest. "They don't know I am a kosher Benedict," he giggled. The subtlety was lost on me, but I clapped my hands and laughed uproariously at the capital joke Cap was playing on some nebulous executives.

He got in bed in our stateroom with a bottle of Jack Daniels. Maybe, I thought I should make an infinitesimal payment of thanks with a small token of minutiae. I asked if he knew that "stateroom" may have arisen in 1844 when Captain Henry Shreve put sleeping quarters on his Mississippi steamboat and instead of numbering the sleeping rooms called them after the states that bordered on the Mississippi and Ohio Rivers. "For a while," I chirped, "These rooms were known as 'states,' but later they were called 'staterooms'."

I couldn't have been more pleased had I been DesCartes and had just told Cap, "I think; hence I am."

"Really," he grumbled and he pronounced "really" as if it were "rally," Pepys wrote about staterooms on British ships long, long before what you said."

My heart leaped up as if I had seen one of Wordsworth's rainbows. (Wordsworth said "rainbow in the sky." Even as a high school boy I wondered where else in the Sam Hill one would likely see a rainbow.) "Oh, you like the *Diary*, too!"

"What dairy?"

"No, di-ary, Samuel Pepys' *Diary*."

"Never heard of it."

"Where'd you get that about staterooms on British ships?"

"From the Archbishop of Canterbury when he was over here studying snake-handling in East Tennessee."

Before I could add additional jots or tittles to learning, he began to snore, loudly.

I went to the main salon where I put a few drinks on Cap's tab. Enroute to the salon I walked on deck briefly, and the sky was blacker than a despot's soul, as menacing as a blow-torch around gasoline. But if danger is the spur of great minds, no one was likely to confuse with me George Bernard Shaw, including irascible Mr. Brown. Burns said "Freedom and Whiskey gain thegither," but I doubt that Burns ever encountered an incredibly violent storm at sea.

I did. While I had never seen a ship founder, I was sure ours would. Everytime it heaved from port to star, and from star to port, I thought it was going all the way over. Glassware rained all over the big room, as if meteorites were pounding from the sky. One heave threw me to the floor. When I picked myself up I saw, out a window, some people on deck in life jackets.

My whole body, from my ears to my ankles, was permeated with the chilling sensation that I was rat number three in the universe and Noah was just taking off in his Ark. But I bounced, bumped, stumbled, and groped to our stateroom. Cap was sleeping, sucking his Charlie Chaplin moustache, and smiling.

I shook him frantically, trying with pathetic desperation to get a life-preserver on him. "Wake up, Cap, wake up," I shouted, "I think this goddam ship is sinking."

Cap opened one eye. He resembled an owl with hog cholera, one that's been subsisting on green lizards, exclusively. "Let the son-of-a-bitch sink," he yawned, "I don't own it."

Tampico was hardly the Happy Isles, but, then again, I wasn't Homer, Achilles, Ulysses, or even Lord Tennyson. As I remember it, Cap left the stateroom only once the few days we were on the voyage. He went to the dining room one night and devoured a massive mess of pompano while I went on deck and threw up in the so-called blue Atlantic.

He sent me back to West Palm Beach from Boca Raton in a taxi, and I never saw him again. I had asked for his home address a couple of times. He grunted, almost groaned, "Let it go, boy. If it's any good it'll probably bounce back. Otherwise, it's better gone."

I suppose he was forty at this time. In the years to come I'd go long intervals and never think of him, almost forget that I had ever been to Tampico. Then in 1958, just after a book of mine was published, I received this telegram, in Oxford:

"Guess you found that same medicine man in Yucatan. Congrats.

Colonel N. Lewis."

I wondered if Cap served in World War II and got to be a colonel? Maybe, he sold some office equipment in Kentucky? Maybe, he just promoted himself? But I am astonished that he remembered I live in Oxford, indeed, if I ever told him. That part of it is as much a mystery as generous, enigmatic, contradictory Cap, or Colonel, himself.

The *Liberator* wasn't as much fun after Mr. Derryberry's death, and Jackson's Lake became a dead sea, a Sargasso, for me. Each week was bereft of its radiant Sunday, a hum-drum span of six phlegmatic days. I stayed on a few weeks after the Commodore's death, after Tampico, but this final interlude was comparable to the Confederate Army's being inundated in the seige at Petersburg, Virginia. It was all over.

I returned to Oxford where, save for a few furtive detours, I have lived, loved and tried to write ever since. In "The

Death of the Hired Man," Robert Frost has two definitions of home: "Home is the place, when you have to go there,/They have to take you in," and "I should have called it/Something you somehow haven't to deserve." I hope, believe, that Frost's second definition applied to my homecoming, has permeated my long residence. Of course, I know the pernicious accumulations of what Thomas Hood called "homemade infelicity," but I hope I have managed to fall into Oxford's arms, periodically, without falling into its hands, as the indicting old dictum about a woman has it.

I have been identified with Oxford, probably more as a writer than as a day-by-day citizen, but I am not Oxford's spokesman, laureate, or apologist. It isn't Oxford, Mississippi, or Frenchman's Bend, or Jefferson, Mississippi, or Winesburg, Ohio, Spoon River, Illinois, Gopher Prairie, or Altamont. And I'm not Faulkner, Sherwood Anderson, Edgar Lee Masters, Sinclair Lewis, or Thomas Wolfe, as much as I cherish Faulkner's and Wolfe's superlative literary equipment.

Rabelais (1494-1553) wrote that Cain was the first builder of towns. I suppose I understand some of Rabelais's implications, and more than a century later Abraham Cowley amended it: "God the first garden made, and the first city Cain."

I have tried to write about Oxford, about the society into which I was born and have lived, in long and short pieces, in poetry, fiction, and nonfiction. In these searchings I act as a sort of unofficial tour-guide on an excursion, particularly on those excursions that go back, instead of sideways or forward.

So, come in. As the folks in Oxford and Granville County used to say, "Light and rest."

I am Oxford's second-best writer. The best one, Len Sikes, now regaling the angels, never published a word. He talked, and he was branded by the unimaginative as an unconscionable liar. He wasn't a liar, though. He found the unvarnished truth lacking in wings, and he tacked on some lovely appendages. Without Len, Oxford would have been as dull as the only razor of the old House of David baseball team.

One night, Len, my father, and my uncle, three damned superior gentlemen, all now fishing with St. Peter, and I, a small boy, were standing in front of Hall's Drug Store. My father said, "It's cold, getting colder." Len looked at my father the way Noah would look at some guy who complained about a brisk shower.

"You call this cold? When I was a forest ranger in Alaska, years ago, we went three months and the thermometer never got higher than eighteen degrees below zero."

There was additional talk. We were riding with my uncle, and my father said, "John, I'm getting cold. Let's go home."

"You call this cold?" Len snorted. "When I was pro-specting for gold in Alaska years ago we went three months and the thermometer never got higher than eighteen degrees below zero."

"Wait a minute, Len," my uncle demurred. "A minute ago when you told that pop-eyed lie you said you were a forest ranger. Now you say you were prospecting for gold."

"God Almight, John, you don't think I'd be that far from Oxford with just one lousy job, do you?"

All three had fought in the First World War, and Len got to telling a tale involving someone's incredible heroism.

"That's not exactly the way it was, Len," my father spoke up. "I was standing right there and saw the whole thing, all of it." "Well, I'll be goddamned," Len said, "An eye witness surely plays hell with historical accuracy."

My father flashed a quick smile of commiseration. He patted Len's shoulder gently: "I guess there are no absolutes left in society, Len."

"Well, there's one absolute left. You can be absolutely sure carrots are good for the eyes because you hardly ever see a rabbit wearing glasses."

None of the rabbits in the ensuing assorted prose, poetry,

and fiction wears glasses, and I usually manage to eschew sworn eye witnesses.

MAN RAKING LEAVES

I saw a man raking leaves
And I asked if he raked to rid
The grass of suffocation, or if
It was merely the time and season for raking?
And if it was purely a matter of personal importance
Perhaps it was to get the streaming bottom leaves
To toss at Spring as furtive calling cards.

But he said he was passing time without a watch,
The same as men scrawling aimless verse or bandaging toes
Or speaking to a jury, or catching fish,
Or singing a love song in tune. Just so.

Just over the shoulder in time, there were many regional
homes such as ours, great, white barns with endless rooms;
but naked, compulsive, lyrical love was likely to be found
around the kitchen range on a morning early in Fall.

The world was young and pink and innocent, no higher,
even, than the ceilings of those cavernous rooms. But little
boys were silver stallions who had continents of yearning to
cover before the inundation of the rough, wry, masculine
winter weather.

In early fall, when the world was a persimmon too ripe for
the tree, our kitchen windows were frosted on either side.
Early November was trying to come inside to warm his hands
by the kitchen range, and the steam from the pots and kettles
was trying to get outside to tell the last birds of the season
about the fabulous riches stored in our house.

On the back porch, ripening pears were misshapen elephants with freckled snouts, all in a cumbersome row, playing an endless game of prairie schooners. Scuppernong grapes were there, too, austere maidens gallantly standing to be ravished into wines and jellies. How, oh how, we marveled, could such tender vessels hold such amazing cargoes?

My father was God Almighty in a shiny blue suit, an all-wise sovereign whose only errors were made deliberately to disarm small children. His muscles were as big as those on the baking soda box and the compassionate candor of his face was a letter of recommendation from the warrior saints of old. My mother was there, too, the high priestess of the pots and pans, infinitely wiser than she ever felt the need to express. She swept and baked and mended as another might play the violin. Each morning when I walked to school I was warmed down inside from the smells of her starches and soaps and the indescribable earthiness of her bosom. And as I walked it was as if the fragrance of dough was in one nostril and the pure earthiness of her bosom in the other.

Insularity seemed sweet as dogwood, as resistant to change as an anvil. Such excursions as we made were to wave farewell to the fields. It seemed indecent, somehow, not to wave good-bye when summer's abundance was stored for winter's exigencies, not to toss some talisman to the fields to give them grace in the long groping months ahead.

I remember it as it was at twilight when the neighborhood's eyes were smarting from the smoke of the burning leaves. There always seemed to be a mist that fell as a seasonal benediction. When the fields were exposed as mercilessly as a picked chicken, and the last bird flew south, we never knew precisely if a bird, or a season, or a way of life was flying over the dark, wet heads of the nervous trees.

THE MAN WHO KNEW JOE HOWARD

Mr. Parkhurst, who was one of the two "city" mail carriers in town when I was a boy, wasn't especially folksy or gay. He toted his sack of mail around, and when he saw a lady he touched the brim of his cap. He said "morning" and "evening" to folks, and I never heard any grown people complaining about his work.

But Mr. Parkhurst wasn't outgoing the way the other carrier, Mr. Farris, was. Mr. Farris was always delivering messages to his patrons from neighbors and from folks up town. Children and dogs followed him around, and during the summer ladies on his route fixed him pitchers of lemonade and dishes of homemade vanilla and strawberry ice cream. In winter they plied him with hot coffee and sausage biscuits. (I remember one time Papa said Mr. Farris's grocery bill shouldn't be any bigger than a damned crow's.)

But Mr. Farris got cats out of trees and children out of the street. He held squawking babies while their mothers fluffed their hair to answer the 'phone. He settled a thousand arguments about which horseshoe was nearest the pole or where some boy's heel really touched down in leap-frog. Sometimes he'd even put down his sack of mail and umpire for a few minutes at the vacant lot, and he might even pitch an inning, being careful to serve up nice, easy balls.

At Christmas, everyone on Mr. Farris's route gave him a present. It took a two-horse wagon or a truck to get all the stuff to his house. To boot, his patrons were always giving him fresh eggs and butter, vegetables and fruit, and if someone killed a beef or a sheep, they saved a big, fine side or quarter for Mr. Farris.

It wasn't that folks didn't appreciate Mr. Parkhurst. It was just that he walked with his thoughts, and these thoughts seemed to be deeper than a well and longer than a railroad track, as he walked around handing out cards, letters, and duns.

Mr. Farris had a fat wife and three children. He played "hiding" with the children after supper, and his fat wife sat on the porch and laughed. They all lived in a white frame house that had a pretty green fence around it.

But Mr. Parkhurst was a bachelor. He lived and took his meals at the "English House," a cross between a boarding house and an inn. It was a two-story clapboard building that had lots of porches and a big parlor for a lobby. The old building ran everywhere, like Mrs. Farris's belly. It was so artless, the old "English House" was, it had a sort of ugly-frog charm to it.

I always heard that Mr. Parkhurst ate whatever was put before him. He didn't ask Mrs. English to fix things a special way. I always thought he must have eaten about the way he carried the mail, and he didn't crack rusty jokes. You know what I mean. Mrs. English would ask some wise-acre, some wisenheimer, "How did you find your pie?"

And, of course, to hell, the fellow would reply: "Why it won't a bit of trouble, Mrs. English. I found it under at little dab of meringue."

If Mrs. English asked Mr. Parkhurst about his pie, or about his snaps or his spoon bread, he always answered: "It's first-rate, and I thank you, madame."

After supper Mr. Parkhurst usually sat in the parlor for a while. He would smoke a few cigarettes, tailor-made ones that didn't have any premium cards, and watch the games of checkers or set-back that always went on at night, but he never played any of the games and he never commented on the games or on any of the moves the players made.

After he had watched for about thirty minutes, Mr. Parkhurst usually walked down to the depot, especially in pretty weather. One of the sidewalks going that way was paved, but the other wasn't because there wasn't much on that side of the street.

Mr. Parkhurst always took the unpaved side, the one less used. It was usually free of people, and about the time night came toppling like a black kite without any string or tail, he would walk along and whistle. The music might as well have come from a victrola, or a pianola. But, boy, could Mr. Parkhurst whistle.

He didn't sharp and flat and have to fake the notes he couldn't whistle, the way virtually everyone else had to do. No sir, he stayed on the tune from start to jump. Whenever I heard him I always saw his tunes as musical threads that ran straight and true from beginning to end.

Almost every night he whistled "Hello, My Baby," "Good-bye My Lady-Love," "Honeymoon," and "I Wonder Who's Kissing Her Now." Naturally he didn't whistle as if he were going to a funeral, but even when he whistled "Hello, My Baby," you didn't picture Mr. Parkhurst cooing on the 'phone with a pretty girl.

Sometimes he whistled "Little Gray Home In the West," and once I heard him do "Too Much Mustard." But usually he stuck to his four main tunes. I never heard him whistle the one about "O, Mr. Sheen," or the one Papa cussed so much, "Yes, We Have No Bananas."

Once, I remember, I asked Papa if Mr. Parkhurst whistled that sad way because he was lonesome or if there was some terrible secret gnawing at his innards. I can still hear Papa: "Don't talk like such a blamed fool, Arthur. People don't have to have reasons for whistling. You sound like those fool analysts who think everyone has to have a reason for every idiotic thing he does. I'm damned if I don't believe this compulsory education experiment will be as big a blamed fiasco as this fool Prohibition experiment the women forced on us." Mother would always tell Papa not to swear in front of me, but Papa would say, "All right, my dear, you are right, of course, but I'd almost as soon turn the country over to one-gallused preachers as these damned women school teachers."

I never followed Mr. Parkhurst down the dirt sidewalk. That was too obvious, and besides, I didn't think he was any Pied Piper. But I might fiddle on the other corner, the paved one, and pretend I was looking at the stuff in the store windows.

For a fact, I did look into the store windows, especially when the moon was dropping yellow puddles all around. There was a wax lady, or some kind of dummy lady, in Bengough's window. Sometimes I thought I saw her touching her hand to her flaxen hair, to her yellow moon curls. She was telling me she was all dressed up in Mr. Bengough's finery with no place to go.

Down below Bengough's was Captain Turner's hardware store. One window was always filled with guns that really looked fearsome, but the moon always sent scampering rabbits that ran right up to this glassed-in arsenal as if to say: "Go along with you. I know your guns aren't loaded."

The big "time" store was on the corner. The window held everything, including a kitchen stove. When I'd go there at night I'd wish for a pan to wash the gold, but then I'd realize all the precious nuggets were nuts, bolts, and castings, by day. If the galvanized buckets were filled with stars, so I could almost dip the stars, there was an old hobbyhorse, put out to glassed-in pasture, that I knew wouldn't win a race at the fair. And when I turned and looked back up the street the summer night had promoted the Confederate soldier on the monument to a full general, by putting four stars on each of his bronze shoulders.

A couple of times I walked down to the opposite corner to cross the street and to double-back up the dirt sidewalk. I slinked up the street that Mr. Parkhurst was sauntering and whistling down. But I doubled-back behind the platform, on the other side of the depot, and I entered the old waiting room that smelled as if it was made from the Ark.

It would have been terrible for Mr. Parkhurst to know I was following him deliberately, spying on him. So, I fooled around the waiting room a few minutes, spitting saliva into one of those huge brass cuspidors that bounced all around, like a dingy roly-poly doll, but never turned over, even when you kicked it.

Come to think of it, I slipped into the depot two or three times, from the back, across the passengers' platform. I remember once I wasted a penny in the chiclet machine, and I wondered what the world was like when the machine was first put there in the depot. The chiclet was so old I didn't even suck off the sugar. I bounced it off the wall, catching it with my hand and then with my cap.

I could always see Mr. Shelton, the telegraph operator, through the window that led to his room, his place, his office, his special realm. But I could hear the rickety-rack, the clickety-clack, the pounding, droning sound of his magic key before I saw Mr. Shelton. The sounds of his key were like horses, freshly shod, galloping down a cobblestone road. Sometimes I almost expected to see sparks flying around the mangy old depot.

Apparently, the telegraph instrument never slept, or even slumbered. The way it went on all the time you'd think the town would fall into a Rip Van Winkle sleep if it ever stopped its incessant spewing and chirping.

Mr. Shelton could have been anywhere from forty to seventy-five, the same way it was with Mr. Parkhurst. He wore a green eye-shade on his head and he wore fancy garters around his striped shirt sleeves. He kept a pot of coffee on the stove, all the time, summer and winter. He was the only man I remember back then who used canned milk in his coffee. And he always had a cigarette in his mouth and one lying on his table, with the lighted end on the table. That part of the table looked like one of those burnt offerings in the Bible.

Of course, to be honest, Mr. Shelton's halo, or eye-shade, was slipping a little bit. Although the daily paper didn't come until the mail was put up each day, some people, not many, had radio sets. They got KDKA, in Pittsburgh. And it came through pretty clearly, on soft balmy summer nights. But people still went to the depot at big election time and at World Series time.

Mr. Shelton would put the returns and the scores, by innings, on the bulletin board, the big one, out on the platform. He would never say anything, no matter how often people asked him how it was going.

Papa said a fool could tell this radio business was no flash-in-the-pan. Papa said Mr. Shelton wouldn't be a mighty man of mystery and awe much longer. The radio was already taking some of the shine from the magic key, but, for a while, Mr. Shelton would be the only man in town whose ears would collect the secrets of the four winds, whose fingers would send messages across the nation.

For a while, when he wrote something on his pad, or when his fingers worked as if they were playing a magic violin, there was a great sense of drama. It might be only a message that said somebody's Cousin Susie was coming on the train to visit next Tuesday, but if you really looked at Mr. Shelton you got the impression he was talking to President Coolidge, directly, or to Walter Johnson, or Ty Cobb, or to Red Grange.

Some folks said Mr. Shelton was the biggest grump since old Scrooge. Some folks said Mr. Shelton wouldn't give you the time of day if he owned the Elgin factory. But he always spoke to Mr. Parkhurst.

Mr. Parkhurst would push back his white straw or his black winter hat, just a little, and he'd say: "How's it going,

Willie?" And then Mr. Shelton would say: "You were in good form tonight, Park," and he might add, "A big one is coming through at 8:05."

This meant that a long freight would be passing through town soon, and after a little polite rag-chewing, Mr. Parkhurst would walk out onto the passengers' platform and on down to the freight platform. Sometimes he'd sit on an empty baggage-truck, and sometimes he would sit on the edge of the platform and swing his legs as he waited for the freight train to come through.

The freight platform didn't have anything around it, any bricks or planks. It was open-air, and usually I would leave the waiting room by the front door and cross the street to the concrete sidewalk and fool around the front of Bengough's as I watched Mr. Parkhurst.

He'd sit there smoking and whistling and looking at the parked box-cars and waiting for a long-one to ramble and rumble on through. Now, I don't mean I went there every night. But ever so often I did this sneaky-pete, and then one night while Mr. Parkhurst was chinning with Mr. Shelton, I went back onto the passengers' platform and walked down to the freight platform.

But, the devil and Tom Walker, it was a free country, wasn't it? Mr. Parkhurst didn't own the platform or the old box-cars, either. I had just as much right there as he did, as anyone did, except for the folks who worked for the railroad. Hell fire and damnation, I'd stay there as long as I pleased.

But when I heard Mr. Parkhurst's leather shoes tapping the broad boards of the platform I knew everything I told myself was hot air, big talk. I could feel my heart bumping. I really could, and I felt as if I were trespassing, in the legal sense and in the other sense, too. My Adam's apple was blocking my throat. My ears were ringing, but my knees were not even a part of my body.

There were some crates, large ones filled with hardware,

near the edge of the platform. I heard a voice but I didn't put any human being with the voice at first. It said: "If you like freight trains, a big one will be coming through after a while."

Mr. Parkhurst had said the words, and he was sitting on a crate. The crate looked like a coffin-box. He was sitting on one and he was using one higher and behind him for a back-rest. He didn't tell me to join him, but I went that way, slowly, using two platform poles for ring-around-the rosy. I sort of used myself in an extra slow game of "slinging statues" and then I saw a piece of wood on the floor of the platform.

I picked up the wood and started whittling with my pocketknife. Mr. Parkhurst admired my knife and when I handed it to him, I sat down on the long crate, four or five feet from where he sat.

The moon was up and full, and the way the beams hung down it might have been a tree filled with ripe, yellow apples. I looked off at the box-cars. Some were yellow but not yellow the same way the full moon is yellow. Some of the yellow ones and many of the red ones were yawning through open slide doors.

But some of the other box-cars, with their doors closed tightly, and with their sealers flashing in the moonlight, were like hospital babies with identification bracelets, or like immigrants, with their tags, waiting to explore the world.

Many of the box-cars were sheep that had strayed a long distance from the fold. I thought they were "poor little lambs who have gone astray," just as the song said, because back then it was a long way from the Pacific Ocean and from Canada and such places to a small town in Eastern North Carolina. The "Great Northern," the "Western Pacific," and the "Santa Fe" ones had to cross mountain ranges, dusty valleys, big rivers, and hairpin curves to get here.

Off to one side stood two "Virginians" that had brought fertilizer all the way down from Norfolk. It almost looked as if the other box-cars had moved away because the two "Virginians" had such rank odors. A little closer to the two "Virginians" was a "Central of Georgia." It had been loaded with tar-paper, and the open door had a few pieces of tar paper strewn around its edges. There in the moonlight the "Central of Georgia" looked as if it were sucking licorice, or, maybe, chewing tobacco.

On the spur-line, the shifting line, an "Orange Blossom Special" stood with its mouth open. Evidently, she had been left waiting at the church. Whoever it was she was supposed to marry must have gone to Kansas, or Texas, maybe, without even leaving a note.

The main line, which really wasn't a main line, was clear of all traffic. It was waiting for the "big one" to come through, and there in the moonlight, I got the notion it was bracing for the impact, girding its steel loins, or something like that.

Mr. Parkhurst excused himself a minute. When he came back from Mr. Shelton's telegraph room he had his pocket watch in his hand. I figured the "big one" would be coming along any time now. Then I saw Mr. Shelton come out on the passenger platform with that staff sort of trick that held the message for the engineer, only the fireman usually came to the steps of the locomotive and held out his arm for the crooked part to go around his arm, that is, the top part that was a sort of curve or semicircle.

Mr. Parkhurst came back and stood on the edge of the freight platform. I joined him on the edge, but I was several feet away from him. He whistled a little bit of "Hello, My Baby." After he had whistled on through the part that said: "So won't you telephone and tell me I'm your own," he asked me: "Did you ever hear of a man called Joe Howard?"

When I started to nod my head he said: "Naw, naw, I don't mean the fellow who runs the battery shop." I told him that I guessed that I didn't. So he told me how this man, Joe Howard, had written "Hello, My Baby" a long time before I was born, back in '99.

48

I whistled, without whistling, without making any music. I almost said "whoop-de-do," the way Mother did when she heard something extraordinary. Then he told me how this Joe Howard had written lots of the best songs, ones like "Honeymoon," "Good-bye My Lady-Love," and "I Wonder Who's Kissing Her Now?"

He told me how Joe Howard didn't live in New York, or in any place, that he was a super-bum who went around singing and dancing and playing the piano, making up songs, and being as free as the breeze and the sun and the moon.

When the "big one" was a mile from town we could hear the bell and the whistle. They sounded like I always thought Judgment Day would sound. And I know the main track quivered, just as if someone were tickling its toes off in the distance.

When she came, high-balling and rattling and having a wonderful fit all along the line, Mr. Shelton got ready with the cradle trick that held the message. And when it went onto the fireman's arm and when Mr. Shelton walked away I thought he was some kind of new Moses, wearing a green eye-shade and garters around his shirt sleeves, and smoking a cigarette.

Mr. Parkhurst counted 104 box-cars, not counting the two engines, the coal car, and the little red caboose. I counted 106 but I probably saw two twice. I am sure it was 104, and there were 27 different kinds. They were all the way from Florida East Coast ones to Burlington ones, from Baltimore and Ohio ones, to Rock Island ones, from Central of Illinois to Southern Pacific, around by Atcheson, Topeka, and Santa Fe, and back up to Clinchfield and the Norfolk and Western.

When I went home everything seemed changed, different somehow. Some of the rooms were bigger and some were smaller, and I looked at Mother and Papa as if I had been gone a long, long time. I don't know how to tell it because it was so unreal. Even the ice in my glass of lemonade seemed to jingle a million miles away.

I remember a brakeman on top of a box-car on the "big-one" and how he waved his lantern at Mr. Parkhurst and me. Mr. Parkhurst waved back, but I waved and yelled "hello" at him. And when I got home the whole house seemed to be moving, to be tilted.

I couldn't sleep a lick. The whistles and the bells from the two big locomotives sang and rang all night. The whole earth shook and I could smell the thick, black smoke, but it smelled the way I always imagined that incense in the Bible smelled.

And, maybe more than anything, I could hear Mr. Parkhurst whistling "Good-bye My Lady-Love," when we left. He went one way and I went the other, but I could still feel the place on my shoulder where he had barely flicked it with his right fingers, just before he said: "Maybe we'll see another big one, Arthur."

I guess we saw about six or seven really "big ones" together. Then one day Mr. Parkhurst got a job sorting mail on a mail train. Every now and then I'd get a card from some fantastic place, such as Kansas City, or St. Louis, and once there was a card from Pueblo, Colorado. But the hell of it was that Mr. Farris would walk up to the porch and say: "Arthur, you got a card from your buddy, Parkhurst."

I wrote a letter to the Postmaster General, but I never mailed it. I thought he ought to know how old Farris was reading the postcards. But I didn't want to be responsible for cutting off old Farris's rations, for his losing his job toting the mail. But I kept the unmailed letter to flaunt it before old Farris or to use it as some kind of blackjack, I guess.

But the cards from Mr. Parkhurst stopped. I imagined all sorts of things, especially when I felt sorry for myself.

Then one day Mr. Farris came up our front walk, wiping sweat off his face, and moaning about his corn and the hot weather. He handed me the "Christian Advocate" and a circular from Sears, or from Sears and Roebuck as everybody called it back then. He looked at me the way a fish might look at an oyster.

"Arthur, I think your buddy, Parkhurst, is dead. I think he dropped dead in Kansas City, or somewhere out yonder."

I lost my temper, and I was spitting salty water when I told him Mr. Parkhurst was my friend, not my dad-burned buddy. I ran around to the back yard and climbed through the coal-shute into the basement.

"Buddy," old Farris said. I can't stand the word today. It's as bad as putting artificial fruit on a growing peach tree. I have to watch myself constantly to keep from being offensive to some innocuous man. Even so, there are many times when I really get irritated when someone says to me, maybe even a friend: "Give me a light, will you, old buddy?" Maybe I've made a fetish of it, but in all the years since I took over Papa's law practice I never let a man sit on the jury if he had the nickname of "buddy" or "pal," or if he combed his hair in public, not that the two are connected.

One day, I don't remember the precise date, I was in this beer joint at Wrightsville Beach, North Carolina, and this old fellow came in and said, to no one and apropos to nothing: "Anybody want to hear old Joe Howard play the piano?"

The unreality that yanked me was greater than it was the night I got home after Mr. Parkhurst and I saw our first "big one." I know it was at least 1940 and I knew that "Hello, My Baby," was written in 1899. But old Joe Howard could knock the plu-perfect hell out of a piano. We got to be friendly, but not buddy-buddy, over some beers, but he was just midly, not more than casually, interested when I told him about Mr. Parkhurst.

Actually, I wondered if this piano-playing old man was Joe Howard, but the papers wrote him up and said he was. And, God Almighty, things happen fast. I got out of law school and into World War II, and then Ruth and I got married after the war, and the two boys came along.

You know what I mean. I do a general practice in the same small town I was born in. Anyway, sometime in the 1950's some neighbors invited Ruth and me to see a special TV show, some extravaganza. (We didn't have a set because everyone said the new models would be so much better. At least, that was good enough excuse.) And who should come dancing out, as big as life and as filled with sass as a jaybird? Old Joe Howard. Everybody thought I was crazy but I laughed too loud to keep the tears from showing, and how the hell could I explain the tears when old Joe Howard sang, "Hello, My Baby," and the other main tunes of his and Mr. Parkhurst's and mine?

Just the other day I was telling my son, who is now in law school, how it was that old Joe Howard wrote the first telephone song, "Hello, My Baby," in 1899, before the car or airplane and how he was still singing in the age of the astronaut. He was born in 1867 and he died in 1962. You can look it up if you like.

I never found out what happened to Mr. Parkhurst. I never see any "big ones" or "little ones" because the depot was moved ten years ago way the hell on the other side of town. I think the old depot was not in keeping with our industrial image. But a few nights ago I heard some TV singer, Dean Martin, I think, sing "Hello, My Baby," and right in our "den" which was Mother's parlor, a really "big one" high-balled through. There were no damned diesels. It took two big locomotives, each with twelve driving wheels to pull 104 box-cars, not counting coal cars and caboose, and there were 27 different kinds, and I noted that an "Orange Blossom Special" had gotten hitched to a red-faced plow-boy called "Laccawanna."

WOMAN GOING TO THE LIBRARY

The murmuring snow's not so exciting
As your white stocking-cap. I think the orange top-knot's
A comet's blazing tail. The red book swinging
In your mittened hand must be some sort of lantern,
And I know your boots crunch the frozen earth
As if it is peanut-brittle.

The wind's mouthy hound, barking fine sleet,
Pressing his huge front paws against your breasts
To provoke a real tussle. By God, I'd join the melee,
Help a lady, but this is a private feud, I know,
And your oscillating hands and feet slice him
Into ribbons of softest down. (I'll just nail
His docile tail to a tree when you move on.)

Now, your bright eyes are sextants, guiding you
And fixing this day in history for all time to come.
I twirl my hand in unseen greeting, and the snow
Freezes my boisterous shout and snaps it as a twig.

But I'm in the right place, at the right time,
And that's what this on-the-spot poem's all about.
Time never runs out, you know, but you and I
Will run out of time, any day now, and out of
Stocking-caps, snowy mornings, and comets' tails, too.

PERPETUAL DRAMA

Man has a thousand signs and tricks by which he tries to read the mind of the weather. The weather is a cat on a pole in the sky, and man is the rustic clairvoyant determining which way the cat will jump and whether this cat will come flailing down, teeth bared and claws whirling, or whether this cat will knock on the door with gentle purrs and ask for a saucer of milk. But many of these grandmothers' tales are singularly accurate.

A red sky at night denotes fair weather, but red at dawning means rain. The same is true of rainbows. The belief is well founded because you see rainbows in the early morning or late afternoon when the low position of the sun is sharply reflected against the clouds. But dew on the lawn precludes rain because dew comes from cloudless and windless skies, usually. A ring around the moon indicates a storm. The ring is really moonlight seen through clouds. High clouds imply rough weather, and the low clouds tell you to fetch your umbrella.

Older farmers say rain is near when a bell or whistle is heard at a distance farther than usual. This saying is reasonable because cloudy skies and humid air push the sound waves back downward and shrill sounds below are bound to carry farther. Old farmers still put stock in the antics of animals. Cows huddle together as a storm makes up, flies swarm in and near the house, and birds fly low.

Pigs are said to squeal in terror at the moon because they have no idea what the moon is, and dogs are said to bay the moon because the dog is lonesome and is trying to arouse a playmate. Some people still hang up serpents to break a severe drought, but most folks find the process too hazardous to prove the point. But if the point is valid, it's too bad all the Chicago gangsters couldn't have been stretched on the palings during Prohibition. If this had happened, there might not have been any necessity for TVA, and the Arizona cow-poke might have to wear hip-boots across the deserts.

But the weather transcends facts and tricks and sayings. It is the author of the little portion man knows of living poetry, breathing history, and personal drama. And if man is but a shadow of the daily weather, a reflection of the personality of bluebell skies or rapacious winds, his attachment to it is so incessant he gets to think of himself as the alter ego of the whole amalgam of suns, moons, and stars.

For, the weather is man's bookmarker, his personal almanac, and his footnote. Whenever man recaptures the past, brings into focus some tender anecdote or some scalding issue, he always sets the stage with the precise nature of the weather on that foreclosed day. And if he is adept at his vocal memoirs, the auditor may turn his imaginary collar against the pile-driving snow, or the auditor may scan the landscape for a water-brook to assuage the gnawing thirst of that festering day when the sun was a pack of mad wolves devouring everything in sight.

In fact, from the intensely human way the teller sets the weather, you may well assume he not only participated in the drama but ordered the weather by telephone and arranged it with his hands when the order was delivered. Thus, the weather is eternally the indelible footnote appended to all local history because it is always in man's face and hair, around his body, and a river in his bloodstream.

The man who doesn't know the weather the day he went to war or graduated from school or went hunting for meadow flowers with his lady-love was, most obviously, singing his song with one tepid lip and dancing his jig with one leg tied behind him.

Perhaps the piano part to the entire piece is that we err when we speak of the "weather man." "Weather men" is more apt, more pertinent. We err again, egregiously, when we speak of good and bad weather. There isn't any such thing as bad weather. It is good weather with various faces, facets, and penchants. It is good weather and hale to the heart and spicy to the soul even when it puts on a Halloween mask and has such a monumental tizzy it falls flat on its face, in the middle of the fit, and leaves a calling card in the guise of a mud puddle.

LIGHT OF A SMALL WORLD

On snowy evenings
When John Turner swings his lantern from barn to house,
The whole night, and one end of town, sparkle in his arc.
Grass stubbble — strings of pearls, or Indian rope tricks, —
Rise up, stare until blinded, draw back into deep-freeze again.
Stones jump, as flying-fish, then swim into passing darkness.
Under the light his legs are twin oaks, barked with corduroy,
And whistling a medley on a Jews'-harp. Above the light
Only his huge moustache, white with years and snow, is
    visible,
But I have learned by heart those deep trenches that love and
    laughter
Left on his face for anodynes for the world's divisive
    treachery.
At the stile he waves the lantern high, but I really can't tell
If he's playing "through-freight" or Old North Church.
Still on the Stile, he twirls an aurora borealis as he calls
His blue-tick hound from foraging, just as God Almighty
Might call a favorite saint for the pleasure of his company.

Where the back lot rolls and tumbles, I thought John Turner
Was a sinking ship, using corduroy for an S.O.S. But now
Along the level ground his smoothly swinging lantern
Has all the trees playing leap-frog over his shoulders.
Near the kitchen door the whole white sky dances on his flame,
As if he'd caught every moth ever bred in creation.
Suddenly, whistling britches put down their music-makers
And all the light in the world goes out. But John Turner's
    there,
All right, and I think he must have broken half the ribs in
    town

When he stomped snow from his boots.
Now, he gives the night to the night, sky to sky, tree to tree:
Milking's done and stock is fed. The kitchen door slams
As if a multi-volumned epic is closing, but I know those places
On his face that care, with all of her insufferable vanity,
Thinks she etched to show her exacting art work, — those
    places
That blue tick hound and I know love and laughter
Left as lovely talismans for a thousand embattled tomorrows.

ALL THE PRETTY LITTLE HORSES

It was getting colder by the minute. No, by God, it was getting colder by the second, by the split second. Doc Henley's hands were still inside his big mittens, stiff even down in that wonderfully thick, heavy, soft wool.

His fingers were strangers inside his mittens, and they were connected to the rest of him the way a caboose one can't see is connected to the car ahead. Even so, he ran his right hand into the side pocket of his big fur-lined jacket. His hand touched, but didn't feel, the package of cigarettes down there. It was like fishing through a hole in the ice. But, then, what the hell. He'd never get a cigarette lighted, not in this wind and in this combination of sleet and thin snow that fell with the downy beauty of a white angel but scratched and tore with the constant harassment of a terrified cat.

He'd have been better off to have left the horse at Tom Grice's store. The slightest movement jarred all the way to his shoulders, and his feet, in his hunting boots, were frozen, sullen anvils dragging heavily down in the stirrups. The woods were lonely and deep, with the gloomiest chill, and not at all like those woods that Robert Frost wrote about in the poem. And this horse was too cold to give his harness bells a shake to ask questions, if he had any harness bells.

He was lost. They were lost. Maybe all trees look alike in the darkness but he was certain he had already passed this spot, ten minutes ago, perhaps, longer back than that. He ought to have walked up the six miles from Tom Grice's store. The horse wasn't even good company. They were lost. It was that simple, or it was that preposterous, or it was that dangerous. His breath came shorter and he felt himself flush. A drop of desperate sweat dabbed his forehead and then it froze.

59

Some idiot had written a poem, away back when Doc Henley was a boy, or he had first read it then, about going to grandma's on Thanksgiving Day. "The horse knows the way/To carry the sleigh/Across the something and drifted snow." Well, this one didn't know its smoking nostrils from a hansom cab. But, then, people don't freeze to death as others walk around the world on some missile's magic apron strings.

No, he couldn't get lost, not really lost, or freeze or die of exposure, not when other men were preparing to go to the moon. That wasn't merely anachronistic. It was outrageous, incredible.

He clucked to the horse. If he didn't get to the store by closing up time, Tom Grice would gather his neighbors and come looking. He whistled to the horse and the shrill echo seemed to freeze in space. Maybe the echo was hanging on the tree as an icicle. But as Doc Henley thought about the frozen whistle, the horse bolted. There was a collision. Doc Henley's head and the right side of his face were banged, cut, and scratched. He saw the twin trees the horse had struck. He saw them over his shoulder, as he dragged the ground, yanking his foot from the stirrup. For a minute he was too stunned to chase the horse.

The whole thing was completely unreal. He really wasn't out here in this interminable maze called Settle's Woods. No, because things like this really don't happen except with face-less people, in nameless places, in random news stories in the papers.

In a minute the crazy stars would stop blinking and the bloody, salty taste in his mouth would vanish. He'd take a drink of that fine local brandy, from the pint that Tom Grice gave him at the store. He slapped around his pockets. Then he remembered. The bottle was in his bag, and the bag was tied to the saddle.

But nothing was broken about him, insofar as he could tell. He stumbled on a few steps, the fine snow, interlaced with sleet, tapping his face as if someone were playing pool with tiny balls. Where to now? Quo vadis? To the path, obviously, and then to the big road, and then to the car, and then to grandmother's house for Thanksgiving. Well, to Helen, his wife, for Thanksgiving.

She had protested this call to Settle's Woods, to Rassy Lance's, when he had telephoned her. She had even baited him with premature mistletoe and the bait was warm and seductive, although the mistletoe was hung only in fantasy. She had fixed all the things he liked especially. They'd start with the hot drinks. And then there would be the candles, and the oyster soup, the two year old ham, the tiny green peas cooked with the small white potatoes, just the way he liked them, the tipsy cake and the coffee and the brandy.

And then the two of them.

She had almost screamed: "Well, let him die if he wants to die."

When Tom Grice had called, Doc Henley knew something like that had happened. He'd already been to jail to see Rassy Lance when they had locked him up for raising hell in the pool room. Rassy's head was more than a mess where it had collided with the glass cigar counter and he had told Doc Henley: "Ain't no use to sew her up, Doc. I ain't fit to live." And in slow, broken stages Doc Henley had learned how Rassy had blown the fifteen dollars for his daughter's "school piece saying dress," but he hadn't meant to at all.

So, Rassy couldn't go home. Not quite all the way. He was in the clearing, a quarter of a mile from home, when his wife found him. She had walked to the store and Tom Grice had called Doc Henley, even if they were pretty sure Rassy was dead. The way Rassy lay in the fine snow and sleet he looked, to Doc Henley, like one of the World War II Japs in the repose of ceremonial suicide, with the big blade of his big knife so far into his heart Doc Henley had to put his foot on the body to pull out the knife.

So, what was his present mission? To call the undertaker in town. That was it.

As he stumbled along in the icy darkness he started to reproach himself for bailing Rassy out of jail. But that was no damned good. The man couldn't ever go home again, if not precisely the same way Tom Wolfe meant it.

His foot knocked down a stick that had been leaning against a tree. There was no sense of contact, and he imagined the impact was about equal to that between a butterfly that is barely wheeling and a big cone of cotton candy. He seized the stick in his right mitten, rather than in his right hand. It was at least a yard long, and it had been peeled. Now the snow stuck to it as if someone had grated tiny bits of coconut.

He felt a little better with this stick in his mitten, although it reminded him of an Englishman he had seen in the big war who raised an umbrella above a lady he was helping to an air-raid shelter, during a real block-buster of a night-time raid.

But Dr. Henley was not quite so alone, and he also had something to part the crusty bushes, to jab at the frozen jungle, to strike at the silvery silence that seemed as ominous as death.

Some kid must have used the stick for a horse back when October, the old gypsy-man, was in these woods looking for James grapes and scaly-barks. But the kid wasn't a wise or prudent master, to leave his noble steed out in such weather. For, the snow was piling up now, soundlessly, but piling up steadily as it measured its growth against the trees and bushes.

Good God. The snow was a third of the way up the stick, at the slight slant with which Doc Henley carried it, Or, to be more precise, the snow was well up to the stick horse's knees.

But the snow certainly wasn't any shock-absorber. No sir, even if it looked to be bridal lace with diamond sequins. His feet might be pieces of wood falling with haphazard stodgi-ness on acres of white powder puffs, but each step shot off a perceptible jar that raced like a short-circuit all the way to his aching shoulders.

Well, he might be able to work a miracle, even without his bag of magic potions, and ride the stick horse to Tom Grice's store. One thing was sure. He used to be able to go from Camelot to Tripoli on any number of stick horses. Indeed, his big problem back then wasn't riding to the Crusades or with Jeb Stuart around McClellan's army. It was getting the precise name for each horse, one that wasn't too fancy or fanciful, but one that wasn't something as phlegmatic as Pal, or King, or Big Boy, or Champ.

And, of course, the complete biography of a spiritual oaf was revealed if a boy named a horse Tony, after Tom Mix's movie horse, and the ones who named their horses Traveller or Little Sorrell showed extraordinary want of imagination, as well as poor taste.

He stopped and made a meaningless outline in the snow. . . . Sometimes the calloused world of downtown could play hell with loving intention. . . . He once had a fine pleasure horse named Rex. Good old Rex. He and Rex had taken many hedges and gullies and they had played "dancing horse" in many luscious mud puddles before Doc Henley, or rather young Logan Henley, had seen the sign in front of the new Rexall Drug Store downtown.

His stable usually held work, fire, pleasure, and show horses. A fairly pliable tobacco stick made an excellent steeple-chaser, and a matched pair of bluff, brown broom handles could pull the whole end of town. He remembered how he usually bored holes in the top ends of pleasure horses, show horses, and cavalry mounts for places for bridles. Of course, some fool or low-down shanty boy might say that the exquisite bridle was nothing but two or three shoelaces tied together, or some raveled suspenders straightened out to a single length.

But spit fire and save matches. The same trash, well-to-do,

or poor-trash, would just as soon ride an iron picket and try to palm it off as a horse. And no matter what they rode, they'd just as soon leave a horse in the gutter as tied under a shade tree. And, they never curried their horses with their papa's old hair brushes, and they never used a discarded but vividly striped shirt for a saddle blanket. And they left their horses outdoors, in all sorts of weather, the same as this kid had left this one to gain whatever succor there was from the bark of a tree.

Not to use fancy trappings was as poor business as it was indecent. Any fool knew ornate trappings were important at horse-trading time, when many boys met in an alley or in a back lot. Of course, every trader knew the poem that said, "You can notch it on the paling/That it's not a wise plan,/To make up your judgment by the clothing on a man/For if you will remember you will often come across/A forty dollar saddle on a twenty dollar horse."

Now the drifts were above Doc Henley's knees. Without realizing it, he saw that he had been carrying the stick almost as if it were a bride across a snowy threshold. There was a hole in the roof of the forest, but it was a bay window that didn't give any view, a bay window all frosted over. He turned the stick in his mitten, two or three times. He'd better do the magic trick, in a hurry. P.D.Q.

Sometimes when Doc Henley and the other boys had traded horses they wore their fathers' or grandfathers' old jim-swinger coats and plug hats. If tobacco made them sick, they crimped up baking chocolate and crammed it in their jaws. And after a while the ground around was stained as if grown men had been chewing tobacco or hulling walnuts.

Suddenly it occurred to him that the damned horse he so foolishly rode to Rassy Lance's might be at Tom Grice's store by now. And any minute now, Doc Henley would see lanterns blazing through the wilderness. The whole place would be a Christmas tree, and the gift would be life and the pursuit of much happiness later on that night with Helen.

The thought quickened his pace, but his breathing became harder. From somewhere he reached back for something to hang on to and he remembered the best thing to do when you are lost is to let the searchers find you. Well, he'd keep that in mind, even if he was not lost.

He usually rode his mounts in regular rotation so as not to show partiality. After all, horses had feelings, too, just as doctors do when some ungrateful bastard calls another doctor. Hell's bells. Everybody knew horses were peevish and despondent if another one was given preferential treatment. And all were cared for with equal diligence and affection. Hell, Logan remembered how he grazed his horses in high sweet grass, poured water into battered pie trays and flower pots, and cut various types of fodder. Once he even spent his Saturday allowance on his horses, the whole quarter, to buy shelled corn from an old Negro man.

He missed the serial, the funny picture, and the popcorn and soda pop, and he didn't even have an extra nickel left for Sunday school the next day.

He stopped a second and smote the stick in the air. His grandmother had said he was a foolish boy who didn't know the value of money. But now, in the deep woods, salty tears came slowly, to freeze quickly, as he recalled how his father had patted his head and his shoulders, had given him a whole row of corn in the vegetable garden, and had told him to read a lot of poetry but to try not to drink too much whiskey when he got grown.

Some horses had to die because some got old and others were cracked up in ugly spills, among the rocks and gullies. When a horse broke its leg, his master shot it with a wooden pistol but never with a cap or water pistol. Then he buried his beautiful friend, but never with mock solemnity, even though he knew it was a piece of wood.

By now he was too tired and too cold to look for Tom

Grice's store. The best thing to do was to sit against this oak tree and wait until all the lanterns made a Christmas tree of the wilderness. He would sit and he could slap his mittens against his sides and his shanks for warmth, and, maybe, after a while he could supple up his hands and light a cigarette. He'd light a cigarette and draw deeply and light another off that one and on and on until Tom Grice and the boys took him home to Helen and to whatever was left of Thanksgiving.

NOR CUSTOM SALE

"Good God Miss Agnes, did I have a girl the summer
John Turner sliced melons in the moonlight, and that
   jazz band
Came all the way from Rocky Mount. Did I have a girl?
I could have put her on my battercake, or in my coffee;
Lots of mints at the church bazaar weren't half so sweet.
You know, pretty from the ground up, but immaterial
As dewdrops, yet all the swift and lilting graces
Of a fawn racing a star. Why, every single time
Her hands took me, heaven was melted butter.

"You say you remember her, remember that Stella
With the movie star breasts and Miss America legs
Who made the oldest men charge as bridegrooms,
Even when they were sitting down?

". . . Actually, her name was Hazel, not much straighter
Than a stick, with breasts no bigger than Christmas oranges,
But her laughter was a water-fall and every breath
An act of love. My heart was a motor-boat
That Hazel-summer and I burned all over
With such a hard, gem-like flame
She could have used me to open a vault."

K-K-K-Katy

Joe was reading on the back porch and Katy was putting some oddments of wet laundry on the line in the backyard. Joe saw her clearly, became wholly aware of her presence, when he placed his book in his lap and used both hands to put tobacco in his pipe and to light it.

He drew rapidly on the stem, putting the penny match box atop the bowl to intensify the glow and to scatter it uniformly in the caked wood. The stem made a slight whistling sound, like a tea kettle. For a minute he pulled hard at the stem, in quick puffs. Now the stem was clenched in his teeth, and his face was as wreathed with smoke as an old locomotive getting up a full head of steam. He inhaled deeply, two or three times, removed the stem from his mouth, and exhaled a line of aromatic blue circles. He sat for another minute or two alternately sending out fast choppy blue waves and deep single files of exhaled smoke. Maybe, Joe thought, he could send Katy some smoke signals.

Now his jacket and his shirt smelled of tobacco smoke. He used his nose as a highly inquisitive bird dog, sniffing all around. By golly, it smelled good, pipe tobacco did. There was nothing like it. From the beginning Katy liked to sit in Joe's lap and say to him: "Blow some on me, Joe. Blow some my way, Joe."

He noticed that Mildred Austin, who lived next door, was putting up clothes on her side of the hedge. Apparently, the two women were talking about a panel group their church circle had just had. Joe wasn't getting all of it, but the gist of it wafted up to the back porch. He'd go out and help Katy, if Mildred Austin weren't out there. But she would spoil it for Joe. Any third person would spoil it for Joe. But Mildred would especially.

But Katy might be right. Joe might be unfair, the way he referred to Mildred as "Mrs. Jesus" and the "book-burner." And it might be downright libelous for him to tell Katy that Mildred's walk was her whole approach to life, that she walked as if she had a fresh hen egg stuck up her butt and she was terrified she might break the egg with a slightly indecorous motion.

Usually Katy did the talking when they were around Mildred. But the other night when he and Katy were extolling Bishop · Pike, Mildred was lambasting him, and saying, with inexorable finality: "Well, the man simply isn't a good Episcopalian." And Joe said: "Neither was the founder of your religion." And Mildred asked: "Who do you mean? Henry the eighth?" And Joe had said: "Jesus."

Now Mildred was speaking a little louder. She was saying it was up to the better element, to the church people and the P.T.A., to do something about all the terrible carryings-on the high school kids were doing, and about all those pregnancies, pot, drugs.

Katy didn't answer. She had a clothes-pin in her mouth. She stood so high on the balls of her toes Joe thought she would step out of her delapidated old brown loafers.

The wind came running in the yard as a lonesome hound barking ever so often to let the neighborhood know he was around. Now it sent a gust to plaster Katy's cotton dress against her body for a few seconds. The wind made the thin dress look as if it were a living part of Katy's torso, legs, and behind. As she reached to put the clothes-pins onto things on the line, her tail did a little impromptu ocean roll.

In reaching up she would lift first one brown leg and then the other, and Joe thought of a gloriously brown little human mule pawing and bucking gently. The shaggy dog of a wind was romping a little through her red hair, the hair that Joe called his sweet-betsy bush when they were alone. But, then again, she was red all over, like a book, was the corny way he always joshed her. She was a little field of strawberries, with sun spots for freckles.

When they had first met, sixteen years before, Katy had prayed that her freckles would go away. Joe said he could make them go away. He could remove them with a broom straw. He would count the freckles, the way old Mrs. Montague counted warts on children's hands with a broom straw and said special words to make them leave.

Joe would tell Katy that at night, but the next day the freckles would be right back. She would accuse him, almost with anger, of being a fraud, a sort of snake-doctor, but he always said he brought the freckles back. Joe told her that without the freckles she'd be a bird without wings, or the sea without waves or salt.

Now she was bending over the basket of wet things. Her breasts weren't pin-ups but Joe knew they were there, all right enough. When he first fell in love with Katy she was terribly self-conscious about her small breasts. Of course, they weren't all that small, but she probably wanted to stick out like Betty Grable and Virginia Mayo.

They'd had this date, and when they had been parked a while, Joe had pulled out all of this jammed up toilet tissue, although he didn't know what it was at first. If Katy had been a cat on a hot stove she wouldn't have jumped any higher, nor have gone into as many weird gyrations.

Joe knew all about falsies, but he had never heard of anyone using toilet tissue. Katy explained, between anguished, outraged sobs — now he recalled her precise, almost incongruously sweet explanation — that she wasn't "overly endowed." She had been in such a flutter she had forgotten to put in anything until Joe was already in her mother's house. So, she had made do, hastily, with the toilet tissue.

Joe kissed away Katy's tears. He kissed and loved away that violent embarrassment that made her normal astonishing redness as vivid in the moonlight as a ball of fire. And he kissed away her horrible remorse when she was heaving but not crying.

He told her that little ones feel just as good as big ones, and after a while when Katy was a red top purring in the moonlight he told her: "Anything more than a handful or a mouthful is wasted."

He showed her, again and again, and gently, deeply, and fully and he explained: "Anything else is sheer waste, sweetie." Later on that night he had confessed how he had almost automatically emulated the tongue-tied, rural swain in the old song, how he had almost exclaimed "K-K-K-Katy" when his fingers went in for flesh and for rose buds and came out with toilet tissue.

Ever since then, in all the years that flew as hungry birds, they had always said, whether it was tomatoes, potatoes, onions, apples, or even watermelons: "Well, little ones are just as good."

His pipe wasn't a corpse, but it needed reviving. He struck a match and lighted it all around, down in the bowl where it had burned to, again putting the match box atop the bowl. The way the smoke seeped out and under the match box made Joe think of the old chant:

Doodle-bug, doodle-bug, come from your hole,
Your house is on fire and your chillun will burn.

The first time they undressed to go swimming naked, one summer night, Joe's throat was as dry as a banker's moral lectures, despite all his contrived savior faire. If he was Don Juan on the outside, he was Henny-Penny on the inside, and several skies were falling and somersaulting inside him.

Maybe, Katy was nervous and ill-at-ease, too. She had gone into the water just before Joe dived in. She wore only a white bathing cap, and Joe thought of Katy as a glorious, animated water-lily cutting the still water into silvery remnants.

When he dived in after her the water was a ton of cold, wet steel striking his loins and snapping his breath, and he had yelled, "K-K-K-Katy" and he wasn't thinking about the old song, either.

Then he fell into the "K-K-K-Katy" habit when they were alone and he was excited or pleased, or when he professed shock at something she did. One night he even called for her at the kitchen door, and her mother thought him more foolish and useless than ever. But Katy merely took his hand in the darkness of the back porch. She didn't try to explain to her mother that Joe was acting out the old song, the part that says:

"When the m-m-m-moon shines, over the c-c-c-cow shed,

I'll be waiting at the k-k-k-kitchen door."

Now Katy was looking at the stuff on the line and scratching the back of her left leg with her right bare toes. She slipped her right foot back into the loafer and repeated the scratching process with the left toes on the right leg. Mildred Austin was whispering, but Joe could hear her bruiting some high school kid's name around, now and then.

He looked at Katy and at the clothes-line. His fishing and puttering around coveralls, a little fat with the breeze, were Humpty-Dumpty leaning precariously from a wire wall, and near the coveralls one of Katy's yellow linen dresses was sweet sixteen and never been kissed. Two bras were swinging at a lively gait. These things had been unmentionables long ago, Joe had heard, and people didn't put them on the line in the daytime. Now they were as brash as women's libbers and Joe expected each to light a cigarette. One of Katy's shopworn, or bed-worn, pale blue nighties was Sweet Little Alice Blue Gown, in need of tonic or something for iron-poor blood, perhaps. He saw a pair of his darned socks trying hard to put their best feet forward, and a couple of his drip-dry shirts looked as if they had just been converted at a revival at the river.

Now the wind was tumbling in from the sunny south as a loud-mouthed bully. But Joe knew the wind was really more

Dennis the Menace. He was trying hard to shake the clothing down, as apples from a tree, but failing in his design, he tossed a handful of sand on the clothes, probably just to say that he had been to the moon, to Mars, and to Venus when Copernicus was in the equivalent of rubber pants.

He looked at Katy and the wind was up and inside her skirt. Joe started to say, "Down, boy," but the wind was like a pigeon that flies into a building and goes in every direction wildly trying to get out again. Katy bent to her basket of clothing and Joe thought of a snatch of a song he knew once. It was what they called "low-down" music. He could remember just two lines: "The lady stooped down to tie her shoe/And the wind blew up the avenue."

Mildred Austin was motioning Katy to that foot stile across the hedge that really didn't run but one way. Joe guessed they were sunning a little. Katy had her thighs exposed, knees drawn up, almost under her chin, but Joe could see them clearly, and he could see a little farther up, too. He knew knees are supposed to be unattractive, but he wondered if much of this feeling didn't come from mothers who got their daughters into the habit of yanking at their skirts?

It must have been the skirts, before the shorter ones, that made women self-conscious. Certainly, women in shorts didn't seem to be self-conscious about their damned knees. So it was probably all a question of some mother's long finger pointing accusingly down the years.

Well, to hell with it. Joe liked Katy's knees. If he had the talent he might write a poem or do some kind of drawing of Katy's knees, not just any knees but Katy's, and what they meant to him, and how they looked and felt.

Some big writer — it must have been Hemingway — went into orbit about the unadorned poetry in some matador's thigh bone sticking through his tight pants and flesh. Joe was certain he would much prefer to write or draw Katy's knees as they were when they were drawn up so expectantly to receive him. And they would make a rare anatomy or art lesson cocked around his back in that way that was, simultaneously, so tender, so lethal, so wild, so wonderful, and so deathless. Hell, Katy's knees were even good to the touch on a cold night when she was all drawn up, cat-like, for warmth, with them against his back or his belly.

Well, it was a damned fine marriage. He was glad of many things. For one thing he was glad it was Saturday. In a few minutes Katy would come in and they would have a sandwich. Then she'd say they both needed a long nap. "Why, K-K-K-Katy," Joe would say, as he called her a brazen red-headed cat. Just the same he'd beat her to bed.

Joe was always grateful for the faceless challenge, for the boy whom he never saw or knew, the one who was first, the one whom Katy loved so intensely before she met him. Joe didn't think she thought about the first fellow often, or anyone else much, for that matter. But he always had to excel because he couldn't be happy unless she was pleased. Of course, he was probably really more experienced than Katy, at the beginning, but he guessed a little experience went farther with a girl, certainly mechanically, than it did with a boy.

It had all been wonderful, even Joe's initial fumbling and trumped-up bravado. And he had felt as relieved as he was happy when Katy had told him she was pregnant. Of course, the old lady, her mother, had raised holy hell, and Joe had backed her into a corner: "Can't you get it through your head I don't have to marry Katy? Jesus Christ. There's nobody else I ever wanted to marry."

It turned out to be a false alarm. Katy told him he was free, absolutely free, and he told her: "I am free only with you, K-K-K-Katy." The strange thing was that it took them two years of marriage for Katy to get pregnant. Of course, Joe had patched it up with the old lady, at least superficially,

74

for Katy's sake. In fact, the old lady telephoned regularly to see if there was anything she could do for Katherine, for little Katherine, and for Joseph.

VISITOR IN TOWN

The winter rain comes up the alley
Between Cousin Hattie's and the old Simpson place.
His hat is down and his collar is up
And he stands there marking time in puddles,
Waiting for the weatherman's instructions, or perhaps
To test the postman's intrepid boast.

Then he goes down Cousin Hattie's hair-lipped hill,
Stiff-legged on icy stilts. But our neighborhood
Is fast asleep and all we hear outside
Is only water making violin strings
Of shorn and leafless limbs.

But I can see him doubling back to press
His wet face against Cousin Hattie's kitchen window
For a handout. But the old lady isn't stirring
And the rain skitters up her solemn clapboards
And he rolls and dances on her tin roof
To sound as if two skeletons are making love —
A shocking thing for him to do to her
But one likely to get a lonely widow's attention.

The mail-order-bride courtship has almost run out of ink amid modern communication systems, but yesterday many men "wrote for" soulmates. Some men knew the galling loneliness of the anonymous tenement life, and others were captives of the desperate loneliness of frontier isolation. H.C. Bunner's classic, *The Love-Letters of Smith*, still evokes the pathos and the ludicrous banalities of the man snowed under by concrete.

The letters of most of the swains ran from the stiff timidity of "Dear Madam, I take my pen in hand," to purling vistas of an abundant life for two, or more. There was a noble eloquence in the halting, misshapen grammar and spelling of some Lochinvars. Others had friends to make functional corrections, and a few copied off grandiose love poems or thundering declarations. Such a courtier was O. Henry's miner who stumbled over a battered copy of the *Rubaiyat* and copied off the celebrated lines:

"A book of verses underneath a bough,
A loaf of bread, a jug of wine, and thou."

But the response of the honoree, a testy widow, was not in measure with the idealism of Old Omar and the miner. She wrote back: "You can have your scandalous picnics by yourself."

It's too bad that Robert Graves, then about five years old, hadn't had a chance to explain that bread is a symbol for wisdom in Arabic, that wine symbolizes ecstasy. Thus, the miner's beloved box-holder couldn't know Omar-Edward Fitzgerald were extending an invitation to a reverent sacrament and not to be an uninhibited bash.

O. Henry probably knew the distinction, although he has been put down by two generations who haven't read his stories. But in today's society, putting down someone whom we haven't read is almost as fashionable as praising those who are so convoluted or dense we don't understand a page they write. If O. Henry was hardly the creative paragon some of his contemporaries said he was, he is much better than today's ice-watery pedants say he is.

SPUR LINE

Addendum

The old woman who lived in the shoe
Came too early for birth-control pills,
And by the singular nature of her habitat
She defied the primitive equivalent of urban-renewal.

Tom, Tom, the Piper's production of love's labors lost,
Wasn't in enough ever to become a drop-out,
And he remains juvenile delinquency in fervent motion,
A thing of consternation to psychiatric therapy,
If a fleet boon to existentialistic novelists.

Little Boy Blue took a cowardly powder.
The haystack was Nirvana with nettle-rash,
Besides which, his horn wasn't blue at all
But rather more Lawrence Welk than Louis Armstrong.

Peter Piper, the pickle picking peon,
Was labor mercilessly exploited, and Sirs,
Even to mumble about a sheep with black wool,
With or without baa's, is heinous symbolism,
And Little Jack Horner, good God Almighty,
What fearful addiction, what personality flaw,
Sent the kid to the Siberia of that odd corner?
And if Humpty-Dumpty wasn't Isaac Newton's precursor,
It never rains in Indianapolis.

THURSDAY MORNING

You should have seen Thursday morning
Swimming that pale blue lake of dawning.
Then the way he came roller-coasting down,
Slinging coppers to green-smocked urchins,
Was Midas without the bad gimmick.

I can almost swear he had a rose in his teeth
When he took the Roundtree's paling fence,
And somersaulted through those yellow tulips
Singing a song about a medicine show man
Who succumbed to his own magic elixir.

When I was about ten years old I knew a boy who was an off-beat. Everybody called him "Huck Finn" and said he lived in Robin Hood's barn. (That meant that the whole sky was his roof.)

He came to school and Sunday school when it amused him or when forced inside by rough weather. He came to Sunday school one summer day, and our teacher said: "Our lesson is about Ruth. Who can tell us anything about Ruth?"

Huck Finn raised his hand. The teacher camouflaged her surprise, the best she could, and said: "What do you know about Ruth, Huck?" "Well, I know he hit sixty home runs last season."

Everybody laughed but I thought it was a good, honest answer. Another time, at the grammar school, our health doctor was talking about all the good men who discovered such bad things. Everyone felt the way the lepers looked in the health posters. The old doctor was telling about a great man named John Morgan, Surgeon-General under George

Washington, and how this Dr. Morgan had discovered puss. Huck said, to no one specifically, "How in the hell could he miss it?" ("Avoid is a better word than "miss," but I am being accurate, and Huck may not have known "avoid.")

Huck, our local Huck, could talk to the little creatures better than he could talk to folks. He was always telling me what some bird or rabbit told him. And the days of the week were proper personalities to him. He said Monday was a woman (he called it "umun") with the eppezudicks. Saturday was a drunk fool and Sunday a girl with the dropsies. Thursday was the equivalent of today's gladsome swinger. So, the poem is Huck's or Huck is the poem.

NOTE

I wrote "Mr. Pussy" before 007 or any of his swinging girl friends came along. An English professor, who has a national reputation, told me: "Your story carries on, quite successfully, three satires, simultaneously." My smile was as buoyant as young Master Keat's soul was the day he first saw Chapman's *Homer*, but I still wonder what these satires are?

For whatever it's worth, I didn't think of Robert Browning's "Pied Piper" until I was half-way through writing "Mr. Pussy." What I am trying to suggest is the fulsome story-teller, who, after infinite palaver, approaches a dramatic crescendo, and then, inexplicably, cuts, bolts and runs. That's what I had in my mind, along with some fun.

Mr. Pussy

This is a tale I've heard told in Oxford, North Carolina, my hometown, a thousand times or more. Some of the people who told this tale were straight along and all right, from the ground up. Some others who swore by this tale swore, also, that the world was flat, or otherwise, eggs would fall out of the nest during the night. Several Sunday school teachers swore the tale was so, but so did many of the ones who voted three times for William Jennings Bryan, and I don't mean in three different Presidential elections.

Mr. Pussy was a drummer, a traveling man. His card introduced him as a "Rodent Exterminator." Despite the grandiose language on the card, the word trickled around from county to county that Mr. Pussy was a cracker-jack rat-killer.

The people who are alleged to have seen him in the flesh said he always wore the dark suits and string ties that used to be associated with undertakers. He wore an enormous black felt hat and a ruffled white shirt. He had a black moustache and long black sideburns, and his eyes were said to be so powerful that they could shine on still waters with the eerie clarity of two stars afflicted with a sullen squint.

Sometimes, when I heard the old-timers describe Mr. Pussy, I thought of Edgar Allan Poe. Later on, as I remembered these descriptions, I thought of Paladin, the soft-talking gun-slinger who used to shoot-up the parlor from television once a week. (Maybe this was because both men handed out such singular business cards.)

Mr. Pussy always came to town alone, whereas the other drummers usually traveled together. The other drummers rode the same train, and when they got to town they clipped in together for a hired hack to make their rounds of the rural stores, after they had called on the merchants in town.

Mr. Pussy carried a sample case, the same as the other drummers. His sample case was a big box, a sort of leather hat-box contraption, with several holes bored in the top. If an uncontrollable epidemic of rats raged in a community, Mr. Pussy might take his sample case and his business card to the town commissioners. The commissioners would hire Mr. Pussy the way health officers are hired today. But most of the time he called on merchants whose stores were over-run by rats or on large farmers whose crops were ravaged by rats. He would offer to do an exterminating job at so much per dead rat head, or he would guarantee to clean out a big store or a big corn crib at a flat rate.

Mr. Pussy always had a newspaper clipping down in his inside coat pocket that told how he had wiped out the rats in an entire country, in some little country down in Latin, or Central, or South America, somewhere down that way. He also had a gold medal which he wore from a velvet ribbon around his neck. The newspaper clipping said that some president or king, or whatever kind of ruler the country had,

82

gave Mr. Pussy the gold medal for killing all the nation's rats. This medal had some kind of fancy inscription. Some of the local people said the inscription was in Latin and some said it was in French, and I think that one old man said it was in Greek. The local Sunday school teachers said it was Latin, that it came, free, at the Philadelphia centennial of 1876. But the three-time losers, the Bryan folks, said, No, by God, it was in Spanish and that the ruler down yonder had it made up for Mr. Pussy especially. The straight along and all right folks said, "O foot," that you could have clippings or medals made up anywhere, but the flat-worlders denounced that as an infernal lie. They yelled: "O, yeah. Unca Sam would put your francis in the Federal pen for counterfeiting."

Because of the nature of his work Mr. Pussy didn't adhere to a regular schedule the way the other drummers did. No. You'd look up one day and he'd be standing there in front of the Confederate monument. He would roll a cigarette with one hand, against the breeze, and he must have had a startling resemblance to a black apparition, or to a gunfighter, as he stood there soundlessly in the shadow of the monument to the dead.

When he made his first step he twirled his big sample case the same paralyzing way a hired gun fingers his holster. And then, like a consecrated hawk to its prey, he'd swoop down on the place at which he had business. He'd put his sample case on the merchant's counter, and display his merchandise the same as the ones who sold snuff, or rubber boots, or lamp-chimneys. He had two samples, and both had collars and tiny chains.

Sample number one was Goliath, a huge yellow tom cat with whiskers as sharp and as sturdy as well-honed nails. When Goliath reared on his mighty hind legs, smote his broad chest with his front paws, and gave his lion's roar, all the customers and loafers broke for the sidewalk. Goliath was the lethal quintessence of King Kong. Instead of purring, Goliath rasped the way tremendous chains rattle, the way a hurricane rasps and snorts.

Lucretia, the other sample, was blacker than all the pits and all the starless nights combined. She was small, but according to all the old-timers, the Bryans as well as the straight alongers, she could do three back flips without touching ground. It was even said that she had been trained for her profession on flying squirrels. Fast and deadly as evil, she could draw herself into a diabolically deceptive ball no bigger than a baby's mitten. Then, with terrible suddenness, she'd strike with the swift accuracy of an arrow.

There, you have the picture: Goliath, the broadsword, and Lucretia, the dagger up the sleeve. One was a brute and the other a winged serpent and each was as deadly as sin in England's grimmest first phases.

After the crowd around the store had quieted down, Mr. Pussy would take a rat from his outside coat pocket. If he was showing off Goliath he would throw the rat the way Mickey Cochrane used to throw to second base. Goliath would spring from the top of the counter, plowing ahead with the force of a Coast Guard cutter. A chair was less than a paper hurdle. Goliath hit it, knocked it to one side, and stormed on without even checking his prodigious stride.

If Mr. Pussy was sampling Lucretia, he would toss the rat as high as the ceiling, and often he would walk outside the store and toss the rat as high as a lamp-post. Then Lucretia erupted angrily as a mean geyser. Usually she met the rat when it was half-way down to the earth. Some old-timers say that Lucretia had the amazing grace of Hal Chase. Many compared her to Tris Speaker when the old Grey Eagle actually outran fly balls. Perhaps, Joe DiMaggio is the most suitable parallel in modern baseball.

After these brief exhibitions, Mr. Pussy always came straight to a contract, to the big hit. He worked it two ways: he would clean up a town better than Matt Dillon and move on. Or, merchants and farmers could order so many Goliaths or Lucretias, and Mr. Pussy's cat farm would fill the orders, by railway express.

The fee was larger, naturally, if Mr. Pussy took charge in person. That was fair, and all agreed that it was meet. The customer not only had the benefit of Mr. Pussy's personal supervision, but it was said, also, that his long experience in the business enabled him to smell a rat better than a temperance sister could smell out booze. They said, they all agreed, that Mr. Pussy's smelling genius worked even when he had a heavy head cold.

Now it so happened — sometime after Guiteau killed Garfield but before Czolgolz killed McKinley — Mr. Pussy was called to Oxford, North Carolina, my hometown, by telegram, mind you, to combat an emergency. The rats had taken over the largest store in town. The merchant tried bribery, cajolery, and cheese and traps but nothing worked. Customers were afraid to walk on that side of the street. But as luck would have it, the store burned down to the ground the night before Mr. Pussy and Goliath and Lucretia arrived in Oxford, N.C. After the fire, most of the rats up and down the street took the hint and left town. (It was believed by some that the rats thought malicious arson had occurred, specifically for their own grim benefit. But this was not the case, as was proven legally when the merchant had to go to court to collect from the insurance company.)

Well, Mr. Pussy was mad as if some smart-aleck had sent him a rubber mouse on Christmas Day. He stomped around town for a day or two, vehemently cussing kerosene lamps and faulty flues, and hick towns that favor horse troughs and wells in lieu of hydrants. Just as Mr. Pussy was about to leave town, forever, he swore, an old man from the Shoo Fly section of our county, Mr. Tarapin-Eye Tulgin, sort of bumped into Mr. Pussy in the E Pluribus Unum Saloon, which was one of Oxford's best, if, indeed, not the very best saloon.

They had a drink or two as they chewed the fat and talked about tricks in general. Then Mr. Tarapin-Eye said he had a sporting proposition to make to Mr. Pussy. Mr. Tarapin-Eye smiled foolishly and he rolled his eyes the way a sleepy fish does under a cloud of muddy water. From the way he talked you'd think all his brains were in his jawbone. Mr. Tarapin-Eye said he reckoned Goliath and Lucretia could kill almost any kind of rat.

Sho, sho, he was sho of hit, but before he could go on Mr. Pussy almost slapped his gold medal in Mr. Tarapin-Eye's face. Then Mr. Pussy vowed that in any reasonable time, Goliath and Lucretia could kill all the damned rats in the whole state.

Mr. Tarapin-Eye joshed along, agreeing, with all his 'sho, sho's," and then he said he'd bet Mr. Pussy was a dead-game gambler. He also said he hoped Mr. Pussy was a better gambler than he was because he had lost one plantation trying to fill an inside straight and he had lost another plantation when he finally filled an inside straight.

They had another drink or two, and as they stood there at the bar in the E. Pluribus Unum, Mr. Tarapin-Eye Tulgin made two or three half-witted bets for piddling amounts, for drinks and fifty cents and so on.

I imagine Mr. Pussy thought the old fellow was addlepated, but since the store had burned, I imagine he was glad for the chance at a little change and some free drinks.

By and by, Mr. Tarapin-Eye said how would Mr. Pussy take to this proposition: He had several corn cribs and a big stable that hadn't room for anything but the rats that were in them. Mr. Tarapin-Eye said he knew he was doing a fool stunt, a drunk trick, but he had a special rat, a pet, a sort of heirloom, he'd put up in catch-as-catch-can, fists-and-skull, no-holds barred, head-to-head fight with either one of Mr. Pussy's cats.

Quick as Lucretia going into orbit, Mr. Pussy whipped out some writing paper and wrote down the terms of the bet, in legal fashion, with all the "whereases." In fact, he wrote so fast he broke his pencil twice. The bartender and a goose grease salesman from Emporia, Virginia, were witnesses to the contract. The contract stipulated that if Mr. Tarapin-Eye's rat whipped one cat, then the other cat would exterminate all the rats free of charge. Conversely, if the first cat beat the rat, Mr. Tarapin-Eye would pay Mr. Pussy $100 flat rate, or a penny a head, whichever was the greater sum.

I imagine Mr. Pussy was afraid something might happen to his sucker. Anyway, he ran every step of the way to the depot and got his sample case. He and Mr. Tarapin-Eye got into the farmer's buggy and rode out to the Tulgin farm. The arena was a pit that was used for cock fights ordinarily.

As saturnine as Mr. Pussy was, he almost busted his ruffled shirtfront trying to keep from laughing out loud when Mr. Tarapin-Eye brought out this rat about as big as a day-old biddy. It had a white beard all the way to the ground, a missing ear, one floppy ear, and large cataracts over both eyes. Its breathing was so tortured it was bound to have been born with acute and incurable emphysema.

Of course, Mr. Pussy wanted to know the joke. He said he had never heard of such a damned outrageous hotel bill. Who had ever heard of anything so insultingly preposterous? The very damned idea. Imagine, just imagine, putting one of his noble cats against a rat that was at Roanoke Island when the settlers arrived?

Old man Tarapin-Eye laughed some, too. He pulled a jug down from a shelf in the stable. Both men drank a little, and Mr. Tarapin-Eye said that even if it was looney, why they'd come this far and they might as well have the fight. Mr. Pussy's retort was some sarcastic cuss words as he lifted Lucretia from the sample-box and snapped off the tiny chain.

When Lucretia saw the rat she must have thought Mr. Pussy was crazy or drunk. She shook, shrugged her shoulders, and emitted a deprecatory snarl, but she vaulted upon the aged bit of meat and beard and she toyed with it as if it were some sort of ridiculous hallucination. But when Mr. Pussy snapped his fingers, she snarled a real snarl and made a ferocious pass, albeit, it was executed with the grace of a ballerina.

Suddenly, the rat did a double back-flip, bounced up behind Lucretia, did a sort of soft-shoe along her heaving back, and then ran around her belly, as if it were a clock, and whispered something in her ear.

Lucretia waddled over to a corner of the pit, sat down, crossed her legs demurely, and whimpered for milk. Mr. Tarapin-Eye, always the gracious host, picked up a milk bucket, but before he could reach the cow in the first stall, Mr. Pussy had killed Lucretia with a pitchfork.

Mr. Tarapin-Eye flung a red polka-dotted bandana to the rat, and the rat dabbed at his cataracts. While the rat was dabbing his eyes with the bandana, Mr. Pussy yanked that tremendous Goliath from the hat-box with such force the chain snapped. He kicked Goliath in the rear, and perhaps for the first time in his life, he raised his voice and he screamed: "Kill that damn rat and be quick about it."

When Goliath went across that pit he sounded like old engine number 97 coming down that fatal grade. When the big yellow tom cat missed the rat and ran into the side of the pit the echo kicked up the dust back in Oxford, several miles away. But he was up in a lethal flash, up on his hind legs, and roaring as wildly as a lion with a splinter in his paw and a terrible toothache besides.

Just as Goliath was about to strike, the rat ran up Goliath's stomach and started doing a miniature buck-and-wing. Whereupon, old Goliath toppled over backwards and laughed himself to death. (There was some type of hemorrhage, no doubt, due to the paroxyms of laughter. Albeit, the death certificate, containing the precise cause of death, is not on record in the register of deeds office, if, indeed, there ever was one.)

Although Mr. Tarapin-Eye hitched up the buggy as nicely as you please, Mr. Pussy walked back to Oxford, kicking at stones in the road, and throwing the sample case in the middle of Tar River. For months he walked around town blindly, perpetually in a palsied trance. He was a fruit jar of whiskey turned to talcum water, an anvil turned to jello. He spent his days, nights, and months stumbling around, always groping pathetically in shadows of inner darkness. During a storm, even a small one, he crawled under stores or porches. The only time he ever gritted his teeth and stopped his shaking was when some kind-hearted person would let him drown an ailing cat.

If he so much as saw a rat trap he shook so violently and foamed so wildly at the mouth he had to be given morphine. Finally, he lacked the wit and the will even to seek alms, but compassionate people left trays at their back doors for him. Eventually, he turned more and more to booze and he died one day in an agonizing delirium, screaming that rats were gnawing on his innards.

Well, I guess you want to know what that pursy old rat said to Lucretia?

Old man Tarapin-Eye always just grinned and said if you can't whip 'em don't join 'em, but kill 'em with flattery or tickle 'em to death. And all sides always agreed that he said that his rat was the very same one whose neice was courted by the froggie. Remember the song:
"Froggie went a-courting and he did ride,
Sword and pistol by his side, Um-huh.
He rode up to Miss Mousy's house,
And asked Miss Mousy for to be his spouse, Um-huh.
'Not without Uncle Rat's consent
Would I marry the President,' Um-huh, Um-huh."

Everybody, flat worlders and straight alongers, knew that was a contemptible lie. Everybody denounced old man Tarapin-Eye as a blatherskite.

Can you imagine anyone with the unmitigated temerity to try to pass off as gospel the nutty story of a rat in a song being a real rat, and one that courted a frog? But that was the trouble with those old-timey story tellers. They could stick to the truth for eight innings, but they'd louse it up in the ninth, just as surely as Mr. Pussy made a tragic mistake when he didn't get right back on the train when he learned the store had burned down the night before.

EPITAPH II

You didn't understand, and I couldn't explain
My inviolable privacy was the chill of my bosom,
The eternal January upon my thighs.
God knows I know now
It was better to burn, burn, baby,
To turn to those dormant Northern Lights
That begged and ached for illumination.

But I had given me my word, my pledge,
To privacy, and in a world where all the doors
Were opened and all the telephones were party lines,
Privacy was my chilly passion.
I took this veil when you weren't watching,
But I never really intended a rosary
Of ice cubes. I put my love in trust
And not my trust in love.

The townspeople called me "faithful", "long-suffering,"
To the formal end. True, some thought me naive,
    unsuspecting.
But now I confess, where there's no one to hear,
I wished I were the other woman everytime.
I cheered you, you and them,
But the price of icy privacy was too great
For any surrendering, even on honorable terms.

ITEM

The two British psychiatrists who say that George III wasn't crazy but had a metabolic disorder, have the most sensational scoop since an Australian physician revealed that Joan of Arc became a militant avenger because of faulty ovaries.

But certain academic historians are reevaluating George's entire Colonial conduct in light of his porphyria. It is evidently essential to exhume an entire era, to apply different lenses to it, if George was sick in body and not in head. However, the new appraisals may not change the result of the Revolutionary War, even if someone reinterprets George Washington's administration in light of his rosewood false teeth.

And this sensational news is not altogether fair to George III. Somehow, porphyria seems prosaic and ordinary. It does not add luster to a crown any more than dandruff or gall stones. A George III, smitten with porphyria, is to monarchs what Phil Scott's glass jaw was to boxing. George comes off much better as a bumbling nut from Hanover, dribbling erratic phrases in broken English. Take away his aberration and you have a fat nonentity who will pose eternally as an iron-poor blood portrait, in knee britches, in history's hall of cop-outs.

Most modern historians construe George III as a third-rater who possessed honorable intentions. He certainly wasn't the despot or dastard most Americans think he was, but antipathy for George III is yet another one of the massive, enduring prejudices we inherit with our mother's milk or pablum. The old bromide that one may as well kill a dog as give a dog a bad name seems to fit the monarch.

All the Georges had execrable public relations. The first two Georges were foreigners, outsiders, to whom all of the conventional stigmas attached, and, simultaneously, the Stuarts had all the sentiment and poignance that devolves upon lost causes. The next two, in a manner to invoke President Herbert Hoover, were cast, unwittingly, in roles far beyond their inherent capacities.

And in company with the hapless Herbert Hoover, the Georges titillated the wits and wags. George I didn't speak or write English, and George II was rollickingly infamous for his hatred of "boets and bainters." George III, often called "Farmer George," thought Shakespeare's gems were "sad stuff." George IV admired matchless Jane Austen and he and Sir Walter Scott were good friends, but he was anathema to all the romantics, idealists, and neo-swingers because he put Leigh Hunt in jail for criticizing him in print.

Perhaps, the real revulsion for the four Georges came at the apogee of the china-closet morality induced by the evangelical movement of the 19th century. The impression we have today was written by Walter Savage Landor in 1855, long after the Georges, but at the crest of the evangelically induced morality:

> "George the First was reckoned
> Vile, but viler George the Second;
> And what mortal ever heard
> Any good of George the Third?
> When from earth the Fourth descended,
> God be praised, the Georges ended."

But if this medical research continues someone will probably discover that "Mad Anthony" Wayne wasn't irascible or impetuous nearly so much as he was smitten by a notable rash of the scalp. Having to wear a powdered wig atop a harassing, itching scalp might make Billy Graham talk and act somewhat less saintedly.

And if some researcher finds out that the British had some

nearsighted, farsighted, pink-eyed, cross-eyed, tarrapin-eyed men on Bunker (actually Breed's) Hill, the lads who go around yelling, "Bang, bang, you're dead," in these gussied-up sham battles, may play hell with Colonel Prescott's ringing admonition, "Don't shoot until you see the whites of their eyes."

DOG DAYS DROUGHT

The street is a funeral pyre,
And the sidewalk is grounded white swans
Caught in the tar-paper of an alien land.

Blistered leaves are fish
Too morose to strike or swim. They hang around
Aimlessly as scorched jokes hunting for punch lines.

Old men scan the sky
As if it were a raffle-ticket
They'd bet their last fifty cents on,

But the sun's a hunter who lost his dogs,
And wild hounds range the skyland damning
To hell the gods that drove them mad.

The crow's caw is a falsetto bellyache
And he wouldn't spit on rotten cornfield corpses,
Not even if he had the spittle to spare.

Twilight's a rose, criminally assaulted,
And the departing sun strikes his tent
As if it had cheated him at cards.

But all the village oracles say
It has always managed to rain,
Certainly up to now,
And old Brother Brokenfield,
Who's to do the main praying for rain,
Is toting his umbrella to Little Zion Church.

The weather, in what remains of small town and rural society, is never merely an external force. This is especially true of the endless torpor of summer, when the parched earth is laid bare as a peevish anvil on which the sullen, perverse sun flails with red hot marlin spikes.

Our people don't talk about the weather as though it were merely related to daily life. It isn't seen as a force that comes and goes by seasons. It is the blood and marrow of life and not merely something that relates to living. When we small town and rural people talk about heat and drought an uninitiated stranger would assume we are discussing the personality of a close friend. The weather is more than every man's double-first cousin. It is his alter-ego. And, it is his ward and his guardian, simultaneously.

The poem is intended, primarily, to describe summer weather. But the poem's conclusion, with the reference to praying for rain, is written to show the continuation of many fundamental precepts and mores. Although small-town Southerners understand the importance of science in the space-age, and although we have pretty generally rejected the essence of the old Monkey Laws, we are still the creatures of habits and customs. We are fundamentalists in ways that most cunningly invite analysis but in devious ways that elude analysis and drive the professors to tranquilizers.

Each community still cherishes stories about prayer meetings for rain. We laugh, but we don't want others to attempt to share the humor. I know many such stories, and the best one I know is true, beyond all peradventure. It was told to me by my father, Thad Stem, Sr. (1884-1959), the best man I ever knew. He was an eye-witness.

About 1900, Granville County, North Carolina, was ravaged mercilessly by an unending drought. My father's home baliwick, Tally Ho Township, was so scorched it doubled for the devil's cow pasture. So, a big meeting was called at Tally Ho Church to pray for rain. There would be short prayers and silent prayers, but the main prayer, the keynote prayer, was to be delivered by an old man named Duncan Farabow. He had the reputation for being the best "outloud" prayer anywhere around. And not just incidentally, he was the only person who brought an umbrella to the big meeting.

Duncan Farabow's eloquent petition was saturated with copious reports relative to the parlous condition of all the crops in the fields. Indeed, a team of agricultural experts all the way from Washington City couldn't have made a more graphically detailed report of a drought-stricken area. But while Mr. Farabow was still giving the Lord the devastated local picture, enormous black clouds chased off the wooly lambs called white clouds.

The wind was the back of creation's hand. The lightning was an electrical artillery barrage, zeroed plunk on the target. The rain, for a while, made the Johnston Flood resemble a gamboling freshet. And all of this dark terror was followed by an immense hail storm, with hailstorms of lethal size.

There wasn't enough tobacco left in Tally Ho to make one roll-your-own. There wasn't enough wheat left to make a single biscuit, nor enough corn for a small hoe-cake.

After the big meeting a fabled lady of Tally Ho, Miss Addie Webb, viewed the carnage and harrumphed: "They should have had more sense than to ask Mr. Farabow to pray for rain. He always does overdo everything."

Miss Addie Webb, the terse commentator, was an aunt of James E. Webb, who was head man of NASA. It must be a far piece from Tally Ho to the Geminis. Or is it really such a far piece, after all?

PAGING PROFESSOR GOOSEBERRY

When Professor Gooseberry gave up his ghost
He laid down his bow. His palsied hands
Had already dropped his fiddle. The funeral
Was the biggest thing since the opera house fire,
And we brought him where
The wind was sweet on April air
(Because a strong element of poetry was implied).
But it was a toss of a fiddle string for top billing
Between dozens of cousins and lodge hall buddies
And assorted unpaid professional mourners.
   (Not to mention poor Gooseberry)
Everybody who didn't make a speech had a part, and
There was enough respectful commotion to make
The wind crawl into the church mouse's hole.
But what I am morbidly curious about, and
I really wish someone would tell me: Is there
Ever any balm for fiddlers in any new Gilead,
Or does everyone, Gooseberry included,
Have to try out for a harp, just for size?

Many Southern boys of my generation were grown men
before we learned that Sidney Lanier's birthday, February 3,
was not a national celebration. Local UDC units had chapel
programs at all the public schools. This was as predictable as
the Saturday night bath or communion Sunday.

We marched into the auditorium while a UDC lady
plunked "Dixie" on the piano. While there was a pling to her

plunking, it was as if an eagle were flying with an anchor on one wing. Then, the program was as predictable as the observation of Lanier's birthday.

We already knew, from previous programs, that gallant Lanier died at 39 from the tuberculosis he caught at Point Lookout when he was a Yankee prisoner of war. One nice lady read a portion of "The Marshes of Glynn," and another lady sang "A Ballad of the Trees and the Master." Then, everyone sang "The Bonnie Blue Flag," although we didn't know whether Lanier wrote the song or whether it was written by the lady who led the singing.

A few of us read Lanier's Civil War novel, *Tiger Lilies*, a pretty fair book but one that never worried Stephen Crane or Ernest Hemingway. A few of us read Lanier's *The Boys' King Arthur*, and many pupils had to memorize many lines from the "Song of the Chattahoochee," never dreaming that "Out of the hills of Habersham/Down the valleys of Hall," relate to two stony counties in northern Georgia.

But no one seems to have known that Lanier, a featured soloist with the famous Peabody Orchestra, was a world-renowned flutist. No one had ever heard, or heard of, Lanier's compositions for the flute such as "Field-larks and Black-birds," "Swamp Robin," "Longing," or "Wind-song." And the same was true of Lanier's unfinished "Choral Symphony" and those exquisite ballads, "My Life Is Like a Summer Rose" or "Little Ella."

It was a long time before we knew that Sidney Lanier was one of our region's first truly professional musicians and composers. And this is bound to be enigmatic since Lanier's best biographer, the late Edwin Mims, taught some of our fathers and uncles at Trinity College, the University of North Carolina, and Vanderbilt. (Mims taught English at Vanderbilt throughout the Fugitive ruckus. Unlike his younger associates who sought haven in the recreation of a mythological agrarian society, Mims was a true progressive.)

Obviously, the distilled essence of music lies in Lanier's poetry. Actually, his poetry suffers from an overdose of music. But as much as my generation was moved by the resonance of Lanier's verses, we simply were never introduced to the whole man.

Sadly for himself, and for the remainder of us, Lanier was born in a thorny time in America's and the South's cultural development. He lived at a time and in a place where there was social as well as economic prejudice against the artist, against the creative spirit. Apparently, no one was listening when a detractor asked Lanier what place music had in this nation. Lanier replied: "Why, music is love in search of a word."

However, I wasn't thinking about Sidney Lanier when I wrote the foregoing poem about poor Gooseberry. Gooseberry's tragedy isn't that his talent was unknown. Gooseberry's constituents knew all about him, but, as they said, "What's that got to do with the price of eggs."

I doubt that any society has ever talked so much about education as ours, but I am sure no society has ever made so much fun of the educated person. In a monstrously cruel manner, that grisly ambivalence is a whole shelf of local history.

LATE POST

Locusts and persimmons fling such anointments
One thinks the corpse of an old field is
    being laid out
But chinquapins fall and strike the earth
As if Judgment Day is beating a million drums.
All the wind's wild, wailing trombones
Exude the sharps and flats of killing frost,
And purple twilight's flecked with the blood
Of many lambs. Night's a lank man walking alone
With a stiff back and a crick in his neck. I know
When our town's a turtle with its neck drawn-in,
Sleet will drive tacks into roofs, fields and dreams
The way a newspaperman writes "30." My heart
Darts and leaps for many strange talismans:
    I wonder how
Thomas Wolfe would be now, at three score
    years and fifteen?
I count the pretty girls I left far behind me,
And I reach for the strong beauty of my father's face
And the sweet power of his hand. My querulous heart
Whistles old tunes turned to rust long ago.
I reach for a wind-up train and the mighty ticks
Of my grandma's clock are louder than the wind.
    Suddenly, here's
The ring of an axe and the smell of good pine wood,
And the sound of my grandma's voice, dear lady, dead
All of these decades: "Make haste, gather chips,
Cousin November's going to strike his tent
And Uncle Winter's coming home."

INSIDE STORY

My tombstone, the inspiration of my beloved widow, Julia,
Has become a miniature Tower of Pisa. It leans and when
The wind blows it wobbles as crazily as Jericho's walls.
The inscription's as crowded as two lovers in a hammock,
To say nothing of two comma-faults and a split-infinitive.
But, bless Julia's soul, she's proud of it and I don't mean
Just having the last word. Four times each year
She brings fresh flowers and tells anyone who'll listen
About the shines she says I used to cut. But here where
It's early to bed and never to rise, only tired bones
Are beneath Julia's precious tottering stone. Confidentially,
My manhood, — creative, virile, and brave, —
Rests in another country, in another grave.

MAY-DAY, MAY-DAY

George's belly was heavy with sweat, although the room was comfortable and he had only a sheet over him. But he was shaking, really writhing, inside and out, as much as anyone so weak could possibly shake.

He pulled his left hand up from his side with his right hand to see his watch. In nine more minutes this bitch in white, his nurse, would have to give him his shot. She was a stubborn chatter-box of a bitch, and George couldn't talk her out of any extra shots the way he could the night nurse.

Where in hell did Ellen find this bleached magpie, anyway? George let his left arm slide off his chest and belly so that he couldn't see time limping along, even backing up on him, making him even more of a half-human receivership of bankrupt minutes than he already was. But even this was an effort. Even his arm sliding down was an effort. Jesus, everything was going down hill. Even the hill was going down hill, and it would be a tight race to see if the morphine and demerol got to the finish line ahead of George's "thing."

Some "thing" it was, and George repeated it to himself as his tongue chased some dry, random spittle listlessly around his scorched mouth.

When George had come to the hospital, Ellen had told all of their friends, "George has got a 'thing'."

Well, now he'd count the do-dads along the top of the wall, and he would pretend the whole wall was the old bank building downtown, when George was a boy, and he'd be the human-fly climbing the wall. But the ceiling was so high his popping eyes had to take the elevator to get to the top. O.K., then, everybody off for the roof garden. George would have a cornice-on-the-rocks, but the cornice-on-the-rocks made him dizzy. Still, if he got sick and puked that would help him pass the time, until the nine minutes were blotted up by oblivion.

But before the waiter could give him his check, and before he could get sick enough to upchuck, some cherubic bees were serenading the roof-top. Tidings from the outside world floated up to the Plains of Abraham. . .That was a damn good one. . .Plains of Abraham. . .Wolfe and Montcalm both dying, and, for good measure, George threw in little Isaac, too.

But it wasn't bees. Instead, there was a rustle of starchy white ebullience. The nurse was telling Ellen how much better George felt. "Yes, we're much better this afternoon. Yes, much better. We retained almost half of our Pepsi, and we. . ."

And Ellen was standing there in the middle of the shadows of this starchy white trilling. Ellen was smiling as happily as if she had suddenly become happy when she hadn't expected to be happy at all. Now, she was fiddling with George's sheet, fiddling the vacuous way a postman whistles when he's delivering junk mail.

Ellen's kiss on his cheek was cold chalk touching a blackboard but not writing anything. Then she backed up a couple of steps as if some incredibly gentle inspecting officer had buttoned a dog-face's button and had then stepped back to the proper distance.

Well, Jesus, she was still a young 38. Young and full. If George had got his shot he might even feel up to dangling his right hand off the bed to touch her leg a little. But he hadn't had his shot, and even if he did touch her it would be like stroking a child that expects to be stroked but who would rather be left alone.

Ellen had started jabbering out the neighborhood news, turning her head, zip-zap, to include the nurse, who was eating up the intimate tid-bits about nothing as if they were ripe strawberries. But, what the hell, it was pleasant enough chatter, laced with just enough disarming banter to keep the central idea of death at bay. There were two or three fast, furtive asides relative to George's imminent homecoming. And as she spoke these desperate urgencies about home-coming, George wondered if she had picked out his pallbearers, if she had thought about the arrangements, to save trouble at the last?

Now she was saying that his big chair by the bookcase lamp was all redone and he would be crazy about the wonderful red color. There was a new stack of records, too, and also, Ellen was next on the list in her book club for the set of books about the naval part of the Civil War and did George want her to get the set next or to wait awhile?

Wait for what, sweetie, he started to ask? Wait for a red bird to sprinkle salt on some kid's tail, or wait for a rabbit to catch and tree a hound?

He noticed, without bothering really to notice, that Ellen had a sly way of sneaking glances at her watch as she talked. Miss White Cloud didn't notice this, obviously, but George did. He knew Ellen had to stay long enough to make her leaving seem natural. Hell, George had that much sense, even in his agony. He didn't blame Ellen. Not really. Life was out in the sun, not in this place.

Now, Ellen was a clock running down. In a minute she'd kiss his cheek and leave. So, maybe, George better take a good look at her. The look might be a sparkling toy when he got his shot and felt a little better. For a while he could lie back a little easier and think of summer skies and yellow roses, and Ellen's long, golden legs with all of the world's knowledge somewhere along them and between them. By God, she was good to think about, a damn young 38, full and ripe, with lots of wonderful saps and juices.

Now, she was quiet, just before leaving. George knew she was waiting to see if he wanted anything, if he wanted to say anything, to ask her anything. But there was nothing he wanted and there was nothing he couldn't leave unsaid.

Besides, he hurt all over. His head was such a storm of pain he could barely squint with one eye.

She had on one of those tremendous hats that never made anyone say: "Where did you get that hat?" She always wore her hats. Nothing ever wore her. Now, he remembered, through all his dark pains, that she once had another hat almost exactly like this one. George had bought that other hat for Ellen when they couldn't afford it. So, he had bought it because they couldn't afford it and because she really didn't need it, either.

The hat was bigger than one of those New England states, and it was as black as the Black Forest is when somebody writes a poem about the Black Forest. George used to pretend that the hat was an awning for him to get under during a storm. He did this sometimes when she wore the hat and the great tropical storm was making up in his eyes. But she wouldn't have the hat on when the real storm began raging.

One time they had filled the hat up with wildflowers. Another time George had asked her to carry the hat in her hand so that he could pretend she was a seminary girl and they were strolling around leisurely on a Sunday afternoon. Then, still another time, they were caught in a storm, a cloudburst, and Ellen had tried to put the hat under her dress to keep it dry. The hat was too big or the skirt was too tight, and George had told her she would get her tail wet with her dress up like that, Old Whale-Tail. And she had made a pretty face at him because she knew he really didn't think her tail was a whale-tail. . .

Whale-tail. That's what they said during the war, in the E.T.O., anyway. Everybody said "Keep your tail down, whale-tail." And because it was stupid and because everybody was so scared he was wetting his pants, everybody laughed nervously, and kept on laughing and saying, to everybody else, "Keep your tail down, whale-tail."

Well George had been much better at keeping his whale-tail

down than he had at dodging their "thing."

Now Ellen was kissing his cheek good-bye, putting a quick dot to an "i" no one would ever read. Then George could hear her high heels clicking all the way to the elevator. He knew she was walking fast because she was crying, not sobbing, just crying like a lady. George almost yelled for Ellen, but the nurse had gone for the shot. Still, he knew she'd come running if he yelled. And then her high heels would answer all the questions they were asking going to the elevator.

With a terrible effort, he pushed up until his back was against the head of the bed. He swung his feet off the bed towards the window. He knew she always parked back there in the back, where the doctors parked, so she could slip in and out without facing people who asked about George and his "thing," his cancer.

A younger fellow was opening the car door for her. He wasn't any boy but he wasn't 38 either. Then the car turned away from the hospital, away from the town. It went up towards Virginia, away from death.

George guessed the fellow must be the new architect, the one Ellen had talked about just before the "thing" came. But back then she was just talking about an interesting new person. Anyway, George guessed that was the fellow. It was hard to tell anything, with all this pain, with one eye, and from this distance. But somehow it was comforting to know that it was a stranger to George, and not one of their close friends, not yet anyway. It could be embarrassing as hell if it were someone who would be on the list to tote George's coffin, someone who might have to come to the hospital to "look in" before the "thing" got him.

DIAL FOR THEOLOGY

I always found it strange
That dogs, cats, roosters, foxes, squirrels,
Lack the soul breathed into me in my mother's womb.
Frankly, I always thought heaven, devoid of wagging tails,
Royal scarlet alarm-clocks and bushy arabesques
Must be Roxy's without any girls. And heaven
Without a lean hound to bay the earth below
Must be similar to being serenaded by a big band
That doesn't have any instruments. Paradise, without one cat
Purring near the front of the throne
Must be a book with the pages uncut.

Conversely, I am reminded, high and low,
That God's eye is on the sparrow, eternally.
But from what I have observed, from my insular post,
I have never noted such celestial surveillance helped any
  sparrows.
I think it would be more to the sparrow's point
If He kept His eye on men with shotguns and rifles,
And particularly on small bastards bearing B-B guns.

"QUIS CUSTODIET IPOS CUSTODES"

The rain had turned itself into ice during the morning, and stalactites were glistening under the eaves when Dave and I were walking home from school.

The TV hadn't said anything about this ice, but the naked tree limbs were already loaded with shivering silver birds. Some of the saplings were bent down, with wind and ice. Dave said the moon would use them for croquet wickets, when the moon came back up again. The grass, especially in vacant lots and unused alleys, looked like old men with white beards, and when the wind came ripping through we could almost hear these old men moaning about their frozen joints and bones.

The Methodist bell wheezed, as if it had forgotten to take its flu shots, and the wind spun the steeple as if he had a string and it were a top. From the way the wind jumped up and down on the tops of the buildings, especially on those made of tin, you'd have thought old Goliath was daring everyone in town out to fight.

The shop windows were frosting over, and you had to make a peephole with your hand. Dave rubbed a hole in one window. He said a topless woman was inside, a mannequin, and that's why the window was frosted.

Some big limbs had fallen from some old trees near the post office. They might have been dead limbs, but the whole sidewalk was piled up with ice, or diamonds, or with bits of broken Sunday goblets. The shrubs along the sidewalks were big collies, scratching for buried bones, probably, but Tick, the dog that just about everyone loves and no one owns, had ducked into an alley between two buildings. Dave said that Tick was dreaming of last July, of the times when he stretched out on the warm grass on the courthouse lawn and waited for Mr. Muller, the shoe shop man, to come by and tickle his belly.

We crunched some ice from the Crenshaw's crepe myrtle, and Dave wondered if it would keep snow from coming, if he would put a jinx on snow, if we went back up town and bought a bottle of vanilla to make a big batch of snow cream? Only, Dave called it "junxt," the same as Mr. Muller, who used to fracture folks at church when he said, "O, 'O, lamp of God," and "Let us bray," until folks got used to it.

Then we saw old man Abernathy. He can look at the sky in April and tell the size of tomatoes in July. He can tell a mushroom from a toadstool, and he speaks several foreign languages, although he was born here in town. His red moustache was white with particles of ice, or almost like a barber's pole, anyhow. He pointed to the sky: "Old Marse will be plucking that goose long before supper time."

Now, Dave and I knew it would snow. We could count on snow the way we count on our weekly allowances. He saw us smile. He said: "Vive la bagatelle. Long live trifles, boys." He pointed to the sky again and then to the frozen earth: "Virginibus puerisque." But Mr. Abernathy knew Father makes us take Latin and he knew we knew it means "For boys and girls." Mr. Abernathy went along, taking pains to be careful, but he hollered back: "Honi soit qui mal y pense." We knew it was French. We don't take French, but we worked on it a while as we watched the Crenshaw's paling fence do all the dances from the frug to the mashed potato, and as it waved at the ice and wind it probably did what Father calls the shimmy, too.

The Lacy's have a small fish pond behind their house, and Dave and I went to see if it was frozen solidly. It wasn't, but after we skated some on the edge, in our boots, all the goose feathers on earth started falling. Dave was as excited as I was. I told him we could pretend we were the man in Jack

London's story we read, the one called "To Make A Fire."

That was okay with Dave, but we decided we'd better get home and see if the runners on our two sleds needed sliding grease. By the time we got home the snow was falling so hard and thick we could hardly see each other. I had my cap flaps down and a scarf over my face, with just enough room to squint. Dave said I looked like a nun who was being punished for swinging too much.

We saw the other car, and we knew Father was home. We wanted to ask him about Mr. Abernathy's French phrase, and we also wanted to know why ponds don't freeze over solidly so that people could cut ice, not that they would cut any, the way Father says his father's father did.

Father was in our big old-timey kitchen — I mean it is bigger than some living rooms in the new suburbs — taking a drink with his friend, Quincy Warren. Father was saying: "It IS slick, Quin. Ruth just broke the world's record for sliding on her tail. Of course, she had the benefit of slacks. I'm not sure if Ty Cobb or Maury Wills held the old record."

Dave is almost 14, and I am almost 13 and we know the word "ass" has many meanings, and I guess we knew that Mother had one, too. Dave and I had already figured out that some thoughts and words are common to almost all parents. Still, what Father said gave me a little turn, but then I remembered when Mother had bought some of those black fish-net stockings and those new dresses that show her knees. Dave had said, as if his thoughts and not his lips were doing the talking: "You know, Mother is really stacked for an old doll," and Father, who is a lawyer, had replied, "The court takes judicial cognizance of the exhilarating fact." But all mother did was to put her hands on her hips and say: "Old?"

We could hear Mother somewhere upstairs singing snatches of "Second Hand Rose," and humming the parts she couldn't remember. But Father drowned out the music: "Before you damned scoundrels go off snow-balling and helling it up in general, high-tail it up to Miss Pansy's and see if she is all right. Be sure all her coal skuttles and wood boxes are filled to the top. Ask her if her lights are working and if the water is running."

Dave started to say something, nothing much probably, but Father grabbed us and shoved us around in that affectionate rough-house way he had. He pointed his long finger: "Pretium laborum non vile. Now scram."

We knew that means "The value of labor is not trifling," the motto of the Golden Fleece, but as we were putting on our things, Dave bowed from the waist and cried to Father: "Morituri te salutamus."

We got to the front door when I remembered to ask Mother about the vanilla extract. She yelled down from upstairs that we had plenty of vanilla. "See to Miss Pansy, and we'll have a bowl of vanilla, and a bowl of chocolate, too."

Dave and I cut across four front lawns to get to Miss Pansy's so that our boots would sink down into the soft snow. We ate a little, holding our mouths open and letting the flakes fly against our lips and teeth. We snow-balled some, and we made a snow man, or a snow midget, almost on the run. When we got to the Roundtree's lawn, Dave slid down their front embankment, which is about five feet high, at a slant. He didn't stop until he had crossed the sidewalk and the grass plot, all filled with snow, that is between the sidewalk and the street.

He rolled over and jumped up like an albino horse. He clapped his mittens over his head. "We're a two-champion family now, Paul. I just broke the old world's record for belly-sliding."

I told him that was fine, just so long as we weren't a one toothpaste family like those finks on TV.

It was dark now, not just dusky dark. The snow was falling so thick and fast you would think it came from anger, if it were anything but snow. The elm trees in Miss Pansy's front yard were all huddled together, probably for what little bit of warmth and cheer they could get from one another. But the way they were huddled up they reminded me of the news pictures of passengers holding hands and praying on a sinking ship, knowing they are going to drown.

Dave and I sort of single-footed down the long grove of oak trees that lead to Miss Pansy's back door. Father calls it "Miss Pansy's boulevard," but Dave and I know, and sometimes Mother agrees, that Father says a lot of things that aren't cool today. But I do think a path between big trees used to be a "boulevard," around here, anyway.

We don't have to go to Miss Pansy's back door. No, sir. But we knew she could talk to us easier at the back, and if she needed coal and wood, and, surely, she must, then we would be close to the shed in the back yard. Besides the only light burning in the house was in the kitchen. It was from a dropcord. It reminded me of a lantern swaying in a ghost town in a Western, especially as I saw it through the thick snow.

Usually, Dave and I go to Miss Pansy's back door so we will not mess up her den rug, only she calls it "parlor drugget." Just the same Father tells people a story that must be true because Father wouldn't make up such a bad story about someone, some old lady. Father came along once, when he was young. Some Negro men were working on the street. Father saw smoke pouring from Miss Pansy's roof.

Father hollered to the men to follow him. He thought they could hold down the fire with Miss Pansy's garden hose and buckets of water until the fire department got there. At least, they could get some of Miss Pansy's furniture and things out of the house.

The men followed Father onto the front porch. Miss Pansy met them at the screen door: "Arthur Moorefield, you may be young, but you know better than to bring darkies to my front door."

So, Father and his friends ran all around to the back door, and Father says that most of the Negro men threw off their hats before they went inside to fight the fire and tote the furniture.

When new folks in town, those who live in the suburbs, kid Father about the strange, cruel world he was brought up in, they say he lived in the "Uncle Tom" era. Father says: "Uncle Tom, hell. It was Uncle Remus, by God. Ipso jure. Invenit."

Dave and I filled all the skuttles and two old tubs with coal, and we stacked the wood-box on the back porch and the one by that kookie old stove of Miss Pansy's that burns wood and has "eyes." We caught her two hens, the ones that lay her eggs, and we put them in a cardboard box behind that crazy stove. We took off our boots, and even our shoes, on the back porch. Even so, Miss Pansy put down some old magazines on the kitchen floor. The illustrations on the fronts were really wild.

She insisted that we "take" tea. We really didn't want it but we drank some, anyway, and she gave us a huge cookie each (she called them "tea-cakes") that looked like the picture of the "Gingerbread Man" in the kiddie book.

Near the kitchen sink, which looked as if it was made of copper or brass, there was a big pan to catch water from a leak. The water leaked down from a big splotch in the ceiling. I guess there had been paper, or something, up there but it looked like my impression of hair pulled out by the roots. The drops of water came down in a flood, the way Miss Olson, in English, says I throw commas around. Everytime a drop hit in the pan the sound seemed like a cracked bell.

Against the far wall there was a cot, away from the leak. It had a pillow and sheets and a crazy blanket filled with patches, or something like that. At the head of the cot there was this record-player that had a handle on the side. I have heard that these old things will not play but one record. You

114

can't put on several at a time. The arm was the wildest thing I ever saw. It looked like the drill in some mad dentist's office.

Dave walked over to that nutty record-player. I could tell he was having a hard time keeping his hands off it and from asking Miss Pansy questions about it. Over at the other end of the crazy stove was a rocking chair, like the one President Kennedy had when I was a kid. A book was lying on the seat, opened. I couldn't see the name, but later Dave said it was *So Red the Rose*, whatever that is.

We told Miss Pansy we'd come back about nine, to see if everything was all right for the long night. She shook hands with us, and her fingers felt as if they belonged to Betsy Ross. She wasn't unpleasant at all, but her old eyes had a long-ago and far-away look. I got the impression, almost, that she was still living, somehow, but had stopped breathing. She stood on her back porch with an old shawl around her head and shoulders. She really reminded me of Peter Quint in that spooky *The Turn of the Screw*, which I don't understand at all. Father told us we wouldn't understand it but to go on and read it anyway.

We had our shoes and boots on when Miss Pansy said: "Remember me affectionately to Maria and the Judge." I really gave a start, and my mouth flew open, but Dave made a shut-up motion. Then I knew Miss Pansy was thinking of Grandfather and Grandmother, dead all these years.

We built a super snow man in our front yard, before we went back into our house. There wasn't anything in the world but snow. It was silent but the silence seemed to shake the earth. I asked Dave about Miss Pansy's cot in her kitchen and that kookie record-player. Dave knows a lot of things. He told me how Miss Pansy had sold off her things, by the sideboard, by the picture, even by the spoon, to keep from having to go to the old ladies' home that our church has in a city somewhere.

Dave said Miss Pansy sold all this stuff at night, out the back door, that she got enough for a grand piano her father went all the way to Baltimore to get for her when she was a young girl to pay her taxes for several years. He explained that there weren't any rugs in her den to get messed up. He said that except for a few clothes everything she had was in the kitchen.

Later that night Mother told me, because I asked her, how Father wrote off in his office to people who wanted to buy fine furniture and spoons, and how Father always made the truck come way after other peoples' bedtime, and how Father always went up to help with the loading and to keep things quiet. But Mother said all the grown folks in the old part of town knew about this and she was sure they would never let Miss Pansy die among strangers in the old ladies' home.

Father said that "Honi soit qui mal y pense" is French, as Dave and I knew. It means "Shamed be he who thinks evil of it." He also explained ice used to freeze solidly on ponds because people had special ice ponds with shallow, still water that had a lot of grass. An ice pond would freeze over solidly but the Lacy's pond might not ever.

I don't know which was better, the vanilla or the chocolate. I think each of us ate about a gallon of both flavors. Anyway we ate enough to get a headache but that kind goes right away. We did a lot of sledding, taking running starts in the street because there wasn't any traffic. Mrs. Roundtree told us we were more than welcome to use her embankment, and it was like having your own roll-a-coaster.

When we had gone out to play, Father told us to stay warm and to have a good time. He said he and Mother would check up on Miss Pansy. He gave Dave and me a kiss on each of our foreheads, but he rough-housed it so that we wouldn't think he was sissy or corny. But I don't think Dave and I would have thought that, anyway. As we started out the front door, he and Mother were standing just inside it. She had her arm around his waist and he had his arm around hers, only his hand was where he said she had made the sliding record.

Mother kissed Father and he bellowed, like a big wolf: "Varium et mutabile semper femina." Mother asked a question with her face and her hands. I think she studied Spanish in school. Father told us: "Woman is ever a fickle and changeable thing."

After maybe an hour or two, Father and Mother came out in the snow. They took a few turns on our sleds, and Mother even went down the Roundtree's embankment. I don't care if she is an old doll, she was as pretty as a swinger in one of the whiskey ads in her white slacks and in her stocking cap with the red top-knot.

Dave and I had a ball all right enough. If there is ever a better snow or a better time, I hope I'm here. The only trouble was I kept wondering if Miss Pansy's hens would lay in the box behind that nutty stove. Too, I kept hearing that leak-leak hitting the pan. Everytime I tried to picture her empty old house, from my imagination, it was like the dream when you get lost in a bat-cave, and I don't mean those kooks on TV. But everytime I got lost in the cave, I'd throw snow balls at Dave. From the way he threw them back and the way he made himself a horse to pull me on my sled, a couple of times, I think he was thinking something, too.

THE MAKER OF DREAMS

Often, the maker of dreams
Is the molted angel who spent his life
Trying to conjure from the daily wreckage
A perfect image to delight the population
That wouldn't have known a perfect image
From a cow's tail, and if they had known,
They'd say, "You can sell anything now,
Even a cow's tail."

HIGH TIDE

After many seasons, spent seeking blackberries
    and playing hob,
April's green horses and January's white wolves
Become identical twins. I'm still committed, of course,
To the old New Deal ticket, but these days I ask,
Almost vacuously, "What's our bastard's name
This time, gentlemen?" Presidents, All-Americans, wars,
Deathless authors, heroes, villains, movie-stars, tycoons,
And men on moons run from faceless to nameless, finally.
(Confidentially, some gray-grilled mornings I lose a decade
As easily as I misplace my eye-glasses.) Quite often
I have a distinct feeling a single week in October
    was infinity,
While three decades were a nickel's worth of time
    on a meter.

But I remember, clearly, an August morning,
When August was eaten up by Dog Days. It was ten
    twenty-two

118

By the Elgin Papa gave me for graduation. My Camel
Had smoked down two-thirds. A crow used a white cloud
For a pillow, and a distant train whistle awakened
The gypsy-man sleeping within me. Albert, our town dog,
Panted in the tiny alley between Bengough's (dry goods)
And the "American Cafe, -Pete Trakis, Prop."
    Around the corner,
Where Doc Henley had his office, sounds of a floating
        crap game
Came erupting. (I really thought it a miniature
    "Anvil Chorus.")
It was Dovey Turner, who married Jimmy Simpson,
    groceryman,
And short-stop on our Oxford team, our clean-up hitter.
Her heels were all the music extant that August day, and
I counted three freckles on her knee, and a small mole,
Just above, when Bengough's whanging fan lifted her skirt.
Her face was fetching, but not movie-star, and her breasts
Filled, but didn't try to home-stake, her jersey. The way
Dovey walked I thought her feet would chew up the
        pavement,
As if it were taffy. Her white hair ribbon was lovely snow,
In a gander month. Jesus, when she turned up Elm Street,
Where the post office used to be, I thought the last ferry
To heaven had left me sucking a Camel. That afternoon
Our Oxford nine played Henderson. I booted two easy balls
Because Dovey was in my eye and loins. Lord, I couldn't
        have hit
Henderson't pitcher with a machine-gun, not that Dovey
        afternoon.

Hell, man, I don't know whatever became of Dovey
     Turner Simpson,
But she made peppermint of an August day, gumdrops
     of a gander month,
Back in nineteen hundred and something or other.
The upcoming World Series and Presidential election
     elude me totally,
But I still hear a floating crap game, a miniature
     "Anvil Chorus,"
And I still see sunbeams playing leap-frog on radiant legs,
And I can touch Dovey's adorable white ribbon,
Any damned time I please.

CIRCUS DAY TOMORROW

It came as a shock, or almost a shock, anyway, when Wesley realized the circus wasn't coming to town on the train. His mind seemed to have cobwebs all around it when he finally understood that school wouldn't let out for "Circus Day."

He had some kind of mental dry grin when he reminded himself that schools don't "let out" anymore. They have holidays and recesses, and he grasped the fact, also, that there probably hadn't been an official "Circus Day" in town since traveling salesmen were still called "drummers," not since there was an annual "Arbor Day," and school "let out" for the afternoon and all the scholars marched to the courthouse lawn.

A local minister always opened the program by thanking God for trees. Then Miss Tempie Bell quoted, by heart, "Woodman, Spare That Tree." A male quartet sang Lanier's "Ballad of the Master and the Trees," but later on Joyce Kilmer's poem, "Trees," with the music by Oley Speaks, was sung in lieu of the Lanier poem-song. Then, Mr. "Five-Cent" Jackson, the President of the bank, made a talk on the "Forest Is the Future," or was it the "Future Is the Forest?" Then Mr. Moorfield, the lawyer, in his bat-wing collar and Prince Albert coat, made a talk on the loveliness of trees. After the music and the speeches, the U.D.C. sold refreshments. Everybody bought a piece of pie or cake or a bowl of ice cream, whether he was hungry or not, because it was an act of patriotism.

Nonetheless, Wesley had made plans, premature and abortive ones, to set the alarm clock for five the next morning. Then he would roust out his sons, Wesley, Jr., and

121

Seymour. He would storm into their bedroom, flip back the covers on each bed and yell, as his father used to yell: "Rise and shine you lazy bums." In fact, Wesley had decided he would add: "Water jack, water jack, ought to be there and half-way back."

He and the boys would put on their jackets and pound down to the depot to see the circus train come in. They would go at such a happy bound their six feet would play the frosted pavement as if it were drums or cymbals.

They would be among the first to arrive. Of course, nobody could get to the circus train ahead of Dock Parker, Jimmy-John Tate, Willie Walker and the ones who spent the night in the depot to wait for the circus train. Just the same, Wesley and young Wes and Seymour would exercise all the privileges and prerogatives of squatters' rights. They would know the animals as well as Noah knew the ones on the Ark. They would learn the names of the clowns, the bare-back riders, the trapeze artists, the lion-tamer, and the roustabouts. And, very soon, Wesley and Wes and Seymour would be privy to, hip to, that is, the strange and esoteric jargon spoken by circus people.

Then when the circus had detrained for the old showing ground in Settle's Meadow, the three would race home, exuding chilly excitement. If breakfast wasn't steaming on the table, Wesley would yell to his wife, Martha: "Good God, woman, are you going to starve us to death?"

Then like three ravenous but benign wolves the three males would make war on a platter of ham and fried eggs, with side dishes of tiny link sausages, hash-brown potatoes, and grits. Martha would make biscuits. They would eat about a dozen each, and they would obliterate a pound of real butter as they soaked up about a gallon of maple syrup and various jellies and preserves. And they wouldn't have any dinky glass of fruit juice. No, they would begin breakfast with huge bowls of steaming oatmeal, quick with golden butter and with cream rich enough to endow a college. . .But, what the hell, it might as well be bowls of oyster soup, with the oysters dropped in at the last second, with piles of croutons as brown as October and as deliciously crunchy as snow that falls with sleet.

After breakfast, Wesley would go up town and work a while. Then he'd fetch Martha and the boys. The four would look out the windows of his second-story office when the fabulous circus parade came down the street.

Each one would wave a balloon from the window, to the parade and to friends crowded and stacked like bright playing cards along the sidewalks and gutters. The four of them would do a spirited ring-around, a big ring-around, when the old calliope was a hooting owl whose enormous throat was the dwelling place of ebullient, magical sounds.

They would all cut-the-buck, Shuffle-Off-To-Buffalo, do a high-stepping wing-ding, or the Swim. For, no matter what a dance was called, it was always a rooster crowing down the stars and calling up the yeasty thunder of the marrow.

They would all eat at the show grounds. The boys would be sea lions with foam on their faces and up their noses in form of cotton-candy. They'd eat hot dogs and candy-apples and swill pop until they had to send for the doctor.

When their original balloons busted, Wesley would get a round of new ones, green and gleaming and yellow and sassy. He'd win Martha a kewpie doll throwing baseballs, and when he swung the sledge, to send the ball up that narrow, metal ladder, why he'd make it bounce off the garden gate of heaven.

It might be better not to go inside the hootch-a-me-kootch-a-me show, but they'd watch the gals dance on the improvised stage in front of the side-show tent. But as the gals shimmied and gyrated, Wesley would think about Martha. She might be pushing forty but she still wore a size ten dress, and he was reasonably sure she was 23 around the middle.

Amid all the hullabaloo of the midway crowd, amid the "wow-wow-wow" screams of the trombone, on the improvised stage, amid the go-to-hell plings of the banjo and the gritty, contagious impudence of the snare-drum, Wesley would pat Martha's pretty tail a couple of times, as the hootch gals bumped and the barker's tongue was a flooding river. Wesley would smile and whisper to Martha, amid the asylum of all the sounds, "It must be jelly cause jam don't shake like that."

She would remember, instantaneously, the line from the old song. She'd wink, subtly, deliciously, twitch her tail against his hip so fast no one could see the movement, but the place that she twitched against would be forever sacred to him and to the big afternoon.

He doubted the barker would say about the leading dancing girl, as the old-time professor said: "She dances first on her right leg and then on her left leg and between the two she makes a handsome living."

No, unfortunately, that wouldn't happen, and the four-piece orchestra wouldn't play that marvelous old stem-winder, "I Wish That I Could Shimmy Like My Sister Kate," — not because of any current strictures, but simply because the musicians wouldn't know the tune.

Then they would all sit together and watch the ingenious performers and the death-defying acts in the big tent. They would roar with the clowns, but they would peep through their fingers when the girl did the triple somersaults on the high trapeze. They would almost swallow their bags and bags of peanuts and popcorn whole, and they would swill down their bottles of pop in two mighty swallows.

Martha would wear a yellow ribbon on her hair. She would smile sunbeams, and her knees, in her short dress, would be as exciting as the flag the embattled farmers unfurled against the breeze, at Concord Bridge, in Emerson's old poem.

And after the final act, Wesley would buy a whole stand of balloons, as many as fifty, perhaps. He and Martha and the boys would use the balloon sticks for swords, for batons, and for pencils to write wild and lovely geometric designs in the air. Some balloons they would pop, in the manner of merry vandals, and some they would free, as birds from a cage. But they would give many to friends of all ages, as the four of them walked home down the middle of the street.

Of course, the crowds would usurp the streets on "Circus Day," but if some interloper blundered in with a honking horn, Wesley would wave a balloon for a red flag, or for a policeman's·billet.

But he had forgotten to remember about time. He kicked his forgetfulness with a silent reproof that wasn't up to total outrage. Hell, there wasn't any damned "Circus Day" tomorrow, no train, no parade. He forgot, too, that Wes and Seymour were already bored with big-time circuses they had seen on TV. And school wouldn't ever "let out" again, not ever.

It wasn't that he didn't love Martha for insisting that the boys meet him after school to go to this ratty circus, and it wasn't that he didn't love her for breaking her golf date, or whatever it was, to go to the circus herself.

It was the simple truth that he could write down the conversation he hadn't heard. "What's so great about a creepy circus, Mom?" Seymour had asked. "It's a drag, Mom. It's for squares," Wes had told Martha.

"I know. I know," she had answered. "But it means a lot to your father. Don't ask me to explain. Just do this for him, and for me, please."

Well, Wesley guessed he'd better make the scene tomorrow afternoon, as the boys would put it. If they were willing to make this sacrifice, and all for his sake, he guessed he could get into shape to make it a real gas, as the boys put it.

He rubbed his right arm. There might not be any kewpie dolls to win, anyway, but there was bound to be cotton-candy, and that could be one of Eugene O'Neill's masks. It would be all right, he told himself, and he laughed, mirth-lessly, when he remembered his Papa's joke about the fellow who said: "I guess it's all right, but if you really want to know, I still think it's a hell of a way to run a railroad."

ENTRIES FROM OXFORD

Oxford, N.C., November 3, 1959:

My father was buried two days ago. It is hard to write about him, but it is much harder not to write about him. I feel that I have to make this entry about my father, about his time of life. What I write will not be a success story, not in conventional terms. He was success infinitely more than he ever attained success.

Right now the woodlands around Oxford are flushed with a poignant fever called Indian Summer, or Second Summer. The earth is so lovely I feel a strange compulsion to walk on tiptoe, almost, to speak in low whispers, for fear any extraneous sounds will break the spell.

My father's old friend, Wallace Wade, the great football coach at Alabama and Duke, drove over for the service. Coach Wade and I stood in our front lawn. He looked around at the trees that seemed to be burning from fires of red and yellow leaves.

I followed Coach Wade's swift, tender kaleidoscope. I half expected to hear the crackle of flames, to smell smoke, because the woodlands seemed engulfed in a glorious red and yellow conflagration.

Coach Wade is not an emotional gentleman, but he said to me, softly, clearly, "It's a nice day for the Major, a very nice day."

I nodded. I understood precisely what Coach Wade was saying. Later on in the afternoon, when we were returning from the cemetery, the smell of first frost was in the air. A large flight of wild geese, flying in a perfect inverted V, was heading south. I lowered the car window. The air was quick with the wild cries of these ebullient transients.

In another part of the sky some tatters of reddish clouds seemed to be old-fashioned post-riders. The fast way these tatters tore down the skyland's turnpike, taking fences here and there, made me think they were cantering, post-haste, to spread the news of imminent falling weather.

If my father saw these scampering clouds, these rough weather portents, he would say: "The weather is about to fall, the way the Roman Empire fell." Or, he might look, with his sharp, gentle blue eyes, sniff all around, and say, "The weather is about to fall the way Old Man Rufe Duncan will fall when he tries to get up his front walk tonight."

The minister had read from the burial service all the words and phrases about resurrection and rebirth. While my father was not a religious man, certainly not in the orthodox sense, he would have said, "The minister's entitled to be heard."

Two days prior to his death, my father had said to me, knowing he was about to die, surely, "Well, what do you think is going to happen to me?"

I said I didn't know. He cocked his eye: "You've never been timorous about expressing your opinions up to now. So, what do you think?"

I told him I didn't think anything would happen to him, one way or the other. He nodded, readily, and he smiled. Then he quoted some of the once-famous lines of the conclusion to Tennyson's poem, "Ulysses," which he had learned by heart long ago when he was a student at Trinity College, now Duke:

"It may be we shall touch the Happy Isles
And see the Great Achilles, whom we knew.

Then he smiled again. He waved his huge right hand the way a judge does when he says, "Call your next case."

I think my father enabled me to have the best of two worlds, although this may not be in the exact sense that Joseph Wood Krutch wrote *The Best of Two Worlds.*

One world is the best of homogeneity as this endures in

the time of the bomb. The other world was the lusty one before "image" became the big dog in the meat-house, when rustic humanism thumbed its nose at political and social expediency. (By "rustic humanism" I mean, succinctly, the perpetuation of three great traditions: Judeo-Christian ethics, Greek aesthetics, and Roman law.)

Before it is too late, before my faded photographs crumble and are scattered by impersonal winds across Time's Potter's Field, I have acute, if vain, urgency to share those puppydog days when children were two-legged centaurs and not self-appointed Napoleons.

As bizarre as it sounds, there was a time when a house was big enough for parents and their children. There was a time when honorable parents were not the permissive captives of their children's whims and caprices and peeves.

I tried to please my father. His approbation was always the supreme accolade. We loved each other deeply, but he never tried to curry favor with me. He always leveled with me as much as a mature adult male can be completely frank with an impressionable boy.

When he whipped me, he never said the whipping hurt him more than it hurt me. Obviously, I was aware of that aphorism, and once, when he whipped me, I asked him if the thrashing hurt him more than it hurt me.

He looked at me as if I were the village idiot: "That's hookum. It didn't hurt me a damned bit, boy."

To attain one's majority, to receive all the cherished privileges of manhood, was worthy of lengthy apprenticeship. But when a boy grew up, finally, to deserve long trousers, to be trusted with his full share of local moral and intellectual responsibilities, his blood raced as if he were a possum with the only keys to the henhouse. I know my blood raced that way.

Today, when so many intellectual red-necks wear button-down collars, when cost harasses merit, to paraphrase Oscar

Wilde, I find myself seeking succor and sustenance in an insular world that was bounded by Wake County on the south and by the state line border on the north. Yet, if my geographical domain was highly restricted, if my physical sorties hardly ever carried me beyond the sight and the smell of the smoke from my father's chimney, I managed to cross many continents of love and excitement.

When I seem to be ensnared by today's expediencies and social flap-doodles, I think tenderly of many folks who are dead and buried but who remain preciously quick to me. For instance, my father, an old-time lawyer, exuded more excitement over a spelling bee, an old ham, the first snow of winter, or from chanting Whitman's "I Hear America Singing" than his current counterpart would get from a weekend visit to the White House.

Perhaps, memory wants to use a blue pencil on the past, but I am positive everything Papa did was pitched to a distinctive tune, even when the music was as silent as the phantom fragrance of lilacs.

I remember those scented, buried summer nights when I went out to catch lightning-bugs in a bottle just for temporary captivity, mind you. I'd pretend the bottle was the tower of the Old North Church, or that I was a flagman, waving my lantern, as I used the front porch banisters for a long line of careening box-cars.

I can still hear Papa's booming voice when he waved me out to the evening's wonderland, as he quoted the last of Whitman's poem:

"At night the party of young fellows, robust, friendly

Singing with open mouths their strong melodious songs."

There was a sampler on our parlor wall, just above the piano. The state motto was stitched there, "Esse Quam Videri." It meant "To be rather than to seem."

I still translate the phrase that way, but there are times when I feel almost as alone as the boy on the burning ship.

130

For, aside from the fact that Latin fetches no green stamps, the ancient and honorable motto is currently construed: "To seem rather than to be."

Hence, you may plumb my desire to share with you a time in local history when life was intensely personal, and much less standardized, mechanized, and by-the-numbers. You see, I remember when buttons were something mothers sewed on the britches and shirts of little boys. Back then one didn't push buttons the way Aladdin rubbed his lamp.

As Emily Dickinson had said about her own father, "Our whole house was filled when Papa was on the sofa." Of course, we called it a "settee," and not a sofa. In that era, when Papa's personality was a benevolent flood, the arms on our settee were decorated by "Antimacassars." There was no wall-to-wall carpeting. Indeed, the word "carpet" was hardly ever used in Oxford. Our settee rested on a "drugget."

We had no electrical vacuum cleaners, and each spring we carried the "drugget" to the backyard to beat it. This was man's work, and Papa pretended that the "drugget" was Judge Erasmus Booker, who, Papa said, thought he was the Old Testament God and every poor white and Negro defendent was Job.

Many times I imagined that the "drugget" was Jo-Jo Tulgin, who won my marbles at school, and who beat my tail regularly just to keep in practice.

Papa would swing his flail against the "druggett" and then exclaim, "Take that, you polecat." I'd swing my flail and yell "Zooks," even if I didn't know what it meant. But "Zooks" seemed eminently pertinent as I imagined Jo-Jo's being knocked on his keester.

When I was big enough to smell myself a little, I imagined that the "drugget" was Brailsford Entwhistle, who stole my girl in the seventh grade, because he slicked his hair with "Stay-Comb." Even worse, he put me down in a big spelling bee by getting Constantinople correctly. . .My revenge was hearty, if deferred, when Constantinople was changed to Istanbul, and old Brailsford's laurel became as rusty as a tool left in the rain all winter.

(If my father had never read Freud, we engaged in the most active sort of psychiatric therapy everytime we walloped that drugget. It was the receptacle for our hostilities. Therefore, my father didn't emulate our neighbor and friend, Mr. Lester, who always mumbled aloud as he walked home from a mean day downtown: "If supper ain't ready, I'm go raise pluperfect hell. If supper is ready, I'm ain't go eat er damned bite.")

Man was a free agent in Oxford, when this century was a gangling colt, and for a short while afterwards. To be sure, God made the world, in seven days. (Papa said God forgot to make Texas while He was fashioning the other states and territories. Papa said God made Texas late Saturday night when he was tired and His mind wasn't on His business fully.)

But God made the world the way Mr. Elgin made a watch. He handed it over to you, in fee simple, and you had the complete running of it. This freedom, if full-throated and open-handed, was a matter of utmost gravity. It was never an abstraction, even when it was outrageously faithless or funny. The pursuit of freedom, happiness, and labor was a sort of pantry, a larder, as well as an inspiration.

I heard a stanza from Shelley quoted many times. Most of the men who quoted it hadn't been off to college, but they respected learning, for the beauty and joy of learning, as if learning were the last dab of fire on earth and a hard sleet was falling:

> "For the laborer thou art bread,
> And a comely table spread.
> Thou art clothes, and fire and food,
> For the trampled multitude."

Shelley was talking about freedom, and his stanza is gallingly pertinent right now as I look around and admit the depressing fact that Oxford is merely an extension of the mores of some Metropolitan place. For, the image, the status-symbol, and things (just "things") are everywhere.

It used to be different, I think. People were turned on differently. I remember one day Papa left a hard-cash client in his office to walk rapidly across the Square to climb the long steps to Mr. Ben Parham's law office to tell his friend that Shelley's father had been born in Newark, N.J. They both knew about Garibaldi's residence in this nation. Mr. Parham didn't know the odd fact Papa had gleaned, God knows where, about Shelley's father, although Mr. Parham got a law degree from Harvard in 1907, or "ought seven," as Papa put it.

Shelley's stanza is balefully germane today when virtually every family in town, including the ones that have artificial grass, seems to be bucking so hard for "Yard of the Month." Almost every lawn in Oxford stands posed as if it is waiting for a photographer from "Life" to come and take its picture.

One wily, sneaky-pete of a wild onion in a lawn brings more embarrassment today than a shotgun wedding did back when yards were for human enjoyment, when they were paeans to love, to sunshine, and to rain. If Blind Pew came to town, he'd know these lawns aren't for leap-frog, marbles, stick horses, one-eyed-cat, treehouses, or Prisoner's Base. For, a grass-sticky void stands where the resounding hosannas of "Bum, bum, Here I come," once erupted from games of Pretty Girls' Station.

Chickens don't run and scratch or leave a raucous cackle for a calling-card when they lay an egg almost surreptitiously in the shrubbery. If a passing dog uses a tree for a rest-station, you'd think the honor of the town has been sullied. And God knows, if a bitch in heat and her boy friend dog used such a lawn for a trysting place, a lot of modern people would expect the C.I.A. to come down and handle the heinous offense, personally.

The last rooster in town is crowing in the dawn in some other place, and the last goat must be butting with Mr. Scratch somewhere south of Suez. But we had a wonderful goat. His name was Miltiades, but we called him Milt since we all voted a Woodrow Wilson ticket, whether or not we were all old enough to vote. Milt mowed the lawn, and he could tell and honest hobo from a free-loading tramp a block away against the wind. He never butted Mr. Farris, the postman, who read all the cards and told you what they said as he handed them over. He never "wet" or "grunted" when ladies were visiting Mother on the front porch; and when he was ailing, he always cried a little when we comforted him, to show his gratitude.

Papa taught Milt to count to five, with his right front foot. Papa said, many times, that Milt could have been elected president of the Rotary Club if he had a place to put his tail. But, then again, Papa said he didn't think Milt liked green peas and calf liver enough to walk down to the hotel to the weekly meeting of the Rotary. But you have to know that Papa never joined anything but the Methodist Church and the Democratic Party and he said anybody could join those. . .

When Milt was as old for goats as Methuselah was for folks, Papa sat up with him three straight nights, so I could sleep and be fresh for school. When Milt died, we buried him in the far, right hand corner of the vegetable garden, and our friend, "Old Dan" Tucker, put a little picket fence around the grave.

At the services, Papa made a sizzling anti-sheep speech. I guess, now, he did this to dry our tears with anger at foolish sheep. He compared Milt to Tom Paine, Thomas Jefferson, Andy Jackson, Mark Twain, and Vachel Lindsay, whoever he was. He said sheep reminded him of the Bloomer Girls' baseball team, baaing in the field and drinking Lydia E. Pinkham's between innings.

If there was anything incongruous about Milt's long,

intimate association with our family, there wasn't a man between Richmond and Atlanta who had grown enough to say so to Papa.

But, I know, too, that one can't really return from the grave. This month my sister, who lives at our old place, won the "Yard of the Month" award from the local Beautification Committee. The sign, "Yard of the Month" will stand in our old lawn for a month. If angels can cuss, I'll bet Papa hasn't raised such hell since Nixon was elected. And if one could "come back," you can bet your bottom dollar Papa would have tattooed Sister's bottom with that sign, before he threw it to hell and away.

Again, I must push on and tell you about Oxford when it was much more fig leaf than white dinner jacket, so that you will know there was such a minister as Mr. Thompson, A.B.D.D.

His successor, two or three times removed, sits on his emotions as if he were trying to hatch out a nest of golf balls. The way this fellow talks one would think he is giving mouth-to-mouth tranquilizing pills. He uses "however" and "on the other hand" the way an undertaker bows from the hips in a well-dressed crowd.

He sounds as if Billy Graham, Norman Vincent Peale, "Dial a Prayer," and "Popular Psychiatry" had been condensed into a capsule by "Reader's Digest." The only way he could ever get his hands dirty is from holding one of the avant-garde novels he reads to show how open-minded he is. . .

But I have to admit this fellow had done a neat job of keeping Jesus locked up in the church, tightly, except for the hours each Sunday morning when people visit Him there. Everyone praises His name from eleven to twelve on Sunday morning. Then, this minister locks up, and during the week Jesus doesn't get out and get into anyone's hair or conscience or cause any trouble.

Now, it's difficult for me to say what kind of church-preacher Mr. Thompson really was, because I associate him with the town, not with his church. I suppose he was ambivalent.

He talked about love a lot but when he did, his face wasn't so long a barber would charge two dollars to shave it. (Shaves cost only about two bits back then.) He talked about love and life. He loved life and he hated suffering and death.

Other people talked, sometimes, about suffering through something if it was God's will. Mr. Thompson (everyone called him "Brother" or "Brer") said God never made you suffer. Hell no. God wasn't a bloody idiot. But God might help you through your suffering.

About his ambivalence: Papa said "Brer" Thompson was a great Greek scholar. Very quietly, he talked about eros, philos, and agape. He didn't use any scholastic blackjack. He just told about the difference.

He and Papa used to write letters regularly, even if they saw each other on the street two or three times each day. I have in possession, at this moment, a letter, and the paper is quite jaundiced, Mr. Thompson wrote to Papa, dated "11-20-24."

Apparently, the two had talked, earlier in the day, about the phrase, "On (and "in") the lap of the Gods." In a bold, uphill script, as if his letters are marching men, Mr. Thompson says:

"I write from Tom Stewart's where I wait with Dr. Henley until the pneumonia crisis is done. Anent our discussion, at the P.O. earlier this morning: The phrase, of course, is from our ancient friends, the Greeks. It means that everything has been done that can be done. The result awaits a power beyond known human control. Betimes, I checked. The phrase is found in the 17th book of the *Iliad*: 'Yet verily these issues lie on the lap of the gods.' Likely, reference is to the pagan custom of placing prayers written in wax tablets at the knees of the

136

statues of the gods. I fear the custom still persists. Will see you at the oyster 'bilin'' if all goes well here. O, yes. A thoughtful Christian has promised me the loan of a big snake for the evening. Surely, a snake-bitten servant of the Lord is entitled to a stiff dram before a 'bilin'.''

Despite his learning and all the quiet conversations he had with Papa, and many others, about Aristotle, Aristophanes, Aristides, Homer, and Sophocles, "Brer" Thompson was as outgoing as a gate that swung toward the big road. He was always joking about his huge appetite. He said when people invited him to supper, their children started cutting turnip greens without being prompted, and the children used a mowing machine. He said all the chickens and hogs ran off and hid in the woods when they heard his steps.

I remember this joke he told on himself: He was (he said) visiting an old lady who lived on the other side of a foot-log. In mid-stream, "Brer" Thompson had a sneezing spell and lost his false teeth in the creek. The water was more than belly deep, he said, but he went on to the old lady's house and returned with a drumstick of a chicken.

He waved the drumstick over the water, and the false teeth jumped up from the bottom of the creek and bit into the meat. "Brer" Thompson put his "Roebuckers" back in and went on his way.

At the time of which I write, he was about fifty, but his muscles were those of the young athlete. His lean face looked as if it had been cut from whitleather, but his eyes laughed and sparkled the way smooth stones at the bottom of a clear brook laugh and sparkle.

He was the chaplain of the local fire company, but such a sinecure was not for "Brer" Thompson. He acted as Captain of Number One Nozzle Unit. He was always "in the middle of the fire" with his "boys."

The bell would ring and we boys thought the whole sky was made of iron and clappers and it was falling. Mr.

Thompson would yell, "Play the Doxology," and he'd run down the aisle, leaping past pews in tremendous strides.

The barber shop was right up the street from the fire house. When the telephone bell, the small alarm sounded, all the firemen who worked or loafed up town would run to catch the wagon, or the truck, after we got a truck.

Many times I have seen Mr. Thompson running from the barber shop to catch the tail-gate of the fire truck. He would bound from the door, throwing the apron back over his left shoulder. As he ran to catch the truck, he would blow the lather from his face, and from his lips, as if the sweetest, fleetest hound of heaven were frothing at the mouth.

If the fire was a big one, Matt Venable, who was our fire chief as well as our High Sheriff, would yell up and down the street: "Dammit, pour it 'em, boys. Dammit, give 'em hell, boys."

And "Brer" Thompson would nod his head and thunder in his great baritone: "That's right, boys. That's exactly right, boys. You do precisely as the chief says."

Not just incidentally, the fire company in Oxford was integrated for almost fifty years, although I never heard anyone make a sociological comment about this. The blacks grew old and died, and their sons, nephews, and younger friends didn't volunteer to take their places. Of course, the explanation could be more devious, more elusive, but that was about the size of it, superficially, anyway.

There were twenty-odd black volunteer firemen when I was a small boy, but by the time F.D.R. came along, black membership was down to four old gentlemen, Cap'n Dave Johnson, the venerable foreman, Cap'n Sam Owens, the assistant foreman, and two other elderly men. I guess Cap'n Dave published the requiem when he told Papa: "Well, there ain't nobody left for me and Sam to boss at fires."

I always thought our integrated fire department was a fine plus for mankind's better portions, but it may have been paternalism, and it may have been merely that the community obtained the services of such excellent fire fighters free of charge. Who knows, perhaps, the younger blacks decided, without actually having to decide, that if the whites owned the buildings, they could put out the fires, too. Our whole racial amalgam was pretty crazy: Many black women fed, even breast-fed, white kids, washed them and heard their prayers. Then when the kid got fourteen years old, the same black woman had to call him "Mister."

If there was a big fire, women brought coffee, lemonade, and sandwiches for the firemen. After the fire, when all the "boys" were on the truck, returning to the fire house, everyone along the street clapped, and many of the men along the sidewalk took off their hats, waved their hats at our firemen.

If the fire bell rang while I was at school, and if the commotion on the street indicated it was a big fire, I'd hold up one finger with my right hand and two fingers with my left hand, signifying to the teachers, always a female, that I had to be excused to do "number one" and "number two" also.

If the fire occurred after school, or in summer, I'd usually reach the scene almost as soon as the firemen. If there was a fire at night, I'd beat Papa to the car and hide on the back seat.

Gradually, I was accepted around the fire house, via a process similar to osmosis. Several times, after fires, when the "boys" were lounging around the firehouse and drinking their "re-wards," the confiscated whiskey supplied during Prohibition by Sheriff Mat Venable, Cap'n Dave asked "Brer" Thompson if one of the thieves crucified with Jesus might have been a black man?

"Brer" Thompson didn't know but he always pondered the question seriously.

Local blacks used to sing a song about the crucifixion. It

was about Jesus's silence when one of the two thieves asked him to speak up and save the three men being crucified. The old song, "And He Never Said A Mumbling Word," asked more oblique questions than anyone in Oxford wanted to try to answer.

There used to be a brick privy between the firehouse and the courthouse, a tiny building which was a lawyer's office prior to the Revolutionary War. Plumbing had been installed by my time but the rank odors had taken on almost heinous proportions since the reign of George III, and the walls, redolent with all sorts of writings, filled me with consternation. The crumbling, old walls were littered with words and phrases not contained in any of our family's dictionaries or reference books.

I ransacked all of my school books, parallel books, and all the books we had at home. Finally I concluded that these esoteric words and phrases must be restricted to Oxford and environs. I used to slip up on the privy the subtle way Ty Cobb stole home by pretending that was the last thing he had in mind.

When I started to the privy, to revel in the lascivious scribblings, I did what I thought of as my saunter. Papa had told me that during the Middle Ages thousands of Europeans walked around begging alms, that the ruse was that they were on a Crusade, "a la Sainte terre," "to the Holy Land." Finally these beggars were so commonplace that whenever a child saw one coming the child exclaimed, "Here comes another Sainte terrer," and that's how we got the word "saunter."

I had sense enough to pretend that I was urinating as I read all the graffiti on the smelly walls, and occasionally I took a drink of water prior to entering the place. One day as I was reading some unvarnished testimonials relative to a local woman's incredible sexual prowess, I urinated, when I wasn't expecting to, because a rollicking bass voice boomed: "Your Pa didn't get to be a lawyer and a fine man reading such trash as this. "Cap'n Dave was standing behind me, and I felt the same loathsome way I would have felt if I had broken wind at the communion table.

But I ask permission to amend this entry, slightly. In 1969 the new Heritage Dictionary arrived in Oxford. And there is wry consolation in learning that many of the words scrawled on the walls of the old town privy, now long dismantled, are real words, are in the big dictionary.

OLD MAN'S FANCY

Love is a hungry hobo
Knocking on back doors
For last night's left-over dreams.

Love is a small boy
Quarantined with chicken-pox, and
Pressing his face against the bedroom window
To look for Lancelot or for men from Mars.

Very often, love is a cat on a fence
Somewhere after midnight, striking
A yellow paw at moonbeams, and being predatory
In a haughty, hump-backed way
About squatters' rights and all the hosts
Of Johnnies-Come-Lately.
And, as I have observed,
Love is also a tall water-lily
Being majestic and unsullied
Above three frogs with boisterous manners.

But, principally, love is a hobo
Blowing a ragtime harmonica at kitchen doors
And making chalk marks on the friendly ones
For tomorrow's ravenous minstrel.

THE MANTLEPIECE

The modern home, virtually the Big Rock Candy Mountain with picture windows, contains services and entertainments that were restricted to the beauty parlor, the barber shop, the public library, the vaudeville show, and the sporting goods store yesterday. But the old-timey mantlepiece is in general oblivion, save, perhaps, for a single, slim, almost surreptitious suspension in the den.

At best it holds a single vase of flowers, and it stands in space as vacuously as if a sick cat had licked her tongue out but lacked the will to pull it back in again. However, when the strongest man in town couldn't lift two dollars worth of liver, a mantlepiece was in almost every room. It was a toll bridge, a pack horse, a plunder room, and an express depot. Indeed, it wasn't hard to get the impression that the house, a sort of after-thought, was built onto the mantlepieces. And, like the Vicar's head, everyone marveled at all it held.

On the average mantlepiece in traditional homes were bottles of cough syrup, chill tonic, castor oil, and citronella, interspersed between hump-backed hills of ancient letters, postal cards, circulars, wedding and birth announcements, all bound up in shoe strings or with wrapping string. An iron box held within its metallic jaws recepits, recipes, newspaper clippings, school report cards, assorted snapshots, old issues of *The Farmers' Almanac*, mementos of the state fair, old watches and coins, a rabbit's foot, a buckeye, four-leaf clovers, a shoe-shorn, Seidlitz powders, and ringlets of hair.

Looking down and zealously guarding a box of shotgun shells, some seashells, a checkerboard, a hymnal, and a seed catalogue were a Cardui calendar, pictures of Uncle Frank taken in his uniform in France in 1918, Joe in his World War

II threads, of papa and mamma at Atlantic City on their honeymoon, and of little Lucy in her first communion dress. There was a big clock that kept time by ear, and the eyeglasses that grandma could never find.

There was enough stuff on one mantlepiece to enable a kid to get a Ph.D. in an exhaustive study of the most fascinating elements of several generations of accumulated, teeming minutiae.

ENTRIES FROM OXFORD

October 19, 1964

When I was a boy, Mr. Ed Settle preached the gospel of pine seedlings from his buggy. This was far into the automobile era, and Mr. Ed kept cars for members of his family. But he always rode around in a buggy. He wasn't six feet tall and he weighed about 475, and he had to go to the railroad freight depot everytime he wanted to see what he weighed.

His buggy was a two-seated carriage with the front seat removed. Even so, his improvised buggy was a tight squeeze. For a petrified fact, his sons and I used to make tents of his old shirts. I swear a small boy could play Hiding in one of his old shirt sleeves.

His belly and his knees weren't even on speaking terms. His stout young assistant, a boy named Aleck, always went with him, to help Mr. Ed in and out the buggy, and to help Mr. Ed make water. Mr. Ed not only couldn't see that far down below his bail of cotton of a belly. He couldn't unbutton his fly or find his hammer. When nature called, and she never seemed to have laryngitis, Aleck reached under the seat for a pail. Then Aleck placed the pail between Mr. Ed's legs and he unbuttoned the fly and found the hammer. One afternoon in front of the music store, on College Street, Mr. Ed had a terrible call from nature, but Aleck couldn't seem to find the hammer.

"Hurry up, hurry up, I'm dying," the old man screamed. "I'm sorry. I'm sorry as hell, Mr. Ed, but I can't find it nowhere."

Sweat was flooding the old man's agonized face. "Well, Aye God, boy, you better find it. You're the last man to have his hands on it."

But if he took his bathroom along in his make-shift buggy, he carried his own piped-in music, too. He always carried a big chromatic mouth-organ, or harp, as the instrument was called in Oxford. The harp was in his right hand coat pocket, summer and winter. It looked big enough to fell an ox, but the music was sufficient to sweeten all the coffee in town.

We boys used to walk beside the buggy to be serenaded by "Ora Lee," "On the Banks of the Wabash," "Wait Til the Sun Shines Nellie," and other sentimental tunes. Then he would switch to such "salty dogs" as "Didn't He Ramble," "Too Much Mustard," "Everybody's Doing It," and "The Lady Stooped Down To Tie Her Shoe" ("The wind blew up the avenue").

The Settles lived a block from us, and sometimes when I had gone to bed, Mr. Ed would be driving home from one of his farms. The whole street would be as quiet as a child spent from play. Suddenly, the deep, purple stillness of the night would be anointed by the sounds of the big harp. I'd lie there in bed as the room filled with the sounds of "Let the Rest of the World Go By," "Let Me Call You Sweetheart," or "Kiss In the Dark."

Then I'd hear Mamma and Papa, downstairs, singing softly, or humming, along with the floating serenade. Sometimes, Papa would yell, "Encore, Ed, encore, please, Ed."

I never heard Mr. Ed speak any reply, but in a few minutes the horse and buggy would be coming up Front Street again. I remember one night his first encore was "A Hot Time In the Old Town Tonight," the fence-rattler that was associated with Teddy Roosevelt and the "Rough Riders," the irresistibly infectious tune that percolated around Teddy Roosevelt his entire political life.

I grabbed a walking-stick that Papa never carried. I used it for a sword and for a rifle, too, as I went charging up San Juan Hill with Teddy, Bucky O'Neil and the other swashbuckling "Rough Riders." I ran through several Spaniards with my sword. Others I clubbed with the rifle butt. Before we routed the enemy I was knocked down several times, but despite the shock and pain I had the bounceability of an especially resilient tennis ball.

When we reached the top of San Juan Hill, Teddy clasped me in both of his strong arms. He almost rattled my teeth out when he hugged me and yelled, "Bully, Sandy, Bully."

I must have made quite a ruckus. Just about the time Teddy was giving me the accolade, Papa yelled upstairs: "That's enough, Sandy. That damned war is over. Leave enough Spaniards for seed corn." (I never was sure just how Papa knew what I was doing, acting out, but then again, Papa had been a boy, too.)

That same night Mr. Ed's second encore was "Pretty Baby," one of Papa's favorites, and he sang the words to Mother, along with Mr. Ed's harp music. The Entwhistle's house was dark, but the lights came on, like a trail of fireflies, in a few minutes, and someone over there played "Pretty Baby" on the fabulous Steinway piano that Mr. Entwhistle had ordered all the way from Baltimore.

For his last encore, Mr. Ed played "Be My Little Baby Bumblebee." I heard Papa buzzing around Mamma downstairs. Then some courting couple on a porch near by took it up on a mandolin.

The way Mr. Ed played the tune made me think every bee extant was buzzing around, sipping clover. One part of the lyrics says:

> "Hon-ney keep a buzzing please,
> I've got a dozen cousin bees,
> But I wantcha to be my baby bumble bee."

Many years later I wrote a short story which I had not given a title. Near the end I remembered that wonderful night. I called my story "A Dozen Cousin Bees." I don't know that the title really came across, but the story did about as well as anything I have ever written.

As I said, one of Mr. Ed's coat pockets held his harp, when he wasn't playing it. The other pocket, which seemed as big as a bushel basket, was always crammed with candy, "Mary Janes," "Downey's Taffy," and a wide assortment of jaw-breakers and all-day suckers.

God knows how many different pieces of candy he gave each day to us black and white urchins.

I see him now giving out candy with one hand and pine seedlings to adults with the other hand. As he handed out his packages of seedlings, he made about a one-minute speech, along the line, "The Forest Is the Future." Anyway, he explained the growing pines were money in the bank, drawing whopping interest. If a young farmer had small children, Mr. Ed told him: "Plant pines and educate your chillun in a show-nuff college."

When he was not playing his chromatic harp or giving away candy and seedlings, Mr. Ed was reading a book. Some of them were kiddie books, things such as *Billy and the Major* and *Miss Minerva and William Green Hill*. And he read so many "Westerns" I think he acted some out in his mind.

One day he told Papa the Sioux — he pronounced it "Sow-ex" — had attacked him and his buggy. He said he had been gut-shot by ten Sow-ex arrows. However, none did more than penetrate the first fold of fat on his belly.

One summer he got hold of a copy of *Gentlemen Prefer Blondes*. He would see Papa on the sidewalk, park the buggy parallel to the sidewalk, and ask Papa all sorts of questions about Paris.

Papa had been in the First World War. Naturally, Mr. Ed considered Papa an authority on Gay Paree, and the old gentleman related Papa's information to the peregrinations of Lorelai Lee.

As he read, a fat dictionary lay in his huge lap. When he saw a word he didn't know he looked it up, then and there. Finding a new word was more nearly a new world than a new

148

thrill or a gem. One such word was the word "probity," and another was "peradventure."

I remember, this very moment, the gentle way that Papa, "Brer" Thompson, and Doc Henley made it easy for Mr. Ed to insert his glittering new worlds, his words, into conversations.

One time Papa said, "Ed Settle is the most omnivorous reader in town." Mr. Ed "looked her up." Then he beamed as if God Almighty had given him His best milk cow. He said the word over and over, smacking his lips as if he were tasting the finest brandy.

Everytime Mr. Ed passed Papa for a week the old gentleman doffed his tremendous straw hat and said "Om-niv-O-rus," adding a soft "t" to the "rus." Instead of saying "howdy", he said "Om-niv-O-rus, Major, Om-niv-O-rus."

He liked the narrative poetry of Scott. His favorite passage was from *The Lady of the Lake*:
> "The stag at eve had drunk his fill,
> Where danced the moon on Monan's rill,
> And deep his midnight lair had made
> In lone Glenartney's hazel shade."

A man in town, Dougald Cameron, had moved from Scotland. He came to Oxford to work for the local branch of the Imperial Tobacco Co., a British concern. Dougald knew all about Monan's rill, as well as other places described by Sir Walter Scott.

Mr. Ed would fix enough lunch to arrest an Old Testament famine. Then he'd take Dougald Cameron fishing. He had a super-reinforced canvas chair for fishing. Then Aleck got the whiskey, the best local brandy during Prohibition and the best Scotch when North Carolina voted in the package stores.

Mr. Ed would sit enthroned for the day listening to Dougald tell about Monan's rill, about Scott's home, Abbotsford, and about the Highlands.

The triumphant, exultant look of discovery in Mr. Ed's eyes made the astronauts seem as if they had discovered their big toes instead of having landed on the moon.

Until FDR called in all the gold Mr. Ed gave an annual award of a twenty dollar gold piece, a "double-eagle," to any local student ("scholar" was the old designation) who learned by heart a long poem. The teacher had to certify the poem was rendered before the class, and Mr. Ed always asked, humbly, for a private recitation.

After FDR called in the gold, Mr. Ed upped the prize to thirty dollars in greenbacks during the few more years he lived. But I doubt that extra ten dollars compensated for the gold pieces.

Each gold piece was more than a glorious diadem. It was a passport. It meant distinction rather than status.

I won one of the last gold pieces awarded. I had it put on my watch chain for a fob. Papa told me not to be ostentatious. So, the "double-eagle" usually rested in a vest pocket, from my watch chain, but I could hardly wait for someone to ask me the time of day or night. When I whipped out the Elgin Papa gave me for my 16th birthday, Mr. Ed's gold piece managed to expose itself. It was as if I toted the moon in my vest pocket. And the Lord knows how many hours I spent twirling the chain when no one was looking.

When FDR called in the gold, I took my glorious fob to the bank, to exchange it for greenbacks. I gave it to Mr. Kennon Taylor, an officer in the bank. My heart was as heavy as the gloom of those grim Depression days. Mr. Taylor fondled the "double-eagle." "The new President seems to be a fine man, a good man, but he can put your gold medal where the monkey puts the nuts."

I didn't tell Papa, not for a while. I knew he would say I was breaking the law, and I knew, also, he would say that if I got arrested for hoarding gold, I would have to represent myself. Lawyers said when a man represented himself he had

150

a damned fool for a client. I knew Papa would think I qualified, all around.

My "double-eagle" was awarded for learning the "Rounding the Horn" section of John Masefield's *Dauber*. The section I memorized must have been at least sixty lines.

Mr. Ed invited me to his house to say the lines to him. He saw on his side front porch, in a swing that had double chains to hold his incredible girth. He filled the swing the way two people always seem to fill a hammock, or the way May grass seems to fill a lawn.

He asked for, and got, a synopsis of the long narrative poem, up to the point where my recitation took over. He nodded his big head as if he had just seen some parallel lines that crossed and criss-crossed. From the way the old gentleman sniffed I am sure the rose arbor was emitting the twang of salt spray.

His eyes scanned the horizon the way the master of a sailing ship would see everything in and out of sight. I was, I am, reasonably sure Mr. Ed was acting out the role of ship's captain.

But about the time I reached the part of the poem that says,

"Up! yelled the bos'un, Up and clear the wreck,
   The Dauber followed where he led,"

it was I who got an urgent call from nature. Mr. Ed perceived my distress. "Jess go there to the banisters, boy, and make water over them. Don't lose time going inside to the water-closet. By God, I want to know how she turns out."

So, I cut loose over the banisters. Mr. Ed rubbed his hands as he waited for me to continue the narrative. I know Mother would have an old-fashioned Methodist fit and fall into the middle of it if she heard I had done "number one" on the Settle's porch, and right in broad daylight, too.

Mr. Ed probably detected my consternation. For, just as I finished he said, firmly, "There ain't a gal in nine counties who can stand flat-footed and do what you just did."

We had a copy of Masefield's *Salt Water Ballads* at home. Papa lent the copy to Mr. Ed. He read it in his buggy, off and on, the remainder of that spring and summer.

He took his family to Morehead City, N.C. or to Virginia Beach for two weeks each summer. He said he "never really saw" the ocean until he read Masefield's book.

When he died in 1939, he left an estate of about one million dollars, mostly in good property and land. God knows what his holdings would be worth in the currency of 1975. However, I am sure his proudest attainment, his most choice possession, was reading Masefield's famous poem "Sea-Fever" over and over, and aloud to himself, in the buggy until he got the whole twelve lines letter perfect.

He never told his family about this accomplishment. He said the poem to his cronies, to Papa, "Brer" Thompson, and Dr. Henley. Papa made him an honorary Doctor of Letters, at Oxford. But the "degree" was not bruited about. It never became cheap by dint of talk-talk.

Dr. Henley said Mr. Ed had the "Chair of Poetry," at Oxford." The old gentleman's eyes danced merrily as April showers, as he laughed and said: "Doctor, you better make that 'settee' or 'davenport'. A cheer wouldn't be big enough for me."

On the western edge of town, beyond the old corporate limits, he owned a lovely grove. Everyone used to call it "Settle's Lane." A private road, maintained by Mr. Ed, ran through this magnificent stand of pines and oak trees. (Papa told me "Settle's Lane" contained 82.5 acres, more or less.)

Weekdays a chain barred the entrance to the road, but it was down on Sundays so people could ride, slowly, or walk through the gorgeous woodland. And he let respectable people in for picnics, for "gypsy teas," as they used to be called. But "Settle's Lane" was posted against all hunters.

Even back then real estate hustlers were trying to get

"Settle's Lane" for housing developments. They might as well have tried to buy the Washington Monument to make room for a filling station. Albeit, Mr. Ed didn't waste his breath trying to explain his refusal to sell the lovely acres to those who couldn't understand.

His explanation was the same, to anyone who asked: "What'd become of the fire horses?"

When Oxford had bought motorized fire equipment, Mr. Ed had bought the two horses that had pulled the fire wagon. They were two wondrous bays, Matt and Bertha. Matt was named for Matt Venable, the fire chief and High Sheriff, and Bertha was named for Miss Bertha Hornbuckle, the telephone central who gave the fire alarms.

Without being at all fulsome, Mr. Ed said the two fire horses deserved a pension, the same as other faithful town employees. So he paid the town $1000.00 for the pair. He built a fence around a big grassy field he owned, just off the lovely woodland.

Aleck, the young man who held the pail between Mr. Ed's legs, fed, watered, and groomed the retired fire horses. I visited these beautiful horses many times, with Mr. Ed and Aleck and alone. They'd eat lumps of sugar out of my hand; but when the fire bell rang, they tore around and around the pasture, just as if they were pulling the wagon again. Their eyes blazed like headlights on a locomotive, and their neighings rolled up and down "Settle's Lane" as if rapid bursts of small thunder were annoucing a freshet.

Whenever there was a local parade, or some big wing-ding, the chamber of commerce or the Kiwanis would say it would be a fine idea to put Matt and Bertha into the parade, to let a new generation see horses pulling a fire wagon. But Mr. Ed sucked his breath and said: "The circus is for freaks."

Matt and Bertha have been in heaven, or wherever it is that good and faithful horses go, for many years, and about five years ago Mr. Ed's lovely lane lost out to the bulldozer. The housing development is called "Shamrock Drive," but I haven't seen a shamrock out there since old man McDuffie passed out about 25 years ago walking home from a three-man St. Patrick's Day celebration in Oxford.

Architecture isn't my bag, but most of the homes in Shamrock Drive seem to be identical twins, to me. I hope this bland sameness doesn't attach to the folks who live in these look-alike houses, but I certainly wouldn't make book on it. One thing is for damned sure:

The election results show that they vote alike. Nixon walked off with the vote in Shamrock. I find this mildly sardonic because the fathers and grandfathers of the ones who live in Shamrock were broke as hell when FDR was elected.

Mr. Ed Settle's granddaughter lives in Shamrock, and her house doesn't resemble the others. It is a replica of Tryon's Palace, at New Bern, N.C., but bigger. The house crowns a slight knoll, smack in the middle of the luscious pasture where Matt and Bertha sported in light-leafed breezes. The estate, called "Brigadoon," covers the 82.5 acres that the lady's grandfather set aside for beauty.

My wife and I just attended a swanky bash at the home, at Brigadoon. It was one of these deluxe parties at which everyone is a guest and no one is company. Everyone was given a guided tour of the elegant premises. The tour started with one of the six opulent bathrooms and it ended with one of the six bathrooms.

Just about everyone was deeply impressed and no one seemed to think it incongruous that he had to visit six bathrooms, whether he needed to or not. It was almost as if Xanadu had materialized, with gold faucets.

These bathrooms have harmonic chimes, portable TV's, health vibrators, health drinks, piped-in music, sunken tubs big enough to accommodate an old-fashioned August Meeting's baptizings, .and, I was told, walk-through showers that wet, soap, clean, dry and scent the body with a series of swift, deft motions.

I really got the impression that it would be a social breech to use one of these lavish places to make water. Anyway, I figured if a kid entered one when he was six, he wouldn't have to leave it until he was twenty-one and wanted to get out and vote.

When the Canterbury pilgrims were entering the third bathroom, I slipped away into the luxuriantly paneled library, much as a player would steal home when the catcher is at the hot dog stand.

Aside from the four-in-one condensed versions of "Reader's Digest" novels, the book shelves were filled with expensive-looking works on flower arranging, landscaping, interior decorating, personality analyses, and treatises on diets and the raising of children.

A special table held some statuettes Mr. Ed's granddaughter had won for prizes at local golf tournaments, and there was a handsome Revere bowl she had won for "Civic Contributions" in 1967. On another table there was a handsome copy of *War and Peace*. It rested in a manner that reminded me of Poe's story, *The Purloined Letter*. I opened *War and Peace*, and the pages were as clean and untouched as a child's innocence. It was balanced, on a hassock, by Norman Vincent Peale's *Guide to Confident Living*.

I had heard our hostess make some furtive allusion to *All You Need To Know About Sex*. I couldn't locate this book, and while I was looking around I heard the entourage going into yet another bathroom.

I thought about Mr. Ed Settle, about Aleck and the pail, and about his insisting that I wee-wee over the banisters the time I was reciting from *Dauber*. I knew he made all the money for this paean to plumbing.

It was easy to imagine the horror and consternation a visit from him would cause his granddaughter. And I already knew what Mr. Ed would think of this mansion. But it hurt too much to speculate on what the old gentleman would think of the brutal demolition of his lovely grove.

ANTAGONISTS

You know, I told him, the crinkly grass
Along our runty road is an old man's goatee.
But he said it's just grass, nor much of it, at that.

And when the path bumped up high and fell flat
On its face in Sweetgum Creek, I said it was Joshua's
        warriors
Cupping the flow. He laughed to explain to me how

The path merely peters out and the creek begins,
The way the forest takes over when the field ends.
Well, then, I asked him, how will this one do:

A bluebird is mightier than an eagle
As one hour in April outweighs all of January
By far. But he would have none of this whimsy-whamsy

And replied that I was chasing butterflies
And he was digging worms, but we'd walk each other home
Through the darkness and let silence make us equally wise.

DOG DAYS DROUGHT

The street's a funeral pyre
And the sidewalk is grounded white swans
Caught in the tar-paper of an alien land.

Blistered leaves are fish
Too morose to strike or swim. They hang around
Aimlessly as scorched jokes hunting for punch lines.

Old men scan the sky
As if it were a raffle-ticket
They'd bet their last fifty cents on.

But the sun's a hunter who lost his dogs,
And wild hounds range the skyland damning
To hell the gods that drove them mad.

The crow's caw is a falsetto bellyache
And he wouldn't spit on rotten cornfield corpses,
Not even if he had the spittle to spare.

Twilight's a rose, criminally assaulted,
And the departing sun strikes his tent
As if it had cheated him at cards.

But all the village oracles say
It has always managed to rain,
Certainly up to now.

And old Brother Brokenfield,
Who's to do the main praying for rain,
Is toting his umbrella to Little Zion Church.

ENTRIES FROM OXFORD

Oxford, October 11, 1968:

Today, profanity, in all phases of society and conversation, is almost as axiomatic as ants at a picnic. The chaste dash ("--g") is gone from literature, and profanity in mixed company, with or without mixed drinks, is as commonplace as chiggers around blackberry bushes.

Hardly anyone whispers swear words, uses pantomime, or says, "h," "d," or "g.d." I suppose this trend was inevitable when books, the theater, the movies, and TV relaxed the old strictures relative to graphic language.

This doesn't bother me, personally, but it annoys me, somewhat, that so many people swear because they seem to think free-swinging talk makes them cool or groovy, per se. What I do object to is the fact, the sad fact, that much current swearing resembles the worst of modern poetry, cubist art, and rock music.

It's a jumble of sounds devoid of verve, spontaneity, purpose, and passion. Much of modern swearing is shorn even of that therapeutic relief which appealed so much to Mark Twain and to his alter-ego, Pudd'nhead Wilson.

I remember long ago Papa's telling me that in Chaucer's time swearing was a privilege, a badge. All the top cats during Chaucer's time had distinguishing oaths, the same way big-name American dance bands used to have definitive theme signatures.

During this same conversation, "Brer" Thompson said that several British monarchs — William the Conqueror, King John, and King Edward I — all had special, identifying oaths.

However, as I understood it, swearing was not a divine

right in the New World. Swearing was the prerogative, if not the privilege, of the eloquent, of the fervent. For a long time each community had some champion cussers, men who could swear for an hour and never repeat the same expletive.

The community used such men the way many of their grandfathers hired substitutes during the Civil War. They sort of took a verbal last strike for someone. If something occurred that demanded profane redress, someone sent for a champ, for a real pro, to do the cussing.

Papa combined the magic of Mark Twain and the bravado of Wagner's overtures. Without preamble or research, Papa exuded righteous indignation, social protest, moral outrage, frustration, or the hellishness of some hurt or offense.

What I object to today is the fact that swearing has been usurped by arrant amateurs, by effete poseurs, by rank dilettanti. Hence, many of the surviving old-time experts are mute for the same reason that Buffalo Bill wouldn't mount a merry-go-round horse and shoot a water-pistol.

Swearing today, with most of the cult, is as vacuous and incongruous as giving a Stradivarius to one of the fiddlers in one of the ersatz hillbilly bands on television.

About 1928, long before civil rights was ever spoken locally, before the phrase was ever used, within my hearing, I was uptown one day, barefooted, when I ran into Papa.

He invited me into Hill's Drug Store for a cool drink. While we were sipping our lemonades, Ramsay Davis, a college senior, came into the drug store.

Ramsay was all the rage, with what Papa called the "jawbone set." A "jawboner" was someone, who, in Papa's judgment, had more brains in his jawbone than in his head.

Anyway, Ramsay had won national acclaim for swallowing a fantastically large number of live goldfish. He had won a Charleston dancing contest, a marathon dancing contest, and he had been so successful as chief cheerleader at football games that one of the cough drop companies had given him free samples of small boxes of cough drops to hand out to his yellers at the Saturday games.

He greeted Papa with "Put her there, Major, old boy," but Papa pretended not to see Ramsay's hand extended. With mock solemnity, Papa asked Ramsay about the great honors he had won at the university, and Ramsay went into profuse details about swallowing the live goldfish, winning the marathon dancing contest, and attracting the attention of the cough drop company.

He winked at Papa and gave this yell, one he had perfected, he said, when he was chief cheerleader at the university.

> "Zim, zam, zee
> Hit 'em on the knee,
> Zim, zam, zazz,
> Hit 'em on the other knee."

Ramsay doubled up laughing. "You get it?" he asked Papa.

"I get it, Ramsay," Papa replied. Then, turning to Mr. Tasker Davis, Ramsay's father, who had followed his son into Hill's, Papa said with terrible anguish: "Tasker, it must have been for this blessed moment, for these cherished honors, for this exalted hour, that Homer recorded his journeys, that Erasmas sequestered himself at Oxford, that Columbus put out to sea, that Whitman wrote *Leaves of Grass*, that Edison made illumination a way of life."

Mr. Davis nodded assent, as if he were conceding he had a frightful, terminal illness: "Yes, sir, I am reasonably sure Gutenberg pointed to this hour when he invented printing, and, beyond peradventure, Major, Hannibal anticipated Ramsay's triumphs, or, otherwise, he would not have troubled to invade Rome."

Another time Papa encountered me on the street and took me into Hill's for a "repast." When we were leaving the drug store, Mrs. R.C. Shaw was walking along the sidewalk.

Her husband was the principal of the Negro high school

and the preacher at the Negro Presbyterian Church. Papa tipped the brim of his hat and said, evenly: "Good afternoon, Mrs. Shaw."

Just Plain Snake Imboden was slouching under the awning, holding onto the awning rope. Just Plain Snake was a blockader. People said his blockade whiskey must be all right since he drank so much of it himself. He was called "Just Plain Snake" to distinguish him from his brother, "King of the Green Snakes" Imboden, who raised such wonderful Green Snake watermelons and other luscious produce.

Just Plain Snake dropped his awning rope. He siddled up to Papa, his eyes sizzling like fresh spittle on a red hot stove. "How come you called at damned nigger um-man 'Mrs. Shaw'?"

Papa said, softly, unemotionally: "Well, Mrs. Shaw's older than I am. She's better educated than I am, and she has more money."

Then, thrusting Just Plain Snake away as if he were afraid he would get his hand dirty, Papa boomed out: "But more to the point, none of your business, you damned low-life miscreant, you two-for-a-nickel jackal, you son of a bitch, net."

Tom Day, the soda water clerk at Hill's, told Papa: "I think Just Plain Snake understands the last part of what you said, Major."

It's been a long time since I've heard anyone append "net" to son of a bitch. Yesterday, "net" meant a real son of a bitch, doubled, and in spades.

A lot of people in town sent for Old Man Rufe Duncan to cuss for them, the same way they sent for Mr. Erk Mayberry to do the main out-loud praying at a meeting held to pray for rain.

Old Man Rufe Duncan was best at cussing things that people referred to as "a sin and a shame." His epithets were "vile uv the vilest," "fiend incarnate," "pot-likker hound uv hell," "not worth a dried apple dam in trade," and he said of people whom he didn't like, "I could whittle a better specimen uv humanity with a piece uv bark and a Barlow knife."

One of his pet words was "egregious." He called it "E-gree-juice." In fact I learned to spell several fifty cent words from the way Old Man Rufe pronounced, or mispronounced, them:

Virtually all politicians, living or dead, except William Jennings Bryan and Al Smith, were "in-come-pete-unt swine." Lazy folks were "non-shall-unt hobbledehoys." Old Man Rufe got the jake-leg from the yellow-jack, when he was in the Spanish-American War, or so he said, and he was forced to spend the remainder of his life "con-val-sing."

I never had any trouble spelling incompetent, nonchalant, or convalescing.

When Al Smith was running for President, several of the local ministers opposed him because they said he was a "wet." Papa said this was a "loathsome deception." The preachers who opposed Al Smith were against him because he was a Catholic, but they didn't have the guts to say so. Hence, they preached against him because he favored moderation of the 18th Amendment.

But being against Smith was sufficient to send anybody "to the bottom cellar in hell," in Old Man Rufe's opinion. One day during the 1928 campaign, Old Man Rufe was making a speech for Al Smith in front of the "Ivanhoe," the local candy store.

There were three or four adults, Albert, the "town dog," and me. Silas, Mr. Virginius Purvis's old horse, was at the curb. Then this minister came up and started putting Smith down. The minister had flaming red hair.

Papa saw me, and he walked up about the time Old Man Rufe denounced the preacher: "You lying, red-headed, knock-kneed, fiend incarnate, you psalm-singing, lily-livered imp uv Satan, you double-dealing, whore-hopping enemy uv mankind, you Judas I. Scariot son of a bitch, net, you."

The preacher turned to Papa for refutation. Papa said, "Let us examine the evidence, good sir." Then Papa repeated every word and phrase in Old Man Rufe's diatribe. When he had finished quoting Old Man Rufe, Papa said, blandly enough: "Well, your hair is red, isn't it?"

Old Man Rufe Duncan was what was known as a "town farmer." He and his wife, Miss Texanna, did own a lot of rural property, but Old Man Rufe was too busy "con-val-sing" to visit their farms. However, Miss Texanna was an excellent manager, and the Duncan's were "good livers." (They had one child, Pansy Alice, or "P.A.," as she called herself, and P.A. was Oxford's first fully liberated woman. I have an entry about her.)

Old Man Rufe reminded me of a jerkily mobile scare-crow. People said he could shut one eye and pass for a needle. Dr. Henley said if he cut open Old Man Rufe there wouldn't be any more blood in him than there is in a fishing worm.

He was so thin his bones rattled like a shackly wagon when he walked around. He carried a handsome blackthorn cane, on account of the jake-leg he got fighting the Spanish down in "Cuby." The cane had a hard point, and I could hear Old Man Rufe three blocks away as the cane went plink-plink-plink on the sidewalk.

Sometimes he used the cane for a pointer. About five o'clock in the afternoon, when he was always plastered, he used it for a baton to sort of direct his own singing and whistling.

He always walked, no matter the weather, and Miss Texanna could hear him singing two streets away, when he started lurching, stumbling, strutting, and wobbling homeward.

His piece de resistance was "Amazing Grace." When Miss Texanna heard the sounds, she'd say to Pansy Alice: "Go open the gate, honey. Your Pa'll be along directly."

When he sang the part that says, "A-maz-ing grace, how sweet the sound/That saved a wretch like me-ah," he'd always shout, "Hurrah fer Williams Jennings Bryan."

Other housewives along the route, knew it was time to get supper ready when they heard Old Man Rufe's yelling out "Hurrah fer Williams Jennings Bryan."

His second tune was "Heaven Will Protect The Working Girl," and I think he projected himself as some kind of knight-errant, some avenging force. For, his cane became a sword, or "swore-wurd," while he sang "Heaven Will Protect The Working Girl."

Many times I saw him stop, lurch, and strike out in all directions with his cane, with his "swore-wurd."

Papa would say: "Hold your trousers up when you walk down Front Street. Old Man Rufe, I mean D'Artagan, has the sidewalk strewn with the corpses of the malefactors of the working girl."

Except on Sunday, when he wore a straw or a felt, he always wore a huge tin hat, shaped like the helmets the American soldiers wore in World War I, but much bigger in the brim. (It was almost a larger replica of the hard-hats construction workers wear today.) Of course, no one had ever seen such hats back then, not around Oxford, anyway.

It was never told, for certain, where he got his tin hat, but he wore it all of the years I knew him, and Papa, and others, said he wore it long before I was born.

He said he had a tinsmith make it when he enlisted for the Spanish-American War, but by my time, he probably forgot where he found his hat. But his cronies tapped on it for good luck, in lieu of wood, I suppose, and others said it kept birds from roosting in his hair. He hated barbers and he never went into a barber shop in all the years I knew him. His hair was as long as many young men wear theirs today. Miss Texanna gave it a few whacks with her scissors, occasionally, when she got him to sit still long enough.

He said he promised his mother, on her death-bed, never to enter a barber shop. When he told of this pledge, his eyes filled with tears. Then he would say, to anyone or to no one: "By God, sah, Rufus Duncan, E-sick (that meant "Esq.") is a man uv his word, sah."

I have seen him look at the sky, towards heaven I guessed, and say, sonorously: "Ma, to my pledged word I'm true. The bastards can't tempt me with gold, ner seduce me with promises uv high office. I spit on them and they bribes and tempertations, dear, dead lady in hebben."

When FDR was elected, people said things would get better. Old Man Rufe demurred: "Lemme tell you somep'n, boy. There won't be no cot ding peace ner prosperity in this nashion until every egg-sucking barba is putt to the swore-wurd."

The Lord only knows why he disliked, or pretended to dislike, barbers so fiercely. I did hear, once, that some barber had beat his time with a girl, long ago, and I heard, again, that some barber had bluffed him out of a big pot in a poker game.

In a hard rain his tin hat sounded as if a game of marbles were being played on it. In a hard sleet or a hail storm his hat sounded as if several hundred woodpeckers were zinging pneumatic drills, simultaneously.

He got so worked up about the theory of the world's being round he would beat his hat, on his head, with his cane. He used to argue with Papa, "Brer" Thompson, and Dr. Henley. Or, to be more precise, they listened to his tirades about the fool teachers who taught that the world is round.

He had an unimpeachable demurrer. He said every night when he went to bed Miss Texanna put eggs in a nest, and, "by Jesus H. Christ," the eggs were still in the nest the next morning.

Invariably, Old Man Rufe said "Jesus H. Christ," rather

than "Jesus Christ," for an expletive. I didn't know Jesus had a middle name. One day I asked him what the "H" stood for. He scratched his tin hat a second and said, "Hubbut," his way of saying "Herbert." Ever since I've wondered if the angels know Old Man Rufe gave Jesus a regular middle name?

Q.E.D. If the world were round, if it turned on its axis, like the "id-jut" teachers said, why the eggs would fall out of the nest during the night. He beamed at his irrefutable logic the way I always imagined Descartes beamed when he said, "I think, hence I am."

One day when I was walking home from school, he accosted me on the street: "Sandy, on your Ma's honor, do 'em id-jut teachers rilly tell yawl the world turns round and round?"

I conceded the fact.

He tapped his tin hat, lightly with his right hand fingers. Then he smiled and he put his hand on my shoulder, gently: "If what them teachers say is so, then God, Jesus, and William Jennings Bryan would be standing on they haids half uv the time, and jess fer your own information, and because I like you, William Jennings Bryan ain't go stand on his haid in hebben half the time jess to pleze your id-jut teacher."

He patted my shoulder, briefly, gave me a nickel, and said, the same way a minister dismisses a congregation, "Now, go long wiff you. Mind your Ma and Pa, don't steal Miss Texanna's peaches withouten permission, and don't never let nobody ketch you in a barba shop."

Old Man Rufe built the first mausoleum in Oxford, insofar as I can determine. It was, is, a handsome marble structure, designed in the manner of a miniature Grecian temple. He called it his "mossy-lee," and he used it, from spring to fall, as a combination office and playhouse for several years. I think the "mossy-lee" was built at least fifteen years before Old Man Rufe died.

He said it was the coolest place in town, next to the ice

plant, and each morning, in pretty weather, he took his newspaper and stumbled and jerked over to the cemetery to his "mossy-lee."

He would sit in the doorway in a rocking chair, read his paper, sing and whistle his songs, and smoke his roll-your-own cigarettes. He was the only man in town who smoked Maryland Club. This was the smallest sack of smoking tobacco and it cost a dime, twice as much as ordinary sack tobacco cost back then.

As soon as he rolled and licked his cigarette paper, he put the cigarette into the grippers of one of those clamp things that men used to wear on their right legs to keep their pants from getting caught in a bicycle chain.

The smoking ring, the clamp thing, was so big you could hardly see the roll-your-own in its metallic teeth, but billowing smoke poured from the door of the "mossy-lee."

I had never seen a French cathedral, of course, but sometimes when I rode by the cemetery on my bicycle I got the impression someone was burning incense.

I was in the "mossy-lee" a few times. I used to deliver some stuff for the "Ivanhoe," and a few times I took oddments to Old Man Rufe, in the "mossy-lee." There was a small table inside which he and his cronies used for checkers and for set-back and poker.

Old Man Rufe kept jugs of buttermilk, which he used for a chaser, and mason-jars of Just Plain Snake Imboden's home-made whiskey. On the shelves, where the coffins went, ultimately, were apples and pears, in season, and there was a huge glass jar filled with horehound candy.

Old Man Rufe dropped sticks of horehound into the white whiskey, to give it color and to soak up the fussel oil. He gave me a stick to suck on, several times.

Women in town were always raising hell about the poker games that had gone on, without interruption, long before Lord Cornwallis marched through Oxford. Occasionally, some irate wife would charge into a game to grab her husband by the ear, but no one ever mentioned anything about raiding the poker games in Old Man Rufe's "mossy-lee."

Although the "mossy-lee" was not used for an office or recreation center in cold weather, Old Man Rufe always ran off a batch of persimmons-and-locust beer in it along about October.

He had a large barrel, with a spigot and a dipper attached, and he filled the barrel with layers of persimmons and locusts and broom straw, alternately. Then he filled the barrel with water and let the persimmons, locusts, and broom straw "work."

Most people in town drank persimmons-and-locust beer for a soft drink, but Old Man Rufe let his get as hard as his tin hat. He and a few of his tombstone buddies slipped over along about Thanksgiving to sample the beer.

Sometimes the sampling went on for two or three days. Miss Texanna didn't worry about Old Man Rufe's being exposed to pneumonia, to any disease. As she explained: "Germs and mosquitoes jess get pickled when they bite into Rufe."

One Thanksgiving Just Plain Snake Imboden passed out in the "mossy-lee" and Old Man Rufe locked him up inside. Whether this was an accident, I can't say. Anyway, Just Plain Snake awakened about ten o'clock at night, and he started bellowing for someone to let him out.

There was a lovers' lane, right by the cemetery, and several couples were out there in cars, courting. Ramsay Davis was there, with some girl. He bolted from the car and ran all the way to his father's house, where he hid in a closet. I don't know about the girl, but I understand that she took off in the opposite direction.

Each fall Old Man Rufe put boards on the concrete floor of the "mossy-lee" "to bed" Irish potatoes. He sprinkled lime all over the potatoes so they wouldn't rot or get frost-bitten.

Just Plain Snake had gone to sleep on the potoates, and when Sheriff Mat Venable came with Old Man Rufe's keys to let him out, he was as white as any ghost.

Some other people, walking home late at night, saw Just Plain Snake as he emerged from the "mossy-lee." They were sure he was a ghost, a "hant."

The true story became garbled. The sparkers swore they heard ghostly yells from the tombs, and the pedestrians swore they had seen a "live ghost."

The whole cemetery became haunted, or "hanted." The adjacent lovers' lane became a briar patch, and for a long time, most of the people in town gave the cemetery a wide berth at night.

Tom Day, the soda water clerk at Hill's, lived just beyond the cemetery. When he walked home at night, he went half-a-mile out of his way, to avoid the cemetery. One day Papa said to him: "Tom, boy, don't you know dead folks can't hurt you?"

"Yes, sir, I know that, Major, but they show as hell can make you hurt yourself."

I was about grown when Old Man Rufe died. When he was laid out in his coffin, his tin hat was on his chest, his long, bony hands clutching the hat. I don't know if the hat was buried with his body, but I never saw it again.

The choir sang, "Amazing Grace," and when they got to the right part, Papa yelled, "Hurrah fer William Jennings Bryan."

Just as we were leaving the cemetery, a terrible storm came up. I thought the salvos of thunder would break every window and glass in town. Papa looked at the black, angry sky, and he said to "Brer" Thompson: "Well, I suppose Old Man Rufe is up there by now, and he must be telling St. Peter all about the barbers on this earth."

ELEMENTALS

Sometimes beauty is too much sugar for a cent,
A hill almost tumbling with loveliness, or
A forest choking with green wonderment.
And the eyes, those wild blue horses,
Trample the brain to dizzy consternation.

And the heart begs for the lean winter afternoon,
The cheerless nocturne smeared in gray with a blunt crayon,
And a lone chimney, bleak against the sky's cold razor,
Or a bell with fog and ice in its throat,
Tolling in the lacklustre distance, or, perhaps,
A vision of a solitary rose amid the fallow field,
And, most assuredly, a lone crow in half-frozen darkness
Heading home with empty purse and market-basket
With a snow-flake for a silver shield
And a hard-luck tale to tell.

JOHN TURNER'S EPITAPH

Many called me "contrary" even "anti-social,"
Because I never reduced to words and phrases
The reasons I had for late plantings and early harvests,
Or for whistling love songs in the rain.
They thought my actions were devoid of reasons
Because I never explained my passion for green and yellow
Was the same as theirs for cards and women and land.
Hence I was "impulsive," "capricious," unreasonably fond
Of doing things for the various hells of them.
(The list would cover the courthouse square,
But I didn't explain the elephant was coincidental,
That I bought that little defunct circus at auction
Solely for the calliope. And the only reason
I limited my playing to stormy nights
Was just to keep down the noise.)

Of course, if I had ever conversed with them enough
To deprecate myself a bit, they would have believed
Everything I would have ever said. But then,
You know I should have been horribly annoyed
If they had taken me at my word.

ENTRIES FROM OXFORD

Oxford, November 7, 1968

There used to be a lot of litigation about dogs and other animals. Farmers were always trying to sue the railroad to recover damages for cows, mules, and horses killed by the locomotive. Mr. Moorefield, one of Papa's contemporaries, brought endless suits against the railroad. In his summations, Mr. Moorefield always pictured the railroad as a diabolical monster seeking innocent prey to slaughter, merely to satisfy its lust for blood.

I remember a particular case wherein Mr. Moorefield alleged that the locomotive had deliberately set fires, by blowing coals from its smokestack, that burned a wheat field, an orchard, and a pen of pigs.

The fires had been set on a Sunday, according to Mr. Moorefield's allegation. In his peroration, Mr. Moorefield accused the locomotive of disturbing the peace of the Sabbath. He said to the magistrate: "Here it was, Squire, a-ringing its hellish bell and blowing its infernal whistle and running around the countryside seeking something to destroy when all God-fearin people were a-worshipping the Lord."

He continued: "It could have unloaded its heathenish fires, done its brutal arson, when it passed Buzzard Swamp or when it crossed Tar River, where there's nothing to burn. But, no sir, it waited until it got to my client's wheat field. It waited for that wheat field the same malicious way General Sherman waited until he got to Columbia, South Carolina to start his fires.

"When it spied that wheat field it started to belching its fiendish destruction. Then it burnt up the wheat field, it burnt up the orchard, it burnt up the creek. . ."

At this juncture, Squire Stovall interposed: "Mr. Moorefield, you didn't mean to say the fire burnt UP the creek, did you?"

"Yes, sir, aye God, I did, indeed, sir. It burnt up the creek, and then it burnt down the creek to get at those pigs it missed coming the other way."

As I say, there was much litigation, usually about the railroad, about cows getting into somebody's corn, about stray dogs that weren't returned by the people who found them, about the sale of blind mules and the sale of horses that had the "heaves."

Sometimes, owners were indicted for keeping vicious animals that attacked people. But Old Man Rufe Duncan is the only human I ever heard of who was indicted for biting a dog.

The Entwhistles, neighbors of the Duncans, had this blooded boxer, Sir Gay. Sir Gay had such a lavish coat-of-arms he could have joined the Colonial Dames, if he had been a bitch.

Almost every afternoon when Old Man Rufe lumbered home to supper, he picked some kind of argument with Sir Gay. Minor altercations between the two were rudimentary, and people said Old Man Rufe came by the Entwhistle's house dragging croaker sacks on which bitches in heat had lain.

According to the story, Sir Gay got all charged up, but alas, there wasn't much he could do with a croaker sack. And I know it to be an unvarnished fact that Old Man Rufe threw Sir Gay choice cuts of meat that were saturated with black and red pepper. Sir Gay yelped as if he had swallowed sheer brimstone but he couldn't slake his thirst for paroxyms of sneezing.

One night the two had a real fight. Sir Gay snagged Old Man Rufe's trousers and coat sleeves, but Old Man Rufe bit a big chunk out of Sir Gay's left ear.

I think Mrs. Entwhistle forced the issue. Anyway, Mr. Entwhistle swore out a warrant for Old Man Rufe, for malicious injury to Sir Gay. Miss Texanna asked Papa to represent Old Man Rufe at the trial. The trial never occurred, but Old Man Rufe explained to Papa, and to others, that he didn't take advantage of Sir Gay. No siree, bob-jackimo-tail. When the fight started, Old Man Rufe got down on all-fours, to give the dog a fighting chance, a sporting chance. And that's how he managed to get the dog's ear in his teeth.

Dr. Henley wondered if Old Man Rufe shouldn't be "put up" for three weeks, since he hadn't had any rabies shots. Old Man Rufe asked why in the hell he needed rabies shots since he wasn't a Jewish minister?

A lot of folks said if Sir Gay didn't have a hell of a case of hydrophobia he'd miss a damn good chance.

I think Papa achieved the best solution to a bona fide "dog case." This man named Coon ran a battery shop. (He was called "Zip," and he accepted the nickname. When he answered the telephone he always said, "This here is Zip Coon doing of the talkin'.")

He was so stingy he wouldn't give you a stale biscuit if he owned the Red Band factory. He was so disagreeable people wouldn't believe he was telling the truth if he swore on a Bible that he was lying.

Anyway, Zip Coon owned this pointer, this bird dog, that he bragged about constantly. One day the bird dog came to the battery shop, just visiting. Three or four loafers occupied all the chairs in the place. Zip Coon looked around and said: "One a you bastards git up and give this here gennelmun a seat."

One day the dog strayed, all the way to Fairport, six miles away. People said the pointer was trying to run away from home, away from Zip Coon. A young farmer named Arch Clay found the dog. He fed and cared for the dog for six months.

When Zip Coon tried to get his dog, Arch Clay wouldn't hand the pointer over until he was paid $2.50 for boarding the dog. Zip Coon refused to pay the board bill.

Now, about this time the boy scouts were trying to raise money for a camping trip. Our scout master, Bill Hunt, went into the battery shop twice trying to solicit for the scouts. Each time Zip Coon ran him out.

I belonged to the scouts and Papa and I were passing the battery shop when Zip Coon asked Papa if he could get the bird dog back. Papa said he could. Zip asked how much it would cost.

Papa said his fee would be $15.00. Zip had been drinking, and he told Papa to get the dog and he'd give him the $15.00. Papa said: "No, I've had a lot of experience in dog cases. A lawyer has to have the cash, in advance."

Zip went to his cash register and he returned with the $15.00. I rode with Papa down to Fairport. He asked Arch Clay if he had the dog. He said he did, and he told about the $2.50 board bill Zip Coon wouldn't pay.

"That's not enough," Papa said. "Here's seven dollars and a half." We put the dog in the car. When we passed Bill Hunt's house, our scout master was cutting his grass.

Papa stopped the car: "Bill, here's seven dollars and a half Zip Coon has contributed to the camping trip. When you put the list of donors in the *Torchlight*, be sure to put his name at the top of the list."

Bill said, "Why, I can't believe it, Major. That devil has run me out twice, just for asking."

"He's had a change of heart," Papa explained. "He's seen the light."

We rode on to Zip Coon's house and we gave him his fabulous pointer. He was soberer by now. He scratched his head: "I bin thinkin'. I b'lief I coulda got my dawg back fer less'n fifteen dollars."

"That's correct," Papa said, "You could have got him back

for two dollars and a half."

"Well, Ah'm entitled to know what you done with the balance of mah money."

"You're entitled to go to hell, but I'll tell you, anyway, free of charge: I gave Arch Clay seven fifty and I gave Bill Hunt seven fifty for the scouts."

He grimaced. He sizzled: "That putts a bad taste in mah mouff. Whatcha you gonna do?"

"You can kiss my tail and see if that puts a better taste in your mouth," Papa said.

INDIAN SUMMER

Old man Morrison's trees are wild Indians
Wearing wilder paints of belly-deep October.
They circle, for a pow-wow in oak and elm tree idioms,
Then fire a billion arrows into those gray, thatched huts
In the skyland's lower settlements.
. . .And hush, hound, hush your barking interrogations. . .
I really think I hear the Tuscarora buffalo hunters
Gently breaking brush down along Buzzard's Roost. . .
Listen hound, listen. . .
Is that a car's backfire, or a flint-lock rifle,
And what does that smoke say against the haze?
Spread the alarm hound, bark the tocsin,
Judgment Day's coming or is it Fall?

Fall is a vagabond lover who infects creation with an itchy foot, one who puts no stock in politics or in walls and ceilings. When the vagabond lover whistles his wild, hypnotic tunes, mankind knows it is sitting on the edge of a volcano.

The heart would pull up all its roots in the mad spell of its sophomoric desire to taste, to touch, to feel, and to smell the tag-end wonders of spending summer. The heart would seize creation as if it were a vine heavy with scuppernongs. And the brain has to take the heart by the hand, the way a wise parent keeps her child from the teeming street. The brain, long on autumnal changes, puts the heart in a high-chair and gives it a small but clear view of the fabulous parade. Even so, the heart cries with the wild geese and a little portion of it eludes discipline and intelligent guidance and flies where white clouds are great clipper ships off to exotic lands of no return, lightly-ladened with spice, and myrrh, and frankincense, and gently embalmed in nights as soft and warm as a yellow rose when only one is blooming.

178

ENTRIES FROM OXFORD

Oxford, April 15, 1970

Obviously, I know more about men than I know about women, more about boys than I know about girls. From a boy's perspective the first really serious romance is a combination of celestial lightning and electric-shock. The boy is Columbus but he discovers a world far beyond the ken of great captains and navigators.

The boy's days and nights are set to flutes and violins but these days and nights are harassed by cold sweats, by chills and fevers that are impervious to any known medications, and antibiotics.

Young Lochinvar is truly a disembodied spirit. He really uses white and blue clouds for flagstones. Even so he steps into quagmires and he is lacerated by briars. The world is his very own merry-go-round. The spotted horses race to the music of his heartbeats, but the gallant chargers throw many shoes. They shy and they toss him into the meanest gullies.

The world is his own love song, but he can't keep the tune because the melody is dominated by the idea of the song, itself. An hour apart from his true-love is a life sentence in solitary confinement, but a whole evening spent together seems to pass as quickly as the clock strikes one.

First love is glorious and heroic and it is likely to be inglorious and tragic. But it is immortal, somehow, even when it passes rapidly and hides its face in a crowd of stars. He may forget her face but the touch of her fingertip survives countless inner and outer hurricanes. First love is beautiful and terrible. It is ecstasy and anguish. But if the "perfect" rose fades and dies and is blown to sea by cold, impersonal winds, the divinity of its fragrance is eternal.

Hopefully, it works both ways. She may not remember his name but the adoration of his voice endures. He becomes faceless, perhaps, but something about the grandeur, or the pathetic desperation, of his kisses goes on. Perhaps, the words of his heart framed, the words his mind lacked the power to express, become a wisp of a benediction. When all else is gone, it may be that the kisses that their eyes once mirrored continue as a talisman.

My first profound romance was with Rose Blatz. We were juniors in high school. We had "home room" together and we sat near each other. I knew her, was aware of her, somewhat hazily, before we were put in the same home room. Then I looked across the row one morning, almost apropos to nothing, and there sat Rose.

In ten seconds I knew exactly how Benjamin Franklin had felt when he discovered electricity. My insides felt as if someone were using them to shoot off all of the firecrackers and Roman candles that our whole town shot off on Christmas Eve.

Rose was a strawberry blonde. Her long hair spilled over her shoulders, a river of cherries. I knew if I ever touched her long hair it would speak, through my fingertips, in all the tongues known and unknown. Sometimes she wore a white ribbon and I thought it was the Milky Way, and again it was a slender moonbeam, pretending to be a bit of yellow ribbon.

We read Milton's "Lycidas," as an assignment, and two of the poet's lines, just lines to me ordinarily, took intensely personal dramatic shape:

"To sport with Amaryllis in the shade
Or with the tangles of Nearera's hair."

We read another couplet from Pope's "The Rape of the Lock":

"Fair tresses man's imperial race ensnare,
And beauty draws us with a single hair."

Papa said Pope got the second line from a proverb written

by James Howell, along about 1620: "One hair of a woman can draw more than a hundred pair of oxen."

I was ecstatically ensnared. Surely, one of Rose's hairs could reach from Oxford to heaven and draw me along to the Pearly Gates.

I thought her eyes were two stars, when only two stars were burning at night, and when she walked she seemed to float, to glide. Some years later, when she was gone, I saw Degas's famous painting of the ballet dancers, and I conjured Rose, walking along the street but barely touching the sidewalk.

I exclaimed: "It's Rose, Rose Blatz, from the old days in Oxford."

Her face beat anything I had ever seen. It was strong enough to surmount centuries of infamy and social injustice, yet it was as thin, as marvelously delicate, as Mrs. Ashton-Brown's finest, hand-painted china cup. There were a few freckles on her lovely face. I thought these freckles were pure gold nuggets, of infinitesimal size. One day I told her the freckles were "faery-dust." I didn't know what "faery-dust" was, but I ran across the expression in Rupert Brooke's poem, the "Great Lover."

Rose laughed softly: "Meshugge," she whispered. From my association with her I knew that meant "silly boy" more than it meant "crazy." Her smile was a sliver of starlight, at high-noon. But when we went walking on fall nights, her forehead, her nose, and her lips seemed to be magnets on which tiny tatters of moonbeams did arabesques, and I always imagined that the yellow slivers were angels seeing how many could dance on a pin-point, that they used the tip of Rose's nose for the pin-point.

She never laughed loudly, even when she was thoroughly amused, but when she smiled her own special smile, I thought it had the magic of a gentle spring rain putting a necklace around the throat of a red flower. If her laughter was slight it as as warm as the south wind is warm when it rolls and tumbles in the light-leaved fingers of late April.

If I was Rose's beau, I was still a shaygets, a Gentile boy. I picked up a phrase from a boy named Hymie Schwartz, whose people came to Oxford after Mr. S. Blatz, Rose's father, had sort of founded the local Jewish community. The phrase was "Shayn vi zibben velten," or "Beautiful as the seven worlds."

One day when Rose and I, and two or three other couples were sitting around one of the marble-topped tables in Hill's Drug Store I said the words to her.

I smiled and I said, "Shayn vi zibben velten," as casually as I would say, "It's a nice afternoon." At any event, that is the effect I wanted, the one I tried to create. Even so I felt what I said because I loved her, because I thought she was as beautiful as seven worlds.

But, of course, I was showing-off, too, feeling my ginger and my mustard. I imagined that I was debonair George Brent, in a movie, speaking Yiddish to Norma Shearer, or to some virgin Queen of Sheba. And I'll admit, now, it was surpassingly exhilarating to talk excessively intimately and to use a language beyond the comprehension of our Gentile friends.

Rose let it pass the first time, and we continued to sip a single cherry-smash through two straws. Economy really wasn't the vital factor for our sharing a nickel drink. It was romantic, intimate, and glamorous for a boy and girl to sip from the same cup. Or so I thought. Indeed, I thought it was swashbuckling.

And it was titillating, even passionate, the way I maneuvered my straw so that it touched Rose's straw at the bottom of the cup.

I had the distinct impression that I was acting out the intransigent intimacy of a current movie, *Jungle Torment*, as I recall the title, in which George Brent lay on the ground in a

182

forest, in a feverish coma. He couldn't swallow and he was dying of thirst. His girl-friend, Heather Angel, I think, sucked some juice from a coconut and then she kissed the life-saving fluid into George Brent's mouth.

Of course, it was Rose who kissed the coconut juice into my blistered lips. I turned to her to thank her for saving my life: "Shayn vi zibben velten," I said, amid the urgency of unutterable gratitude.

She whispered testily: "Shemen zich in dein veiten haldz," or "You ought to be ashamed of yourself down to the bottom of your throat."

Rose's rebuke stung more sharply in Yiddish, and, thus, she didn't wash our personal laundry in public at Hill's Drug Store.

I touched her knee, tenderly, impulsively, to let her know I was sorry, but, evidently, she thought I was using the anonymity below the marble-topped table as an excuse to get fresh.

"Shmuck, Shmuck, Shmuck." She repeated the word three times, with increasing asperity.

On the way to her home, I explained and I apologized. When I turned to leave, she said "Shalom," and I knew she really wanted to be at peace with me.

After dark, when we took our leave of each other I always said "Gutte noch," but I always said "Shalom," by day. In our county there is an Old Salem and a New Salem church, and there is a large farming community in Salem Township. When I was going with Rose, I used to tell my Gentile friends that we appropriated Salem from the Jews, and shalom, but, as I recall, I didn't make much headway.

Sometimes when Rose had to recite at school (we stood to recite) or when she had to write something on the blackboard, I might whisper "lots of nochos, Rose," wishing her good luck. If I whispered, I still said "lots of nochos" clearly enough for the words to be distinctly audible. If she did well on her recitation, and she was an "A" student, I whispered, "Mazel-tov, Rose," to congratulate her.

Rose visited our home many times, especially in the afternoon, after school. Usually she walked home with Sister and me, but Mother introduced Rose as "Sandy's friend," rather than as "Sister's friend."

We listened to the victrola and I taught her to dance by putting pieces of newspaper on the parlor floor and doing what was known as "the Box." We ate ladyfingers, gingerbread, and Lady Baltimore cake, which Mother and Sister made, and we washed the food down with homemade drinks such as "vanilla floats," royal raspberry acid (an early do-it-yourself version of Kool-Aid) and with locust-and-persimmon beer.

(I was never sure why "acid" was appended to "royal raspberry" and other "fruit drinks." "Acid" was the juice that accumulated when raspberries and other fruits were boiled for preserves. "Acid" was poured into pop bottles. The bottles were capped and stored in the basement during winter. The next summer "acid" was mixed with water to make a drink. I think the proportion was one part "acid" to three parts water.)

(We made a big batch of locust-and-persimmon beer each fall. The process was simple: We placed alternate rows of locusts, broomstraw, and persimmons in a large wooden barrel. Then the barrel was filled with water, and the wooden barrel-top was banded on. Each barrel had a tap, a wooden spigot.)

(The taste was delicious, just sharp enough to make you want to smack your mouth. Of course, this "beer" would get as hard as the bank president's heart if it "worked" long enough, but Mother always tapped ours "before it actually lost its virginity," as Papa put it.)

Rose ate supper with us, ever so often. But when Mother invited Rose "to take pot-luck with us," it was on nights

184

when we were not having pork chops, sausage, or ham. The first time Rose ever ate with us Papa mumbled the blessing. The only audible word was "amen."

Mother spoke up: "I couldn't hear a word you said, Alexander." Papa replied, "I wasn't talking to you, my dear." Then their eyes met the way a key fits a riddle. Mother understood that Papa thought the Christian blessing might be awkward. From then on, Papa mumbled some incoherency whenever Rose "took pot-luck" with us.

I visited the Blatz home more often than Rose visited ours, and although I hardly ever stayed for supper, I developed a taste for chopped livers and Gefilte fish; albeit, I almost turned in the fire alarm the first time I ate the fish, cooked in the skin and almost aflame with red horse-radish.

Rose and I studied together, two or three times a week. She thought of herself as a "greenzy kuzziny," as I got the phrase, or the "green cousin," in relationship to Oxford's mores. When we were alone, I called her "Cudin Rose," because just about everyone in Oxford was related, in some nebulous fashion, back then. Even if the old designation, "kissing-cousin," or "cudin," as we called it, was likely to be a polite euphemism, the wide use of the term illustrates the extensive and intensive sweep of our tribal nuances.

People in Oxford rejoiced to sing an old song, "It Ain't No Sin To Hug and Kiss Your Cousin," and endless smooching, and more, was done in the guise of family fealty. Just as it was impossible for two people to sit in a hammock and to remain physical strangers, one could always establish some "cudinship," with an attractive girl.

Even before the other Jewish families settled in Oxford, the second floor of the Blatz home, a white clapboard house on McClanahan Street, was set aside as the Shul, the sanctuary for minyan and discussion.

When Mr. S. Blatz first brought his family to McClanahan Street, he closed his store, "The Emporium," each Saturday, on the Sabbath. Traveling men who were Jews came to the improvised synagogue. Then after some Jewish families settled in Oxford, Mr. Blatz was the "undeclared Rov."

Mr. Blatz wore a frock coat, whenever he mounted his jerry-built pulpit. Perhaps, he was too absorbed in his "davening," swaying slowly from the east to the west, amid profound meditation, to realize how ruinous it was for him to close "The Emporium" on Saturdays, in Oxford. Saturday was the big day for shopping.

All the farm families came to town to shop, to see the sights, and to socialize with their Oxford friends and relatives. All the stores stayed open until ten o'clock Saturday night. Late Saturday afternoon, virtually all the town folks took their mandatory "Saturday baths," dressed-up, and went "down town," to shop and to chat with the people from the country.

Ere long Mr. Blatz understood his "mish-mosh," his fouled-up mercantile state of things. I am positive the phrase wasn't "mish-mash" because it always rhymed with "pish-posh" whenever it was spoken by any Hebrew in Oxford.

I suppose Mr. Blatz was about fifty, at this time, but he seemed as ageless to me as a rugged oak tree. He was short and his dark eyes blazed from his bearded face the way a cat's eyes blaze in the darkness. Mr. Blatz's beard was so heavy and black he reminded me of one of the prophets in our illustrated Sunday school lessons. When he smoked one of his Fatima cigarettes I thought he was half-Moses and half-burning bush.

I was invited to Passover two or three times, although Mr. Blatz did not put one of the little black skull caps on my head. But I learned the difference between Rosh-Hashanah and Yom Kippur, and about the ram's horn and the Book of Judgement.

In turn I told Rose about local history, about our institutions and families. It was hard to untangle the maze that devolved upon what Papa called the "Gentile Sanhedrin."

Rose had more trouble with local names than she had with irregular verbs. It was hard to explain that "Taliaferro" was (is) called "Tolliver"; that "Morton" was Motun"; that "Currin" was "Kern"; that "Herbert" was "Hub-but"; that "Alexander" was "Eleck-zandah"; that "daughter" was "dorta"; that "Tuesday" was "Chewsday"; that "business" was "bidness"; that "Mary" was "merry"; that "supple" was "soup-pul"; that "syrup" was "sir-rup."

Whenever we talked about local names and mores, I thought· of Rose as a lovely Ruth, plunked down in a strange land. If she came to accept most of the quiddities of our bizarre nomenclature, a sign on Main Street remained hilariously enigmatic. The sign said: "Andrew Beauchamp-China and Silverware."

"Of course, "Beauchamp" is called "Beech-um," here and in many other places. Rose would look at the sign and if someone happened to say, "Why, hell-low, Mistah Beechum," Rose acted as if she had heard Eleanor Roosevelt was subbing for Sally Rand.

Just the unadorned sound of the word "Beech-um" became a marvelously pulsating private joke for Rose and me. When we were delighted by some spontaneous joy, or when we worked out a difficult problem in solid geometry, we said "Beech-um" in unison.

As we said "Beech-um" in spontaneous unison, I got the impression we were throwing champagne glasses against a fireplace, the way characters did in some of the British novels and in some of the British-type movies. As I have said, Rose never laughed uproariously, but "Beech-um" sent her delectable little freckles turning somersaults.

She was enchanted with an old saw that children chanted as they played hopscotch, frog-in-the-middle, farmer-in-the-dell, and hiding:

"Hacker backer soda cracker,
    Hacker backer boo;
    Hacker backer soda cracker
    Out goes you.

Rose loved to chat the meaningless words, although she was quick to point out that "goes" in the last line should be "go." Papa had told me the same thing, several years before, but I always said "goes" so no one would accuse me of being too big for my britches.

Rose agreed that it was better to say "goes," in public. To say "go" might make her a "shlimazl'" an unlucky person, a loser, in today's parlance. According to Rose, as she got it from her father, "When a shlimazl kills a chicken, it walks; when he sells umbrellas, the sun comes out; when he sells shrouds, people stop dying." As I heard the word it was pronounced "shli-moz-zl," to rhyme with "thin nozzle."

My friendship with Rose, and my part-time job with Mr. S. Blatz, which I will get to directly, led to several changes of "Jew-tile," and I had a few minor altercations and one real fight, with Jo-Jo Tilgin. Jo-Jo broke my nose, but it was Mother who fainted, not I. The fight occurred near the "Ivanhoe," and I sat on the steps to the candy store while Dr. Henley set my nose with his fingers.

Mr. Matson brought me a glass of short-beer to "bolster-ate" me. He said I had fought for "the scattered nation," but I didn't know what he meant. Too, the short-beer made me sort of tight.

Mother didn't see the fight. She fainted when she saw my bloody face and shirt. Papa said: "Our boy is like the late Union General, Ambrose Burnside. He will fight, even if he never learns how."

Rose must have heard about the fight, but she never mentioned it. When I had to explain the cause of the fight, I said Jo-Jo had called me an ugly name. That required no explantion since it could mean only one thing. I certainly didn't want Rose to know that she had been involved, even obliquely, in a street brawl, but I am sure she guessed the real reason.

I learned about Chanukah, the "feast of lights," the eight day Jewish celebration that usually came in December but which came before our Christmas. I gave her a present at the commencement of Chanukah, and she gave me mine on Christmas Eve. But once or twice, we gave presents to each other at Chanukah and at Christmas.

Because of Rose I was the only Christian in town to see Christmas things early in September. About the first of each September Mr. Blatz and Rose studied the fat catalogues put out by two big wholesale houses in Baltimore. These were the catalogues from the celebrated "Baltimore Bargain House" and the famous "Butler Brothers."

Mr. Blatz ordered the Christmas "necessities," which were luxuries, too: shirts, dresses, ties, britches, coats, hats, and two-pants' suits. But Rose picked out all of the dolls, books, and toys which she thought would appeal to youngsters. Mr. Blatz deferred to her tastes completely. After all, Rose knew Gentile children. She went to school with them. She knew many things, such as the fact there was no word pronounced as "Beauchamp."

When the Christmas stuff came, the scuppernongs might be getting ripe but the persimmons were not pink around the gills and the trees were still girls in green skirts too tight at the hips. I helped Rose unpack and check the Christmas stuff. Then we stored all of the gleaming oddments and the pungent, earthy-smelling books in the Shul, on the second floor of the Blatz home.

Long before fall came to town to put up his yellow circus tents, I was blowing "Christmas" mouth-organs and Jews-harps in the synagogue. Long before frost put the first faint moustache on the corn shocks, I was shooting Christmas marbles, being careful to keep them uncracked and glistening, and although I was too big for such kid shenanigans, I played with a long toy hook-and-ladder truck. It was the first hook-and-ladder I ever saw, toy or otherwise. I ran the hook-and-ladder all over the floor of the Shul, putting out raging fires and rescuing helpless, pretty girls and children, if they didn't pop chewing gum in my ears as I was hauling them down the ladder.

I remember that I forgot to clean and dust my knees. Papa looked at my baggy, dirty knees, I mean the cloth in my britches. "There are only three ways a boy can mess up his trousers around the knees, the way yours are messed up."

I didn't say anything and he continued: "We can eliminate praying, in your case, I think. That brings us to shooting craps? My boy, are you a devotee of that form of gambling?"

I told him, truthfully, that the only times I had ever handled dice was when I played parchesi with him and Sister.

Then he said, sadly, or perhaps, with poignant resignation: "If you find yourself the defendant in a bastardy charge, I want you to appear as your own counsel. We lawyers have a saying that goes this way, dear boy: 'If a lawyer defends himself, he has a damned fool for a client.' And I think you will qualify, Sandy."

I started to tell him I had been playing with the toy hook-and-ladder, but I guess I feared being called sissy more than I feared being called a carnal sinner. Playing with the hook-and-ladder not only seemed less defensible. It was privileged communication. No one but me knew that Mr. S. Blatz's stock of Christmas items came to Oxford before autumn started whetting its grind-stone.

Rose loved our local weather. She told me many times she was lucky to live where the four seasons had distinctive personalities all of their own, even though they merged into one enduringly exciting whole.

She loved the early spring mornings when every tree was a glee-club of birds, when the singing of one small, hidden bird in a boxwood seemed bigger than the bush, itself. She loved to wander among the forests, flowers, and creeks, but there was never any insatiable impulse to own these wonders, to summarize them in precise definitions.

Rose was content to let nature spread itself without any overt help from her. Thus, she was eternally the bug-eyed pilgrim, the ebullient young seeker. I stumbled across something in a copy of Walt Whitman's *Specimen Days*, lent me by "Brer" Thompson, that revealed Rose in all of her innocent intensity:

> "You must not know too much, or be too precise or scientific about birds and trees and flowers and watercraft; a certain free margin, or even vagueness — perhaps ignorance, credulity — helps your enjoyment of these things."

She loved the great, white wolf called winter, too. She spoke of this lean-rawboned time as "the good shivering." She avoided the skaters on the ice-ponds and all the hosannas and hullabuloos, but she made snow men that were first-rate genre art. She was wild for the taste of snow cream, when I taught her how to make it.

She hated rabbit-boxes. Once she said she wondered how it would be if rabbits made "boy-boxes" to trap live children? Of course, hog-killings were brutally profane, for Rose, and everytime she smelled the odor of sausage in our kitchen, I was permeated with such a sense of impropriety I almost felt I was an unredeemed sinner. I am sure my sense of outrage was specious. As soon as Rose went home, I laid into sausage as vigorously as Macduff and Macbeth laid into each other.

Rose attuned to summer's lazy, hazy indolence, to the endless torpor of the parched days and to the endless rapture of the deep, purple nights. I don't think she really ever let go on a hay-ride or a gypsy-tea, as combination picnics and swimming outings were called, but she could never get enough of local flower gardens. Just about everyone in town planted flowers, and in the immaculate stillness of the night, when silence seemed to be pristine wisdom, the town smelled as if all of the perfume and spice ships in the history of the East had smashed up in Oxford.

She liked, particularly, the long twilights, when late afternoon was a gorgeous diva giving one "farewell" performance after another. Finally, when twilight was a dappled fawn being chased, but never really menaced, by the dark hounds of nighttime, Rose liked to walk our streets and hear the tots singing and shouting, "Ain't No Buggar-Bears Out Tonight."

Warm weather and days as long as Tar River galvanized small kids with ringing bravado. Everywhere they ran and shrieked, "Ain't No Buggar-Bears Out Tonight."

I knew full well, and Rose understood thoroughly, that this was the same kind of courage many grown men got from pulling hard on Just Plain Snake Imboden's rot-gut.

Each shadow was a snake-pit and the shrubs were lions and tigers, but these children-eaters were kept at bay with the blacker magic of taunting songs.

Rose told me about the Evil-Eye and how the Jews placated it. I told her of my fear of lightning storms, how when I was little, my grandma forbade any sounds, any playing, even any reading during a storm.

I knew, beyond peradventure, that any extraneous sound, even an inadvertent swish of a sleeve against a wall, would send the lightning upon our miserable heads. I explained to Rose that everytime a lightning storm ended I always felt that miraculously, and without deserving it, I had somehow managed to escape a ghastly death. I told her I had always felt as if I were a gentile Lazarus.

She asked if I had concurred my pagan fear. I lied boldly. But she knew I was lying, and I'd be lying now if I said I don't pray for temporary lockjaw to smite the big-mouthed heathen who gabble during intense lightning storms.

A few two-for-a-nickel hills are visible from Oxford; and

when these were heavy with the first misty garments of the evening, Rose said the hills were going somewhere. She said these hills had been walking steadily, if barely perceptibly, since the beginning of time. They would never get where they were headed, but they would keep on shuffling along.

If a cloud gave our hills a hump, Rose said they were camels. If they were really black and arched, I said they were cats, like Edgar Allan Poe's, but Rose didn't like cats, or Poe, whom she referred to as "Meester Tintinnabulation." So, we compromised and let the moving hills act out a dog and pony show.

We sauntered around at night when every lawn was a sachet bag. I'd tell Rose about our beginnings, as I had heard about them. Sometimes I was so caught up in the drama of the early days I was almost hypnotized by my own poignance and eloquence. My voice, and my heart, throbbed like the organ at the picture show.

If you can imagine David's getting thoroughly choked-up on his own harp playing, you can fix me in my role as personal historical dramatist to lovely young Rose Blatz.

As I told her how civilization came to Oxford and environs, by dint of long rifle, Bible, and fiddle, I was pretty sure Rose was prepared to hear the Tuscarora braves dancing in Mr. Ed Settle's gorgeous woodland. Surely, she expected to see a deer leap Mrs. Ashton-Brown's heavy iron fence and then go flying down Spottswood Street.

What I didn't know, I improvised, but the first time she asked me about slavery days I felt that she was holding me personally responsible for all of the terrible sins of my father.

The Confederate Monument puzzled her. It amused and angered her, too. I think I defended the monument along the lines of Henry Timrod's:

"Stoop, angels, hither from the skies!
There is no holier spot of ground
Than where defeated valor lies.
By mourning beauty crowned."

To Rose, the monument was a memorial to inhumanity and stupidity. "When you grow up and ged good sense, the monumund will remind you of your sins."

Rose made excellent marks in English, especially in the vocabulary tests. She read the dictionary every day for sheer delight, as if it were the most enthralling continued mystery story extant. And her melodious voice had a definite Southern accent, although it wasn't burdened with magnolia and mushmellons. But she never quite got some words down precisely, ones such as "get" and "monument," but these vagaries merely intensified her charm, made me love her even more.

It amused her that birds nested on the "Monumund," and she asked why the "U.D. and C's" didn't explain to the sparrows that they were committing a sacrilege. These "damn dumb birds" always left bits of straw and thread, as footnotes of their tenacy, when they flew off to Florida.

Occasionally some demented woodpecker would go ra-ta-ta-tat on the bronzed man, but many birds used the man and his pedestal for a public "garden house."

In summer, the old soldier's forage cap was always besmirched with bird-droppings. I still remember the towering embarrassment that seared my tongue when Rose asked me why little boys and girls made sandals of big magnolia leaves and wore them on their barefeet in summer. The magnolia sandals, of course, were to keep bird and chicken-do's off the feet when you played in the yard.

Some children tied the leaves around with strings, but a real expert put the twig between his big toe and the next toe. When I was small, or pre-hobbledehoy, I wore out several pairs of sandals in a summer day. I carried extras in the hip pocket of my Bell Buckle overall britches, the same way many adults carried half-soles, which they affixed with glue.

Sometimes when I put on new sandals, I pretended I was a horse being shod. Mr. Matson caught on, and many times he backed me up to a power pole or to his chair in the "Ivanhoe" to shoe me. He was a smith and I was an infinite variety of horses. Traveller, Little Sorrell, Dan Patch, and that white beauty Buffalo Bill rode in the wild west show.

I, and every other boy, had to crimp up his toes to hold the twig tightly in place. Papa said I would get a club-foot, the same as Lord Byron's, but he said all other resemblances ceased, especially poetic similarities.

One night Rose and I stole by Boot Ransome's flower beds. We came as close to walking on air as mortals can come. We held hands, automatically, as if we were making ourselves into a single cloud, or one disembodied spirit.

We were intruding. We hadn't asked permission to gaze, to smell, to be anointed and enchanted. We stayed just long enough to learn that Boot's violets were the real eyes of the summer night.

It wasn't at all the same as looking at the sparkling gems and the radiant silverware in the jewelry store window. Those splendors were on display for sale.

At Boot Ransome's flower garden Rose and I really felt that we were trespassing on Eden, on Eden's first, immaculate night. I really think the old man heard us. Papa said old Boot couldn't hear a silver dollar hit the sidewalk five feet away, but he could hear a seed turning in the soil at the other end of the county. As we were leaving the wind came through the beds, a colt kicking up his heels jauntily, but wearing velvet in lieu of iron shoes. We were almost drowned by waves and waves of frankincense and myrrh, Rose and I. And as we were drowning so gloriously I thought of something "Brer" Thompson said:

He quoted Henry Ward Beecher: "Flowers are the sweetest things that God ever made and forgot to put a soul into."

"Brer" Thompson told Papa: "Beecher got it wrong. Flowers are all soul."

I usually pretended to pull a star for Rose to wear in her

strawberry blonde hair. Once I plucked the Big Dipper. She said it was too heavy for her head, that it was as gaudy as Mrs. Ashton-Brown's tiara.

However, a lone star, particularly some obscure star, was just fine for her hair, she told me, smiling warmly.

A few times I actually put a flower in her hair. Once it was a white rose. Again it was a bit of hyacinth. Once it was one of Mrs. Ashton-Brown's gardenias. I broke the commandment. I stole it for Rose. I was ten feet tall. I was Jimmy Valentine, O. Henry's marvelous thief. I was Francois Villon. I was the Highwayman, in Alfred Noyes poem, and Rose was Bess, the landlord's daughter. But, of course, the British soldiers didn't put a finger on me.

One night I broke a twig of blooming pear. She put the white astonishment in her hair. We went to the drug store for ice cream. I was sure everyone in front of the drug store and everyone reading magazines and lounging around inside was looking at the pear blossom.

Everyone knew Mr. S. Blatz didn't have a pear tree, and everyone knew we had several. Actually, I don't recall that there were any overt raspberries, but, inwardly, I was Jess Willard, "the great white hope" of the Jews. I snarled so rancorously in my guts my ice cream melted ten times as fast as it did normally. Or so it seemed to me. In my shell I was lashing out mercilessly, savagely, at every idiotic face. "Take this. Take that," my granite fists were saying.

Nonetheless, when we had finished our ice cream and when we were back in the sweet anonymity of the night, I felt as if I had been in the fiery furnace with Shadrach, Meshach, and Abednego, but had stayed a few days extra, after the Hebrew lads left.

I was enveloped by a strange dualism which I do not fathom completely to this day. Even as a boy I watched myself do everything I did. I was looking over my own shoulder, eternally, making notes on everything I did. I am sure I have missed a lot of loot because of my penchant for tiny dramatizations.

When I saw Rose to Mr. S. Blatz's front door, after our leisurely nocturnal strolls. I usually made some kind of goodnight speech, but she hardly ever said anything. Thus, the leave-taking was more filibuster than dialogue. When eloquence ran down, the way a wind-up train ran down, I'd give her a furtive peck on the cheek.

I suppose she thought anyone who talked that long, that ardently, without pausing for breath, was entitled to some commemorative momento. . .Most likely she said, to herself: "A lung un leber adf der noz," or "Stop talking yourself into an illness."

There were many times, though, when she slipped in the door, smiled through the closing crack, and was gone while I was still silently polishing the prologue to my good-night oration.

But one night we really did some hugging and kissing. It was in our flower garden, in a swing under the big rose trellis. Between kisses I told her she was the true "cudin of my heart."

She called me "Cousin Silly," but I guess we did turn-on a little, even if there was never the most remote danger of Rose's losing anything she brought with her to Mother's flower garden.

It was strange and unreal. One minute the crickets were having a quilting party, rattling their knitting needles so loudly my ears rang. The next minute I couldn't hear the merry hell-raising of the insects for the fury of my own breathing and panting.

I asked myself if my panting was what adults called passion? I asked myself if Jimmy Simpson panted so painfully when he was expressing his physical enthusiasm with his beautiful wife, Dovey?

When we left the trellis and started to her home, I whistled snatches of "Love Divine, All Love's Excelling," if not in the precise mood that Charles Wesley intended his song. I was as strong as "Old Dan" Tucker, or Galahad, because my heart was pure.

But did Rose know this? Did she think that I had been fresh with her because she was the daughter of a Jewish immigrant? Suddenly the nosegays in my insides turned to large hailstones.

I squeezed her hand, too hard, trying to be protective. She freed her hand from mine, but I put my arm around her shoulder to show that she was, truly, "the cudin of my heart." She shrugged loose. "Drai mir nit kain kop," she said, "Stop bothering me," and I knew I was being heavy-handed because she censured me in Yiddish.

That night I couldn't sleep for sour apples. I could hardly wait to see her again, to make matters right, but the sun seemed to have gone on strike. The small birds that chirped in each sunrise must have been aged crones when dawn finally came to Oxford the next morning.

I waited until eight o'clock to spring into action. I looked around on our back porch. Cantaloupes and roses would make a nice subterfuge. I put five or six of Mother's best canta-loupes into a basket, and I stuck several long-stem roses around the melons.

I would tell Rose that Mother was sending this stuff to Mrs. S. Blatz. I walked too rapidly. I broke into a sweat. I stopped a couple of times to sniff myself. My socks were wet. My sneakers gave off squishing sounds as I churned along.

When her exquisite innocence filled the door-way, I knew exactly what Papa meant when he said a man like Just Plain Snake Imboden could give hell a bad name, if he went there enough.

I intended to say, "OY VAY IZ MIR," or "Woe is me," the only Yiddish I knew to approximate my chagrin. I expected her to tell me I ought to be ashamed of myself: "Shemen zolstu zich in dein veiten haldtz." To my amazement, she kissed me, lightly on the lips, smiled, and said, explaining her morning kiss, in relationship to the night before, "Ir gefelt mir zaier." That meant I pleased her.

We held hands a second through the crack in the open screen door. She whispered, "Neshomeleh. Tei-Yerinkeh." I think both meant "sweetheart." I am sure I could not have stood the sublimity of her saying "sweetheart" in English.

I ran a block, much faster than Man o' War. I still had the cantaloupes and roses in the basket, in my hand. I ran back, and placed the basket inside the screen door. I didn't want to see Rose again at the moment. One can't improve on heaven, and I was afraid any extraneous sound would make the dome of heaven fall and bury Oxford in broken bits of glass.

Fall, fat, full-bellied autumn, the old minstrel, the eternal gypsyman, was Rose's favorite season, principally, because we had the streets and the world more to ourselves. People were inside. Children were at tables, playing parchesi, or "Authors," instead of chanting "Ain't No Buggar Bears Out Tonight," on lawns.

Fall was always opulently succulent back then, and Rose and I began the annual pageant with scuppernong grapes, marveling that anything so tiny could contain such continents of ecstasy. I shook down ripe locusts and persimmons for us, and we hunted along the creek banks for the nests of scaly-barks, the local hickory nuts that had the essence of Eden inside their tough shells.

She never went to a corn-shucking, except vicariously, but I told her about the big-meal that rewarded the shuckers for a hard day's work, how the tables held some of everything that ever had feathers or fur or scales, that ever grew above or below the ground. I told her how the fellow who found a red ear got to walk home with a pretty girl, without any chaperone.

I found a red ear of corn everytime I told Rose about somebody's having a corn-shucking.

When the gleaned fields were books stripped of their bindings, and the wind came by playing enny-meeny-minny-mo with creation's bare ribs, smoke started pouring from local chimneys, as troups of acrobatic black cats or as a host of gray foxes fleeing the howling wind's pack of hounds.

Rose almost made an anthology of local poetry, in form of smoke. She exuded from her eyes, and even from the tip of her nose, her incessant enchantment with our chimney smoke. I think of this today, sometimes, when most chimneys are mere flues, long fingers that point accusingly to the sky as if trying to get someone's attention.

Back then, before smoke was a known menace, almost every chimney in Oxford seemed to have an incense and a tableau all of its own. The smell of fresh pine wood was a galvanizing, hearty greeting to company coming. Oak belched smoke that was a warm, fragrant epilogue to an evening around the upright piano, or a rousing trip around the world aboard that exalted charger called *The National Geographic*.

When grate fires were lighted, or re-charged, early of a zingingly crisp fall morning, scented smoke came tumbling wildly as a covey of baby birds flying more from exuberance and liberation than from skill. When fires were prancing red ponies, the smoke was a black banner defying the demonic threats of the great white wolf of winter, who waited, almost ready to pounce upon Oxford, just over the horizon. A bit later on in the day the smoke smelled like good pipe tobacco.

Frequently our Oxford smoke was wrinkled, the way Papa's face was wrinkled from incessant smiling. And when the sun called it quits and punched his time-card for the day, the smoke was as old as the serpent, without the original serpent's avarice. It crawled around in the sky on its perfumed belly, as if to erase the memory of that earlier upright reptile.

Well, that was a deeply personal time, even if the scope of human involvement was limited. But we were really excited by picayunes. Rose and I had never seen an art museum but we used our imagination to translate chimney smoke into a kaleidoscopic gallery of intimate pictures, framed with love and longing and with all the heady spices that grew in the forests.

When frost was a billion white rabbits "skinning-the-cat" on the trees, leaping walls and fences, and scampering everywhere, Rose and I walked out at night. When the moon was dropping yellow puddles all over Oxford and the starlight was dribbling fireflies along the darkened hedges and lanes, we were the devisees of November's nocturnal splendor.

She had a muff and matching hat, made of gray rabbit fur, which she wore with a blue coat. Another muff and matching hat were velvet, but the ones made of gray rabbit fur have outlasted all the ensuing changes in fashions, in my heart.

I'd usually forget one of my gloves, on purpose. If Rose didn't notice my bare hand, on nights when the wind was a giant turtle biting down, I'd blow on my knuckles. The muff was "Ganaiden," the Garden of Eden, Paradise. My cold, cruelly neglected hand was "Kabtzen in ziben poless," a pauper in seven edges, a very poor man.

For a block or two Rose pretended not to notice my bare hand, although my huffing and puffing on it was as obvious as that done by the wolf on the straw house in the story about the "Three Little Pigs."

But, ultimately, my labored histrionics were rewarded: Rose made room in the muff for my bare hand. And I can still feel that soft fur, and Rose's fingers, and those chilly nights when the moon was an old steam-boat chugging down the sky's big and majestic rivers.

I felt, and I still feel, the exultation Balboa knew when he discovered the Pacific Ocean. Of course, Keats confused Balboa with Cortez in his immortal poem, "On First Looking

Into Chapman's Homer." Today, the computer would throw a fit. It would say Keats was crazy as hell, because of his error in identification. But the poem retains its matchless exaltation, although Keats has been dead one hundred and fifty years.

The computer gives an immediate analysis of sea-water, but it can't remotely suggest the abiding essence of Masefield, Conrad, and the others who wrote so well about the ocean and the men and the ships that traveled the ocean.

I'm sure the computer can zap up dozens of definitions of love, but it couldn't define Rose and me, two innocents at home, in a hundred years.

I think Rose was something I somehow didn't have to deserve, as Robert Frost said about home in "The Death of the Hired Man." Reverence has nothing to do with deserving. In a glorious sense, she remains eternally in the public domain for me, the way that late April, white orchards, the sound of violins, the poetry of Whitman, and first frost remain in the public domain, remain in the tenderest sort of protective custody.

If he is superlatively blessed, every boy, every young man, has a love-affair with some adorable Rose. In time she becomes as immaterial as the shadows that go pussy-footing in June, but apropos to nothing, she returns, sporadically, to get divinely mixed up with the salt on the table, the mown grass blades, the heroics of the children, and even the most fervent kisses of the wife.

She wasn't a Christian and she never thought in terms of any Christian heaven. But she had more than enough soul, in the old and in the present sense, to go to any heaven, without dying.

I leave her standing there, in Oxford's innocent days before the image came to town like plastic apple blossoms. She stands there in her dotted Swiss, her hair ribbon, her sachet teasing the breeze. Or she stands there in her muff and hat, made of matching gray rabbit fur, in her blue coat, and I know that much of my better portion stands back there, too, on a deliciously nippy fall night, my cold, blue knuckles asking to come inside the muff.

Mr. S. Blatz had peddled, from his back, and then from a wagon, seven years before he saved enough money to open "The Emporium."

Just prior to immigrating to America, Mr. S. Blatz spent three years in the Czar's army. He slipped away, walking much of the time at night and hiding and sleeping in the woods by day, until he reached Le Havre. Some Jewish society got him a boat ticket to Buenos Aires.

Mr. S. Blatz was never sure why his ticket was to Buenos Aires, and I certainly don't know. He worked in Brazil for two years to save enough money to come to New York.

He told me, once, how the first Jews to reach America had come from Brazil. In 1624, twenty-three Jews landed in what is now New York, aboard a ship called the *St. Charles*. Rose and I called the *St. Charles* the "Jewish Mayflower." I wrote a piece about the *St. Charles* which Captain Wade ran in the *Torchlight*. For a few days, Papa called me Lord Beaconfield, who had been Benjamin Disraeli, and Dr. Henley called me Harry Heine.

From Ellis Island Mr. Blatz came almost immediately to Yanceyville. His companion on the trip down was another Jewish immigrant, who became Mr. I. Ferguson. Nervous and possessing scant English, he told the Irish immigration official, when asked his name, "Fergesen," or "I don't remember." So he went down as I Ferguson. Mr. Ferguson came to Oxford, a few years after Mr. S. Blatz came. Mr. I. Ferguson was a jeweler. He was always in a hurry, and he used the Yiddish, "Ich eil zich" so often that many Oxonions called him Mr. I. Ickelzich."

Several years before Mr. Blatz came south, a warehouse had been built at Yanceyville, ostensibly to supply stocks of goods to immigrant Jewish peddlers. Apparently, this warehouse was established by Mr. Fels, who attained national celebrity as the Philadelphia philanthropist. There is little doubt the warehouse was established solely to give immigrant Jews a chance in the new world.

Terms were generous and credit was easy. Apparently, Mr. Fels was satisfied to break even in the operation of the warehouse. For almost a year Mr. S. Blatz peddled from a pack on his back. He was given an itinerary, a map of sorts. The map kept him from getting lost in the vastness of this strange, new land. It told him where to expect friendly or vicious dogs, where springs could be found, and which families allowed a peddler to stay overnight in the house, in the barn, and which families wanted no over-night guests.

Triple stars were placed beside the names of families who purchased stuff regularly, and friendly dogs got double stars. Unfriendly families were marked with triple "X's" and dogs with double "X's."

For the first year, Mr. S. Blatz subsisted almost solely on hard-boiled eggs, while rambling around toting his pack. Eggs were Kosher, and hard-boiled eggs wouldn't spoil. Conversely, chicken would spoil, and there was no rabbi along the way to kill fresh chickens. For many years, around Oxford, many people called hard-boiled eggs, "Peddler's fruit." In time, Mr. Blatz learned that the by-ways of Caswell, Person, and Granville Counties, the terrain he peddled, were loaded with all sorts of luscious berries.

For as long as I can remember, raspberries, huckleberries, blackberries, and dewberries have been lumped together in one word, locally, "jewberries." Every spring dozens of small boys come by my home hawking "jewberries," or pails brimming indiscriminately with all types of the local fruit. Some etymologists of regional folk-words say "jewberry" is merely an accidental corruption of "dewberry," but other students of local idioms ascribe "jewberry" to the old-time peddler.

204

Mr. Blatz would pick berries until he overflowed one of the galvanized or wooden buckets he carried for sale on his wagon, when he graduated from back pack to wagon. Placing the bucket between his legs he'd munch berries and read his Talmud, as his horse, "Freddie," drove himself.

At first, Mr. Blatz referred to this placid mare as "Ferd," the Yiddish idiom for horse. But kids construed "Ferd" to be "Fred" and I suppose they made it "Freddie" the way "funny" is fun, with a tail to it. Anyway, Freddie, often "Freddie Blatz," was the only mare around with such a name.

Children, of all races, made Mr. S. Blatz's way much easier for him. When they spied him and "Freddie" and the covered wagon, the shout went up, "The peddler's a-coming."

Fathers and mothers might say there wasn't a cent on the place, and there was always the excuse of drought, or too much rain, too much hail, boll weevil, or tobacco wilt. But Mr. Blatz learned quickly the wisdom of saying that even though he didn't expect the parents to buy anything he couldn't deprive the children the thrills of looking at his wares.

He laid out the stuff, and he identified each item as some proud conductor might call the names of exotic whistle-stops: "Colognes, t'hamburgs, t'threads, nee-duls, pinz, bud-duns, t'side combs, rib-binz, theme-buls, stick-pinz, t'sweet soap, reach combs, chell-you-loidt collars, ent t'zizz-zers."

Mr. S. Blatz wore a black derby hat, a jim-swinger coat, a stand-up collar, and a silk four-in-hand, perhaps, on instructions from Yanceyville. But this attire certainly set him apart from the hucksters who came chewing gum or match stems, wearing begrimed wool hats, who were always coatless in warm weather, and who, in all seasons, let a single collar button do the work of a shirt collar and tie.

Mr. Blatz wore a big stick-pin in his tie, and on the little finger of his left hand a tremendous glass ring sparkled in the sunshine. He sold lots of the same stick-pins and glass rings.

The rings cost 35 cents each, and Mr. S. Blatz never pretended these rings had any value, but many poor boys bought them for engagement rings. If someone said a certain girl had been "Blatzed," it meant she was spoken for, wasn't up for any passionate grabs.

His luxuriant black beard was always neatly trimmed. The beard barely exposed the dark, swarthy face beneath it. His face, flashing here and there through the beard, reminded me of a hootchie-koochie dancer. Many farmers saw Mr. S. Blatz as a stepping straight from the Old Testament. Many asked him to supper, hoping to get the nuance of a perplexing bit of scripture explained.

He gave away a few favors, now and then, usually small mirrors, for women and girls, and sticks of licorice for children. But once he had all of his glittering oddments laid out, many an adamant and "impoverished" wife raided her egg money, her "pig" — in reality an earthen jar and spelled "pygg," before piggy-bank came along — for the change to buy a few yards of lustrous hamburg lace, or a yellow top for a boy who was out of his mind with expectation.

He always opened a bottle of cologne, the same bottle, until it gave out. He would dab the stopper to a little girl's hair. The scent seemed to linger, in the child's mind, to become for all time a vital part of the odoriferous seduction of honeysuckle.

He laid out bars of sweet soap almost as if he were laying-on hands. The strongest wind from the west couldn't blow away the aromas. As the multi-colored bars lay in their cases, children saw them as perfumed pink clouds, scented green waves, or white clouds redolent with myrrh. Surely, surely to God — to ours and to Mr. S. Blatz's God — if these delectable bars of soap were put on flowing water, they would turn into those Nicean barks which so delighted Edgar Allan Poe.

At this particular juncture most country people made most

of their own soap — lye soap — from animal fats, hickory ashes, and water. A less stringent brand, called "sweet soap," was made by cutting down the lye content.

Dr. Henley said Mr. S. Blatz brought the pleasure and the hygiene of bathing to our country friends and relatives. He sold them pretty bars of soap. The soap cried in bright colors and pungent scents for use. So, those who had restricted their bathing to "bird baths" and to "big baths" in creeks and mill ponds during hot weather, started heating water for "standing up" baths on the back porch. And those who had restricted bathing to heating water for the tub on Saturday night, started bathing on Wednesday night, before prayer meeting.

Beyond question Mr. S. Blatz was the founding-father of hair shampoo, in our rural section. He introduced "Golden Girl," a package of flakes. The flakes were mixed with water for the shampooing.

He gave away, as "favors," some ornate hair combs, the big-toothed kind women used to wear.

Papa said women wouldn't call attention to dirty, unkempt hair by advertising it with a big comb. So, everytime Mr. S. Blatz gave away a comb he won a permanent convert to the new-fangled shampoo, "Golden Girl."

After laying out the soap, he usually put out the cotton goods. They smelled like a bed, freshly made with clean sheets. As crisp as watercress salad in a brook, the cotton goods seemed to speak of a quiet, gracious sanity far beyond the ken of the searing fields, the back-breaking toil of the tobacco rows, the stench of sweaty over-alls, or "over-halls," and the constant urinations and defacations of uninhibited mules and horses.

Some girls bought cotton goods on one of Mr. Blatz's visits to make a dress to go with a parasol they had bought from him on a previous visit. With other girls, it was the opposite way. Brighter than the most radiant hues of Camelot's tents, these parasols always reminded me of exotic birds pirouetting in mid-air. They were like luscious cones of tutti-fruitti on sticks, these bright parasols were.

Mr. S. Blatz even sold silk stockings, but only inter- mittently. While silk stockings were plentiful in my time, Mother said the first pair she ever wore was to her own wedding. She hadn't had any when she was in the May Court at Greensboro College.

Even when I was a boy there was some suggestions of the lascivious to silk stockings. I remember the talk of the town was a pair Ramsay Davis gave to P.A. Duncan for a Christmas present, and Miss Texanna made P.A. return the gift to Ramsay, as being an unbecoming token to a young lady. . .I'm sure P.A. didn't give a damn about the amenities or any such jim-cracked morality. Jimmy Simpson said P.A. told Ramsay that Miss Texanna said for him to put the stockings where the monkey put the nuts, but, of course, Miss Texanna didn't say that.

Whether a family bought oddments or not, the scents and colors remained, in fancy. Hence, when a child looked into her mirror she usually managed to see a fleeting glimpse, at least, of Mr. S. Blatz. His fabulous caravan remained long after the wagon had gone. When a boy spun his glistening yellow top or drew raucous music from his harmonica or jews'-harp, he could still see Mr. Blatz, in the yellow gyration and in the spirited screeching, long after the wagon had vanished into that impenetrable snow storm made from the dust of a sandy, summer road.

Pots, pans, and buckets were lined-up on each side of the canvas that covered the wagon. These things were tied to a rope, and the rope resembled a trot-line across a stream. The assortment of pots, pans, and buckets dangling and floundering reminded many folks of fish, hooked on a trot-line.

They were flying-fish, the same as Kipling's and musical fish, to boot. The pots, pans, and buckets, the iron skillets, and the old-fashioned coffee pots, kicked up a sprightly racket. Everytime the wheels rolled, these utensils used each other for cymbals, drums, and glockenspeils. When Mr. S. Blatz headed his mobile mercantile operation into Oxford the cacophony heralded him ere the wagon hove into view.

When Per-fess-or Max Schmidt heard the approaching sounds, he always clapped his hands, as if he were a superlatively happy child playing "patty-cake, patty-cake, the baker's man." He called the clinking-clanking sounds "The New World Anvil Chorus," and he always started directing the pots and bands, with his hands.

The creaking symphony in brass, tin, wood, and iron reminded "Brer" Thompson of a nursery rhyme, which he quoted with great feeling, and mirth, when Mr. S. Blatz, was all sound and no sight:

"Gay go up and gay go down
To ring the bells of Oxford town.

Orange and lemons
Say the bells at St. Clement's.

When will you pay me?
Say the bells at Old Bailey?

When I grow rich.
Say the bells at Shoreditch."

As Papa stood, eagerly awaiting the appearance of the wagon and Mr. S. Blatz, snapping his fingers and patting his feet to the delightful hullabaloo, he quoted something from Ambrose Bierce, who vanished into Mexico about 1914:

"All the wagon bells make a solemn din —
A fire-alarm to those who live in sin."

Actually, Bierce had "church" where Papa inserted "wagon," but Papa would shout the couplet and, turning to "Brer" Thompson, say, evenly: "Anytime you are ready, I'll be happy to receive your confession."

I suppose the sounds from the pots and pans created the same effect in town that the cologne, mirrors, tops, and other oddments created out in the country. But I know it is no trick of time or nostalgia when I say that the rolling convert salvaged for joy many a listless afternoon already rued to a bad crop, or to those terrible local ailments, the "jimmy-jaws" and the "eppezudicks," which remained adamant to Dr. Henley's science.

Mr. Blatz drove his wagon around the courthouse square much as the circus wagons paraded around town before the big show. Then he parked the wagon in Ransom's Alley and set-up shop for a day or two, at a time.

In Oxford, the parked wagon became the "Jew Store" before Mr. Blatz opened "The Emporium." Inevitably, some of the regular merchants disliked him because "Blatz gets the hard money." That is, he didn't sell anything on credit, and he didn't pay any taxes, save for his privilege tax, his peddler's license.

I forgot a fabulous item. As Mother would put it, I clean forgot the clocks. Mr. Blatz must have had at least two of every kind and design of clock manufactured, from metal alarm clocks, to cuckoo clocks, to big "mantelpiece clocks."

I never knew his system of winding these clocks, but some cuckoo or imitation "Grandfather" was always striking an hour. One clock struck twelve as another struck five, and others clicked, clucked, and spewed simultaneously.

People loved to ask Mr. Blatz the time of day. At such times his bearded lips broke into a vague facsimile of a smile: "Vell, vot time do you vont?" So saying, he would point to the wagon. Then he'd take out his heavy gold pocketwatch — it had a heavy gold chain and a winding key — and he'd swing the watch the way Svengali is supposed to have swung his to hypnotize the Czar's children.

Perhaps, the local Sunday school teachers missed a trick by

not taking their classes to Mr. Blatz's wagon when they taught the lesson about the Tower of Babel.

Old Man Rufe Duncan was Mr. Blatz's first real friend in Oxford, and it was through Old Man Rufe that Mr. Blatz rented the store on Spring (originally Gum Spring) Street. Miss Texanna owned the building.

Mr. Blatz passed the cemetery in his wagon many, many times, and Old Man Rufe waved to him from his chair in the door-way of the "mossy-lee." Then one day Old Man Rufe stumbled from the "mossy-lee" to hail Mr. Blatz. Later on, when he told of this meeting, Mr. Blatz said he didn't know if Old Man Rufe was the devil or a local version of Pharoah. He said he would have hollered for help but he couldn't think of the English words. It would be futile to use the Yiddish, "Machen a g'vald." Hence, he thought it was wise to say a few words. ("Zog a por verter.")

Old Man Rufe included Mr. Blatz in the "mossy-lee's" coterie, post haste, and the total number never exceeded five. Old Man Rufe was about the only Gentile who always addressed Mr. Blatz by his first name, "Saul."

I learned from Papa that it was Old Man Rufe, amid some spell of unparalled lucidity, who suggested "The Emporium," as a store-name, and the slogan. Baldy Moore painted a large sign that said:

"The Emporium
Clothing and Shoes For Ladies and Gents
Terms Strictly Cash — No Mark-Up or Carrying Charges
S. Blatz, Prop."

The sign was written in gold letters, in what Baldy Moore proudly referred to as "My best Spensorium Scrit."

Some of his first customers were people from his old peddling route, but many came in because he looked and talked differently from the remainder of us. But the real key to his limited mercantile success lay in the fact that he was the first merchant in town to allow Negroes to try on shoes and items of clothing for size.

Papa said Mr. S. Blatz was blessed by a lovely defect. Papa said Mr. Blatz was "color blind." Even so, some irate merchants called Mr. Blatz "a Christ-killing son of a bitch," more especially when Negro trade was gravitating, perceptibly, to "The Emporium."

He was the first merchant in Oxford to sell things for amounts such as $1.98. This sounded a lot cheaper than $2.00. Although the sign in pseudo-Spenserian script said "Cash," Mr. Blatz learned quickly that during the long, listless summer months cash was as short as the bank president's sense of humor. So, he was forced to let some items go, "for something down and the balance in the fall."

Papa gave him a list of notoriously bad credit risks, and highest on the list was Just Plain Snake Imboden. One day Mr. Blatz sold Just Plain Snake a pair of incredibly high-class and incredibly expensive patent-leather shoes, low-quarter ones that cost $4.98. Just Plain Snake paid $1.98 "down," and walked out with the shoes in a box under his arm.

Papa told Mr. Blatz he would never see Just Plain Snake, or the elegant shoes, again. Mr. Blatz smiled, almost through his beard and moustache: "The Just Snake vill return, be backt zoon. I puddem two leff shoes in dat box."

Not long after the opening of "The Emporium" Mr. Blatz went to Baltimore and he returned with Mrs. Blatz, his bride. It was told that Mrs. Blatz was a "mail-order bride," but Rose told me that her father had known her mother, as a young girl, in "the old country."

Rose was born a year later. I always heard that Mrs. Blatz, Miriam, was never seen in public during her pregnancy. No, Mr. Blatz bought a Model T Ford, and each night, after dark, he took his Miriam for a spin around town.

Soon, there were six Jewish families in town, and although some of the gentile ladies paid calls to Mrs. Blatz she was inconspicuous in Oxford. She never "stayed" in "The

Emporium," although Mrs. Ferguson "stayed" in her husband's jewelry store, Mrs. Lehmann "stayed" in her husband's furniture store, and when Mr. Fox opened the biggest, most up-to-date department store in town, Mrs. Fox always "stayed" there.

As I said, Saturday, the Jewish Sabbath, was the king-bee in local economy. In time Mr. Blatz learned the mandatory necessity of keeping the store open on Saturday. And I became a Shabbot goy, or his Saturday, or Sabbath, stand-in.

I worked in the store on Saturdays, along with an older man, Tobias Tate, whose regular job was selling lightning rods around the countryside. It was said that Mr. Tate had been struck by lightning two or three times when he was installing rods on roofs, once with such severity that his gold cuff links melted.

I don't know if all of that was true, but he had a definitely scorched appearance, and when he walked he looked as if a gaunt, human Tower of Pisa were in motion. Some folks said he smelled "sulphuric," but when I worked with him in "The Emporium," he smelled strongly of bayrum and that pink dusting powder used in pool rooms, the powder usually referred to as "whore's dust." Just the same, people avoided him, most seculously, when the weather looked stormy.

Obviously, after Rose was big enough to "stay in the store," my acting as the Shabbat goy was a ruse to be near her. I'd come by late Friday afternoon to help Rose cut all of the paper and twine for Saturday's sales.

The store was heated by a coal stove. The hump-backed stove-pipe ran a good forty-five feet, way up high, to a hole in the far right wall. It reminded me of the biggest, blackest caterpillar in the entire history of the insect world.

You had to put a pan of water, some vessel of water, on hot stoves back then to humidify the air. Otherwise you caught a "head and nose cold." ("Sinus" wasn't in vogue in Oxford at the time.)

Most merchants put water in old coffee cans, but Mr. Blatz used a variety of kettles. Perhaps, these kettles were left over from his peddling days, but I remember several different ones. One was aluminum, or, maybe zinc. It got to be magnificently tarnished — silver hair streaked with gray, just like "Mother Macree." One was iron, and blacker than molasses. I thought of the black kettle as "the ram," after a ditty Dr. Henley used to say:

"Richard had a rakish ram,
As black as black molasses:
He butted Richard in the rear
And gun him psorasis."

Another was copper. It jumped up and down as nimbly as Sheriff Matt Venable doing the "clog" dance. I told Rose the copper kettle was the sun, getting hot, turning up his damper, and flexing his muscles.

But she was more entranced by the sounds of the kettles. Sometimes they hissed, as if a paused locomotive were gossiping. Sometimes they were peanut roasters chanting strident rhythms. Again, they were cotton gin whistles screaming twelve o'clock on Saturday, and often they were hunters calling their hounds through silver-plated fingers. Sometimes, a kettle would get religion and shake and cavort and yelp in Holy-roller tongues. Sometimes the vapor was a silver stallion prancing to the window to see the sights.

Ever so often the steam was a water-moccasin, according to Rose, hissing and crawling on its belly and getting ready to bite me because I had such "lascivious" thoughts.

I got bitten, repeatedly, but I can swear that snake bites are not antidotes for certain thoughts.

In cold weather we built a big fire Friday night. The coals weren't touched until Mr. Tate or I arrived on Saturday morning, although Mr. Blatz'd give the fire a chunk, or put in extra coal, when he came by Friday night at nine, on the dot, to cut out the light that burned on the outside of the store.

If the people in Koningsberg set their watches by Immanuel Kant's daily constitutional, everyone in Oxford knew it was two minutes to nine when Mr. Blatz walked past the "Ivanhoe" on his way to cut the front light at "The Emporium."

Fellows lounging around, playing mumble-de-peg on the courthouse lawn or singing beneath a lamp-post, would yawn, automatically: "Well, there goes Mr. Blatz. It's bedtime, already."

Mr. Blatz was a "Yeshiva Bucher" and I construed that to mean a man of learning or one who loved solitude. If this image seems incongruous with the image of a small town merchant, Mr. Blatz spent all of each Saturday reading and meditating.

He sat behind the counter, in a chair, reading, thinking, and lighting one Fatima off another one. I am sure he never needed more than three matches a day.

American newspapers fascinated him. He read everything from the *Torchlight*, to *Grit*, to the metropolitan papers. The first rotagravure section I ever saw was in "The Emporium." The bright pictures seemed to walk and talk.

Papa said Mr. S. Blatz had the quickest aptitude for languages of anyone in town, and I am sure he absorbed a wide, diverse, and bizarre range of local idioms from his friendship with Old Man Rufe Duncan., Too, he dropped in the "Ivanhoe," once or twice a week, enroute to cutting out the store light, and this was comparable to special studies and a Ph.D. from Harvard, in colloquialisms.

He was, I think, more interested in American schools and colleges than anyone whom I ever met, up to 'that time. He was always asking Rose and me about the local school, and what it was we learned and how the subjects were taught. He said the same questions to Papa, Dr. Henley, to "Brer" Thompson about colleges.

He knew, already, many of the things Rose studied. Rose

would ask, mystified: "How do you know these things, Tata, my father?"

"My child, long before you came into my life I was watching history being made." Thus, he related Oxford in terms of Russia and Brazil, and the other way around.

He was the first Jew in town to become a Mason, and although I am not a Mason, I understand much memory work is entailed in the ritual of being admitted. But even before he became a Mason, he was contributing small sums to the Masonic Orphanage, according to Papa.

He required Rose to write letters in Hebrew, or, perhaps a mixture of Yiddish and Hebrew, to her relatives in Europe. This must have been Oxford's first cultural exchange program.

But Rose was an American. I think Mr. Blatz reminded her of this almost everyday. English, not Hebrew, was his primary tongue, but Hebrew was the well-spring of her soul, the soul of her lavish heritage.

Today, when the word "soul" is thrown around the way citronella used to be used in mosquito time, it amuses me that Rose had a way of designating people as "soul"; "tongue," and "hands." Poets and musicians were "soul"; lawyers were "tongue"; and merchants were "hands." But I'm sure her father was "soul." And, of course, it was beautifully clear that "Old Dan" Tucker who had the strongest of all hands, was sheer "soul."

The other Jewish business men and merchants prospered, but Mr. Blatz, the scholar, didn't prosper. The family moved to Baltimore the year I left Oxford for college. Rose and I wrote each other for a while, but I think I spent so many words trying to prove that a mixed marriage would work out I made a case against mixed marriages. Perhaps, I protested for unadulterated love too loudly.

I never saw her again. All of that happened long ago, in another world. But if it is "long ago and far away," as Kipling said, in "Mandalay," it is not entirely "shoved behind me."

Last December I was out one day seeking holly and mistletoe in the woods. The canned reverberations of "God Rest Ye Merry Gentlemen" were still upon my ear when I remembered Chanukah, the "Feast of Lights."

After all these years, I remembered that Chanukah, unlike the festivals of Succoth, Pesach, and Rosh Hashana, has no Biblical origin. It commemorates the victory of the Jewish Maccabees over Syrian despots. It was this fight, one for religious freedom, that rescued Judaism from extinction. I remembered that the Jews light candles eight days. One is lighted each evening on the nine-branched memorah, "men-AW-ra," or "candelabrum."

A ninth candle, the shames, or guardian, is taller than the other candles and is used to light the others. This is done to show that one can give love and light to others without losing any portion of one's own radiance. That's what Rose, and her family, did for me. In a long life, blessed with many loves, and many loves infinitely more active than my first love, Rose endures as the ninth candle, and the spiritual radiance grows with the years.

EPITAPH I

I think his name was Smith,
But it might have been Johnson or Abernathy.
He managed to elude cyclones and snakes,
Without actually dodging them, and once
He had a fast, red conversation with a cardinal,
Between dental appointments.

The sun warmed his back,
He got cold in the snow,
And sometimes he laughed out loud.
The wind that scratched his face
Was spice on his love-making occasionally,
And once he got a second place prize
For saying a piece at the schoolhouse.

Death took him on the installment plan
Which figures, without any figuring,
And his obituary notice filled space
The way he fills that hole in the ground
That says his name was Smith. (But one
Can't be sure; for it might have been
Wilson or even MacGruder.)

In 1815, a minor French sage, Charles Fournier, predicted:
"In the future all wars will be replaced by cake-eating
contests between gastronomical armies."

Unfortunately, this prophecy hasn't been iced, but it
would be wonderful to read about a general in a big apron,
waving a huge wooden spoon, as he led troops wearing bibs
and tuckers. The chief of staff, shelling walnuts or shredding

coconut, would be told to rush the angel food division to the front, to flank with the upside-down corps, and to hold the chocolate, lemon, and orange cake forces in reserve.

Undoubtedly, the medics would stalk the battlefields with bicarbonate of soda, and the casualties would be carted off in bakery trucks. The artillery would fire salvos of whopping ten-decker wedding cakes as the mortars went plip-plop with raspberry tarts. Of course, mix-masters would be the equivalent of motorized troops.

And, some ingenious nation, maybe this one, would come up with a secret weapon, to wit, the pie. Pie throwing would be added to cake eating, and this would be the first time any war correspondent died from laughter. With the faces of both sides of the fighting men dripping with egg custard, victor and vanquished might be well-nigh inseparable. And when the air forces dropped pie-from-the-sky, especially those luscious cherry pies, the sanity of the world would make peace emotionally mandatory.

Then the boys would come home and parade through pie crusts and cake batter, in lieu of ticker-tape, and in the days of future years one tyke would brag how his daddy got the purple heart for a coconut cream wound. But his pal would reply: "Oh, yeah. My old man got the Congressional Medal for acute indigestion."

ENTRIES FROM OXFORD

Oxford, September 15, 1970

"Doing your own thing" is verbally and emotionally irrepressible today, but so much time is consumed in proclaiming this rarefied intention I wonder if much opportunity is left for execution?

However, a timeless spiritual puts the question much more succinctly, much more pertinently: "Everybody talkin' 'bout hebben ain't goin' there."

Conversely, "Struttin' Bud" Davenport was "doing his own thing" years before the phrase, as such, was ever spoken. He epitomized the buoyant essence without being overtly aware that he was doing anything.

If boredom is the ultimate evil, as Schopenhauer contended, "Struttin' Bud" must have been an angel, with arms and legs, using an imaginary baseball in lieu of a harp.

For, life was an orchard heavy with rich, red apples, and "Struttin' Bud" was smitten with an incurable appetite. His days were entire months of incessant excitements. He transformed idleness into a pulsating art.

Additionally, this bona fide off-beat was kind, generous, and tolerant. He was as natural as an inquisitive puppy given the total run of a sun-speckled morning. Indeed, "Struttin' Bud" was a happy, open-handed contrast to Oxford's uptight wheeler-dealers of this hour who are sure, as "Mr. Dooley" suggested, that God would do precisely as they do if He had the true facts of the case.

Some people in Oxford equated "Struttin' Bud" Davenport, who pitched so many imaginary baseball games, with Peter Pan. They said "Struttin' Bud" was an adult who never grew up, one who lived eternally in what would now be dubbed as some sort of Disneyland.

Others said he was a crank, but I never heard anyone say he was an out-and-out nut. A few put him down as an innate eccentric. I am not certain. It has occurred to me that "Struttin' Bud," revolting from a drab world, made of life an incessant, effervescent charade.

Perhaps, he began by playing a role, the same as a character in fiction. Perhaps, with time, he succumbed to the role completely. It may have been that the role became primary as the physical world, the little monarchy of Oxford, became hazily secondary.

"Struttin' Bud" was wealthy, as rich as cream, as the saying used to be. Obviously, a poor man couldn't have got by with his shenanigans, with his aberrations, if one insists on a stronger term. It is monstrously unfair, but we tolerate willingly the "idiosyncrasies" of the wealthy even as we berate the "idiocies" or the "tomfooleries" of the poor.

At the time of which I am writing – Oxford of the pre-image era – "Struttin' Bud" was in his forties. When he was eighteen he had entered a poster in a competition the Big Bull Company, the famous sack-tobacco firm, was running to advertise its famous product.

"Struttin' Bud's" poster won, and his painting is the one that used to decorate the barns, billboards, and blank walls of the nation, the one that showed a majestic bull rearing on his hind legs while a love-smitten cow, separated by a fence, gazed with unvarnished admiration.

In lieu of a cash settlement, "Struttin' Bud" took his fee in stock. The stock became incredibly valuable when the sack-tobacco firm was amalgamated in the huge tobacco trust.

He didn't quit "art" after his financial triumph. From then on he painted and sketched for fun. For instance, he decorated one wall of the fire house with a huge painting of Bertha and Matt hitched to the wagon. He painted a good likeness of the two horses, but Pete Wood, the driver,

221

resembles a caricature of W.C. Fields.

I hardly ever saw him, on his pitching rounds, when he wasn't carrying a sketch-pad. Sometimes he would stop and use a mail-box or the fender of a car for a drawing board. He sketched rapidly, and as his pencil or piece of charcoal raced, he mimicked the person whom he was drawing. He rolled his eyes, twitched his face, puckered his lips, wiggled his nose, grunted, sighed, whistled, or did whatever it was that his subject did subconsciously.

I have read that Dickens and Sinclair Lewis mimicked the salient features of the characters whom they wrote about, that both authors looked into a mirror continually as they put down the unusual features of a face or a voice.

I am sure this was a reflex-action with "Struttin' Bud." Sometimes he sketched from the "Ivanhoe," and he laughed aloud when he thought he had captured some distinctive nuance. I've heard him clap his hands, ecstatically, and dance a little jig when he was pleased by something he saw and drew.

I have some of "Struttin' Bud's" street and "Ivanhoe" work. He gave it to Papa, and Mother gave the drawings to me when Papa went to the Happy Isles, to see the Great Achilles, whom he once knew, via Tennyson.

My collection shows "Old Man Rufe" Duncan ensconced in the doorway of his mossy-lee; Mr. Matson and Mr. Hasbrook toasting Miss Lillie; Mr. Ed Settle in his huge buggy; wonderful Old Dan Tucker going to work on his bicycle; the President crossing College Street and walking as if he had wet his underwear; Miss Bertha seated at her switch-board; Doctor Henley toting his satchel; several of Papa; and there is one of the porch of the whorehouse, with Miss Opal surrounded by her male coterie.

Several times "Struttin' Bud" went to the annual State Fair in Raleigh, where he set-up as a sidewalk artist. He made charcoal drawings of some of the people, from all over the state, who attended the fair. I understand that his usual charge was fifty cents a portrait, although Papa said "Struttin' Bud" gave away far more than he ever sold.

This always amuses me. I wonder how many of these on-the-spot drawings have survived, and I wonder, even more, how many of the sitters, or walkers, ever realized that they had been drawn by Oxford's eccentric millionaire?

His house, unlike any other I have ever seen, had copious examples of "Struttin' Bud's" artwork. Several of the walls of the enormous rooms were filled with murals. Much of this reminded me of the convoluted paintings of Dali, whose works I saw afterwards.

"Struttin' Bud" may have been the first artist to incorporate baseball bats, bases, gloves, and other paraphernalia into larger works. An entire wall, of what "Struttin' Bud" called the "talking room," had baseball equipment floating around the way diverse objects cavort in seances.

I suppose one would say that "Struttin' Bud" had "surrealism" imposed upon "representational" art, although I am positive he never heard either spoken or ever saw either in print. The representational work in the "talking room" was a sort of distorted kaleidoscope of Oxford personalities. Some of his figures were pygmy-sized and others were taller than the tallest of today's basketball players. The pygmies were fat, with huge heads, and the elongated ones had pins for heads.

However, Mr. Matson's features were fairly distinctive, but the scalped portion of his head was green and the crazy pigtail was red. He stood in a blizzard of white bases, looking down at several dead bodies. Several of the bodies wore bandanas around their faces, and I assumed these were the Dalton boys, but one, bearded and haloed, with the strings of a sack of Bull Durham flowing from his shirt pocket, had to be Lord Tennyson. For a petrified fact, the gentle Lord smoked Bull Durham.

The opposite wall was cluttered with big-league ball

players. The figure of a pitcher winding-up, at least ten feet tall, must have been Walter Johnson. "The Big Train" towered over Ty Cobb, painted hook-sliding into home-plate; Babe Ruth swinging at home-plate; John McGraw, throwing a tantrum, to one side; Tris Speaker, making an over-the-shoulder catch in centerfield; and a fast double-play, executed by Tinker, to Evers, to Chance.

A man in a blue suit held a whisk broom in his left hand, a tin cup, with pencils, in his right hand. The wizened face of the blind umpire always reminded me of my mental conception of Blind Pew, in *Treasure Island*.

The crazy house was built in 1911 when "Struttin' Bud" was twenty-one or twenty-two. He called the house "The Bull Pen," and he always smiled to indicate the double-meaning, but Mrs. Davenport, nee Ethelene Talcott, called it "Xanadu," albeit, I never heard anyone allude to "Struttin Bud" as Kubla Khan. Anyway, "Xanadu" was the official name given to the place in the book, *Famous Homes and Gardens of North Carolina*.

Many local people called it the "Nut House." It had three stories, in addition to a tremendous basement, or cellar, as basements used to be called. There were sixty-odd rooms, not counting those in the cellar. These included a ball room on the ground floor that was approximately 180 feet long and 100 feet wide. There was a theatre, of the same proportions, on the third floor. Each of these had four tremendous fire places, although the whole house had central heating, one of the few in Oxford to have that feature, at that time.

Xanadu had the only elevator in town. Marcus Downey, "Struttin' Bud's" yard-man, a strikingly handsome young black, doubled as elevator operator. There was a closet beside the elevator in which Marcus kept his "elevator suit." Whenever Marcus operated the elevator he slipped into a bellboy's cap and jacket.

Papa said Marcus's "elevator suit" resembled the cap and

blouse worn by British admirals, and the sobriquet, "Admiral Marcus," stuck to the young black. Once, a magazine writer, who spent a night in town enroute to Pinehurst, heard allusions to "Admiral Marcus," and thinking he might pick up a lively, unexpected feature story, rode out to Xanadu to interview the "retired admiral" about his naval experiences.

The whole house, including the wings and appendages, covered 3.4 acres. The exterior of the house was made from graystone, quarried in our region, and the roof was made of light red tile. "Struttin' Bud's" barn, containing stalls for his milk cows and prize bulls, was connected to the great-house on the east. The barn sloped to one story, as did the stable, on the west wing, which contained stalls for the master's riding, walking, and trotting horses.

There was a riding-ring, approximately 150 yards south of the house, and just beyond the ring was "Struttin' Bud's" race track. The race-track had a covered grandstand, on one side. About twice a year the Davenports held a horse show, with sizeable cash prizes for gaited horses, walking horses, buggy-horses and the like.

When I was a boy, when paved roads were still scarce and when portable vans were virtually unknown, special trains came to Oxford for the semi-annual "Horse Show." "Struttin' Bud" was the ring-master, and he always wore a top-hat, a natty jacket, tight, sleek britches, and heavily polished riding boots. He had a specially made ivory-handled buggy-whip, with a red, silk snapper. He loved to crack it, and he made it sound as if Chick Hafey were hitting those sizzling line drives for which Hafey was so justifiably famous.

Semi-annually, the Davenports held the "Xanadu Cup Races." These came a week after the horse-show, and hefty prizes were given for the top three horses in the mile and a tenth race, and in the trotting contests.

Locally, the race-meets were called "Epsom Salts," an obvious take-off on the famous British racing course, Epsom Downs.

The cellar contained a large kitchen. "Struttin' Bud" kept two special cooks on the job, in the cellar kitchen, each morning to make breakfast for hoboes. The "specialty-of-the-house" was pancakes, and often there would be a dozen, or more, hoboes in for breakfast.

"Struttin' Bud" loved to flip pancakes and catch them on the griddle when they came down. Sometimes he went to the basement kitchen to give the two cooks a hand. On these mornings he wore a billowing, white chef's cap, the very same as the man used to wear on the "Wheatina" package. Once, I heard him tell Papa that he had flipped and caught, three times in a row, without a bobble, pancakes that went at least ten feet into the air.

Papa agreed that this must be a national record, and speaking of records, he asked if "Struttin' Bud" had ever read Owen Johnson's story, "The Great Pancake Record," the one in which the Tennessee Shad endeared himself to his fellow students by getting a holiday by dint of eating so many pancakes. "Struttin' Bud" hadn't, and Papa lent him the story. Until then Clarence Buddington Kelland, creator of Scattergood Baines, another big pancake devourer, was his favorite writer.

But "Struttin' Bud" was so taken with the Johnson story he wrote Johnson, in care of his publisher, asking him to pay a visit to the "Bull Pen." However, if Johnson ever made the pilgrimage, I am unaware of the fact.

Nonetheless, "Struttin' Bud" established the annual "Owen Johnson Pancake Eating Contest." For several years he put on an annual breakfast for the kids of Oxford. By the second year the breakfast was integrated, and it was the first fully integrated social event in the long history of Oxford.

He gave $50.00 to the boy who ate the most pancakes, $25.00 to the runner-up, and $15.00 to the third boy. Papa said "Struttin' Bud's" annual pancake contest anticipated Huey Long's "Share the Wealth" political gimmick: The grocery store, Jimmy Simpson's, sold large amounts of flour, eggs, bacon, and so on; Mr. Hill, the druggist, sold barrels of purgatives; and Dr. Henley and the other physicians spent at least three days making house calls to the homes of the contestants.

I think every kid in town attended the third annual breakfast. P.A. Duncan had written a blistering diatribe in the *Torchlight* in which she rocked "Struttin' Bud" because little girls weren't admitted. To be precise, girls were never excluded. I suppose "Struttin' Bud" thought his contest was unladylike, but he was happy to send the word to the little girls.

By the fourth year every room in the basement was filled. "Struttin' Bud" cooked, flipped pancakes with amazing dexterity, and he and Mrs. Davenport helped wait on the tables.

Along about the sixth year Papa and "Brer" Thompson suggested to "Struttin' Bud" that he extend the contest into an annual scholarship for some deserving boy or girl. Although the eating contest continued until "Struttin' Bud's" death, the "Owen Johnson Scholarship" was established, as a separate entity.

Papa and "Brer" Thompson told "Struttin' Bud" that the scholarship should bear his name, or Mrs. Davenport's. But he wouldn't hear to it, and the "Owen Johnson Scholarship," an annual grant of $1000.00, continued until fairly recently. Papa served as trustee for many years, and he, Dr. Henley, and "Brer" Thompson were on the committee to make the annual selection of a bright, needy student.

The hoboes called "Struttin' Bud's" fabulous cellar "Big Rock Candy Mountain," or the "Rock," for the sake of brevity and expediency. Among its other unusual features, the cellar had ten shower baths, and these were the only ones in town at that time, save for one in the back of Bill Rick's barbershop and two at the high school. The two at the high school were not available during summer, and as I can testify, personally, they never seemed to emit any hot water during winter, during the last portion of football season and during basketball season.

All the hoboes were required to take soap-showers before breakfast. At first, some hoboes demurred, but ultimately, the showers became an added inducement.

Many of the hoboes, hot, dusty, and dirty from the road and the by-ways, or saturated with soot, cinders, and ashes from riding the rods, exulted in "Struttin' Bud's" showers to such an extent he decided he should share this opulent luxury, to have some "shower bath parties" for his local friends.

After all, the ladies of the town had "showers" for brides and babies constantly. Nonetheless, the "shower bath parties" didn't catch on with the grown men, save for a few perfunctory, polite acceptances. Just Plain Snake Imboden went a few times, but his brother, the "King of the Green Snakes," said "Snake's" taking a shower at "Struttin' Bud's" place was bound to prejudice the hoboes against the place.

But kids went fairly often. I guess those showers were status-symbols for us boys, but the icy water, after the hot water and the soap, was supreme exhilaration during Dog Days when the sun sent mad hounds prancing across the sky.

"Struttin' Bud" had a bowling alley in the basement. It had three lanes, and he let us try our hands at bowling when we went for the showers. I always showered first and bowled afterwards. That gave me a valid excuse for a second shower. Papa said that "Struttin' Bud" did more to exemplify "cleanliness next to Godliness" than all the revivals held in the state.

The showers were in a big bath room, and a cake of ice was always placed at the bottom of each urinal. The hoboes called this "pissing on ice," but the term denoted privilege, status, or high living, rather than the obvious. The phrase encompassed the whopping free breakfasts, the deluxe handouts, the entire amalgam of "Struttin' Bud's" largesse.

For years I assumed that the term was local, or certainly confined to hoboes. Many years later I purchased a copy of the *Dictionary of American Slang* by Wentworth and Flexner (Crowell Publishing Co.) and I found the old phrase as a synonym for "living high on the hog."

The "Winter Garden" was on the first floor of the great-house, next to the stable. It was solid glass on two sides. The floors were made of the finest tile I ever saw. There was a pool in the center that had lily-pads, all sorts of bullrushes, mossy little islands, and fish, tropical fish, allegedly. There were several frogs, and I am sure these were local frogs.

Even when I was used to the sounds it gave me a start to hear, apropos to nothing, apparently, several giant bullfrogs, going "Knee-deep, Knee-deep, Knee-deep," amid surrounding so splendiferous as Xanadu's.

The "Winter Garden" ran the depth of the widest point of the house. Hence it was better than 100 feet and it was as long as the ballroom and the theatre. It would have taken a botanist to have classified all the flora, fauna, trees, flowers, and shrubs in the place. I was in the "Winter Garden" many times and I always felt as if I had walked into a jungle such as W.H. Hudson described in his classic, *The Green Mansions.*

"Struttin' Bud" said he fished in the pool, especially when he wanted fish, freshly caught, for breakfast. But this privilege was not extended to the people in Oxford. But it was told, reliably, that he and his wife went skinny-dipping in the pool, especially in the winter.

Occasionally, there was a rumor down town of a skinny-dipping party. I imagined such parties were literal translations of the wildest Roman orgies, even if I had no real way of knowing.

Ramsay Davis made some loose-lipped allusions to sporadic skinny-dipping parties, but I think he did this for two reasons: Obviously, he had never been invited to one, and, in his role as a perennial candidate for office, he was making a palpable appeal to the "moral element."

One day, when Ramsay was muttering some snide, oblique references to "Struttin' Bud's" alleged naked swimming parties, "Brer" Thompson spoke up, as if Ramsay weren't there: "The scriptures don't say anything about this, but I rejoice in thinking that the Master, and the twelve, after a hot, dusty day spent trudging those rough paths, could hardly wait until evening so that they could pull off their robes and dive into the Sea of Galilea. And they went swimming the same way they came into the world, the same way Michelangelo painted the saints on the ceiling of the Sistine Chapel."

I never knew whether or not any skinny-dipping occurred at Xanadu, but, ever so often, one of the rural Baptist ministers got permission to hold a baptizing in the pool in the "Winter Garden."

I didn't intend to neglect Mrs. Davenport. Ethelene, or "Lene," as her friends called her, was good-looking, without being beautiful. Whenever I think of her features, I think of Merle Oberon, the former movie star. Lene had the same high, strong cheek-bones, the same delicate skin tones.

Her hair was long and dark. I heard Papa quote Martin Luther to her one day: "The hair is the finest ornament women have. I like women to let their hair fall down their backs; 'tis a most agreeable sight."

But one didn't see the long, black hair very often. Lene wore wigs, an infinite variety of them. She played many roles. Consciously, or subconsciously, she must have put on the wig that attended some specific facet of her personality, her creativity.

She sculptured a lot, heads mainly, and she always wore a blonde wig above her smock. She spent many hours in solitary meditation. When she lay on the grass in the trees,

230

"to get the true harmony of nature," she usually wore a rust wig.

Occasionally she had a showing of her sculptures. Most of her heads were modeled on characters in Greek mythology. Hence, most local patrons were unable to judge the accuracy of the likenesses. The best example of her work I ever saw was called "Aphrodite." Something about "Aphrodite" reminded me, pretty strongly, of the lovely face of Dovey Turner Simpson, the wife of Jimmy Simpson, groceryman and short-stop on our Oxford nine, our clean-up hitter.

Lavish refreshments were always served at Lene's exhibitions. Hence, her art-work always drew a sizeable crowd. I went with Papa and Mother once, when the piece de resistance was a copy of Venus d'Milo.

The torso of Venus, mounted on a stand, was draped with a velvet covering. At the dramatic moment, "Admiral" Marcus Downey, dressed in a cut-away, striped trousers, spats, a bat-wing collar and an Ascot tie, pulled the cord. When Venus was revealed Mr. Caleb Entwhistle nudged his wife so hard he almost knocked her down. "Great G-hos-e-fat, Mattie," he yelped, "somebody's done broke off boff her arms."

(This artistic faux pas was not so egregiously gauche as Mr. Entwhistle's calling his wife "Mattie." She was "Mattie" when they had married; when they had outdoor plumbing, but in the financial rise from outdoor plumbing to finger-bowls, she had become "Matilda.")

Lene sculptured, communed with nature, and she had "quiet hours" long before Oxford ever heard of the "Oxford (England) Movement." But the theater was her first love, her real joy. Four times a year she produced and directed plays that were put on in the theater on the third floor.

Sometimes she starred in these productions. At other times she did what she called "Interludes." These were impersonations of people such as Isadore Duncan and Ellen Terry, but I think the best ones were the "Interludes" in which she simulated wind, rain, flowers, passion, grief, or anger by her actions.

Her triumph must have been "The Saga of the Oak Tree," in which she began as an acorn, came up as a sapling, developed a trunk and great leafy branches. At the end she crashed to the floor so hard I thought Jack Dempsey had put the wood to Jack Sharkey. The felled oak depicted man's inhumanity to his environment, and I must confess I never saw anyone take a hard spill more gracefully or more convincingly..

"Struttin' Bud" always made and painted the sets and he acted as stage manager.

Occasionally, Lene hired some road company that was playing in Raleigh or Durham. A few times road companies were brought in all the way from Richmond. I think the actors liked to come to Xanadu. They were paid well, and, of course, they were treated handsomely.

I didn't see them, but two of the first shows brought in were *Hitchy-Koo* and *Irene*. The latter introduced "Alice Blue Gown" to Oxford. The song captivated our town completely. It may be a bit sugary, but it's still a good tune. In fact, I heard Lawrence Welk play it the other night. Jimmy Roberts and Norma Zimmer sang the duet, and I remembered all the stories of Lene Davenport's fabulous "Alice Blue Gowns." It was said she had a bluish wig to go with the gown, but that may be apocryphal.

When I was a small boy, I went one night, with my parents, to see a road show production of *Sally*, with Jerome Kern's exquisite song, "Look For the Silver Lining." When Sally sang "Look For the Silver Lining," as she bent over her wash-tub, I slobbered all over my Sunday shirt. I was so enveloped with empathy, so galvanized by the words and the music, I wanted to go out and do and die for something, for someone, for some adorable, deprived Sally.

Of course, it wasn't manly to cry, except at funerals, but I lost some of my sense of shame when I saw Mr. Ed Settle whimpering into a silk handkerchief that seemed as big as a small tablecloth.

Lene's transcending coup was getting the immortal Irish tenor, John McCormack, to Xanadu. A special Pullman brought him down from Richmond, where he was making a guest appearance. Papa told me that Lene paid John McCormack a thousand dollars for one evening.

McCormack was billed, justifiably, as the rightful successor to the divine Enrico Caruso, at the "Met." As I recall, we had just two days to prepare for McCormack's concert. The guests, whom Lene invited, had a special session at the Woman's Club, with Per-fessor Max Schmidt, the German gentleman who taught music lessons in town. He played all of his operatic records, and we did our best to bone up on Verdi, Puccini, et al.

McCormack's singing was as resonant, as sweet, as rich as Keats' poetry. His voice was as intimate, as pulsating as the most passionate kiss, but he sang only two arias. There we were, cocked and primed for the complex hurricanes of opera, but what we got was "At Dawning," "Danny Boy" and some other Irish ballads, and "Memories," the song written by Gus Kahn.

I am astounded that John McCormack had ever heard of Charles Wakefield Cadman, who wrote "At Dawning," Percy Granger, who arranged "Danny Boy," or Gus Kahn. But the singing, if the antithesis of top-hat, was delightful, exquisite, simply enchanting.

Mrs. Ashton-Brown was appalled. She said McCormack had insulted our sensibilities with those popular songs. But I agreed with Papa. He quoted Anatole France: "It is better to understand a little than to misunderstand a lot."

During all the years that "Struttin' Bud" served free breakfast to all those hoboes, he served supper every night for one man. Each evening, at precisely five o'clock, never a minute before or after five, "Governor Poly," old Mr. Polycarp Marshburn, walked from his room located over "Tull's Billiard Parlor," and started the trek to Xanadu to supper. Come to think of it, Mr. Marshburn was the only person in town, aside from Mrs. Ashton-Brown and the Entwhistles, who had "dinner."

He always wore a frayed suit of tails, an opera hat, and he always carried a gold-headed cane. In cold weather he wore an opera-cape. If he had an overcoat, I never saw him wearing one.

In winter, when the gloaming came earlier in the day, I imagined that "Governor Poly" was a bat as he skimmed along the sidewalk. He had a habit of flinging out both arms, about every twenty yards, and this intensified the bat-image as he walked along in his ancient evening clothes.

He ate in a small room on the ground floor which "Struttin' Bud" fixed up as a dining-room, just for "Governor Poly." A waiter brought his dinner from the kitchen, and Admiral Marcus, dressed in a butler's uniform, served the meal. Apparently, "Governor Poly" ate the same food every night: A double porterhouse steak, a side dish of asparagus tips, a huge side dish of hash-brown potatoes, and for dessert he had a large piece of deep-dish apple pie.

According to Admiral Marcus, "Governor Poly" ate everything served him, and he sucked down the steak bones when he had eaten the meat. He could have had more, and he could have varied the meal. Apparently, he got exactly what he wanted, and in the precise amounts.

Before the meal, Marcus served him two large Scotch and sodas and an El Producto cigar. Even then, El Productos cost two for a quarter. He smoked his cigar as he had his two high-balls.

He was served wine, during the meal, and brandy with his dessert. When he had finished his dessert, his deep-dish apple pie, Marcus brought him two more El Productos. He took another hefty Scotch high-ball with his second cigar. The third cigar was for the trip back to his room over the billiard parlor.

Apparently "Governor Poly" had little contact with the Davenports, but this was in deference to the "Guv," to his important work. For as long as I knew him, and before I knew him in the flesh, he was writing a, or rather "the," comprehensive history of the state.

The magnitude of his work was so absorbing, so demanding, he never left his room save for his walk down to Xanadu for supper. I understand he had a little coffee-lace for breakfast, but he confined his eating to the one meal each evening at Xanadu.

Even when I was a boy, the appellations, "Governor Poly" and "The Guv," were pretty foggy. Newcomers and visitors assumed that "Governor" was appended in the British sense, a mere salutation, that "the Guv" was some sort of local joke, that Mr. Marshburn was a "guv" somewhat in the manner of Crighton, the butler, in Sir James Barrie's play, *The Admirable Crighton.*

Actually, he had been elected lieutenant-governor of the state about forty years before this time, when he was twenty-eight. I believe he was the youngest man ever to be elected lieutenant-governor. Strangely enough, he was never really keen on politics. He was elected at a time when there were no Democratic primaries, when candidates were nominated in convention.

He had inherited a large farm, and he was one of the early leaders in the Grange and in the Farmers' Alliance, even though he was strictly a "gentleman farmer." He had never attended a convention before he went to the one that nominated him for lieutenant-governor, and he went solely to nominate some man for Commissioner of Agriculture.

His speech, totally devoid of political rhetoric and

bombast, captivated the delegates by dint of its effervescent contrast. Then, when an impasse developed in the nominations for lieutenant-governor, some of the weary leaders turned to this disarming young man who made such an attractive impression in his brief, maiden speech.

This occurred late at night, after countless, futile ballots. In other words, young Marshburn found himself in the same position as a crap shooter who picks up a pair of dice with nothing but sevens on them.

Republican opposition in the general election was nominal only, and Polycarp Marshburn, Esq. became "Governor Poly." Albeit, it seems he never went to Raleigh except when it was necessary for him to preside over the biennial sessions of the State Senate.

He had lost his farming interests, his capital, and his inheritance when his land was ravaged by the wilt, by downy mildew. "Struttin' Bud" paid his room-rent. He could have taken a room at Xanadu, but I suppose less stigma was attached to separate quarters, and, besides, no one ever interfered with his writing, ensconced as he was over the pool hall. I was in his room once, with Papa, and there was no place for anyone else to sit down.

Tremendous piles of papers, ledgers, old journals, maps, and assorted bric-a-brac completely usurped the room. There was one chair, at a drop-leaf desk. In a corner there was a rickety wash-stand, with a bowl and a pitcher. I understand "Governor Poly" got his drinking and shaving water downstairs, in the pool room. Apparently, he showered at Xanadu, ever so often.

I always understood that "Struttin' Bud" cared for "Governor Poly" because his father and the old gentleman had been close friends. He was with us, in my time, almost as a ghost and an echo. He nodded amiably enough, on the street, when he came out for his brief appearance each afternoon, but, otherwise, he was immaterial as a shadow, as the permeations of lark-spur.

He had no interest at all in politics. Papa said he was the only ex-office holder extant who didn't even trouble to vote, much less to stage a political come-back. To my knowledge, no one ever sought "Governor Poly's" political opinions or advice and he never dispensed any. But there was absolutely no derision in his nick-name.

His life's work was never published. I am not aware that he offered it for publication. The manuscript, in his own handwriting, very small letters always written in an uphill slant, runs to more than 5000 pages. It covers, in detail, every facet of life. The portion relative to the Indians and the Colonial period runs more than 1500 hand-written pages.

The manuscript, in a packing crate, stayed in the vault in the county clerk's office for a long time. Now, it is under the aegis of the Oxford Historical Society. Despite staggering problems in editing, I should think "Governor Poly's" immense manuscript would make an interesting study for some aspirant to a master's degree in history.

I'll never forget two of "Struttin' Bud's" most memorable stunts, although he didn't consider them "stunts," certainly not in the normal context of the word.

A "tramp" pitcher, "Stuff" Malone, came to town. Our regular baseball players were amateurs who worked at something else for a living, but the fans did pass the hat to get up money for pitchers.

"Stuff" pitched for Oxford one summer, averaging eight or ten dollars a game. Our catcher, George Hargrove, said "Stuff" had the widest assortment of curves he ever saw. In fact, the other teams couldn't touch "Stuff." He was striking out fourteen to eighteen men each game. Then one day some of the Henderson players accused "Stuff" of working on the seam with a victrola needle.

The umpire's investigation disclosed a flat surface on the seam. As any player knows, Jane Fonda could be a whizz pitching a ball that has a flat surface on the seam.

From then on, the umpires searched "Stuff" before he took the mound, and from then on, he was just another pitcher.

Simultaneously, South Boston, Va., also in our semi-pro league, had a pitcher who was caught doctoring the bill with paraffin. He, too, was rendered virtually impotent, via official searchings.

"Struttin' Bud" decided it would be terrific fun, and a most interesting experiment, to have a game between Oxford and South Boston in which "Stuff" was turned loose to use his victrola needles and the other fellow was given free use of his paraffin cake.

The game was played in Oxford the day after the season closed officially, and I'll guarantee there never was one like it, not from Abner Doubleday's time down to the Mets. The game went five innings, before the other 16 men quit in disgust. No hitter, on either side, got to first base. No ball was knocked out of the infield.

Jimmy Simpson hit the longest ball of the day, a pop foul that went half-way down to third base. Hitters went to bat 30 times, and 23 struck out. The longest grounder hit almost got to the pitcher's box. And there were some fine hitters on both teams.

I saw this bizarre game, and there is no doubt in my mind it would have been a double-no-hitter if it had gone nine innings, or eighteen innings, for that matter.

The next year Tom Day showed me in the *Sporting News* that "Stuff" had won ten straight games, without a loss, in the Pacific Coast League, a league that was just under the majors back then. According to the news story, several big league teams were trying to sign "Stuff."

Along about the middle of July "Stuff" showed up in Oxford. Somebody asked him what happened. He answered: "Well, it seems them ball players and umps out yonder is fa-miller with the gramaphone, too."

The superlative stunt was the time "Struttin' Bud" bet Tom Day five bucks that he would serve fresh snow-cream on July 4. Tom ransacked all of the available almanacs before he put up his five dollars. There was no indication of snow in Oxford in July, nor had there ever been any snow in July.

Toward the end of June, when the town was panting from the ravages of a real heat-wave, "Struttin' Bud" passed the word around town that he would have a "Ben Hur chariot race" at his race track on July 4.

Tom Day made circular signs around his head, around his white cap: "Maybe so, but when's it go snow, Bud?"

"Struttin' Bud" smiled innocuously and told Tom not to miss the chariot race.

I guess a third of Oxford went to the race track at Xanadu on July 4. Just Plain Snake Imboden was peddling white booze from a wagon that was filled with turnip sallet, and the "King of the Green Snakes" Imboden was giving away luscious green-snake watermelons.

After a while, three chariots, each pulled by three of "Struttin' Bud's" horses, charged from the run-way. He drove one; Lene, in a sort of Julius Caesar wig, drove one; and Admiral Marcus drove the other one. She was dressed like Cleopatra, in the movie, and "Struttin' Bud" and Marcus wore the same garments Mark Anthony wore.

As I recall, Lene won the chariot race.

Right after the race, all of the Davenport's butlers, cooks, maids, and handy people came to the race track pushing wheelbarrows. Each wheelbarrow held several freezers of snow-cream. "Struttin' Bud" pocketed Tom Day's five bucks as if it were the Hope Diamond.

Papa, who was in on these stunts, told me that "Struttin' Bud" bought the three chariots from Ringling Brothers, or from one of the big circuses. He had put his entire force to gathering snow the February before. The snow was made into ice cream. The ice cream was packed into freezers, and the freezers were stored in the ice plant in Oxford.

Captain Wade had both stories on the front page of the *Torchlight*, and some of the wire services picked it up. The snow story was garbled, a bit, in translation, and for a while some of the more facile of the sensational journalists were equating Oxford with the "Big Rock Candy Mountain," the place that had the lemonade springs and the gum-drop trees. But, then again, as I have already noted, the hoboes were calling Xanadu "Big Rock Candy Mountain" long before "Struttin' Bud" Davenport put on chariot races and served snow-cream, in Oxford, that wonderful, crazy July 4.

next year, with luck

His eyes are yellow glass marbles, burned hollow,
And his bones a squeaking shambles of rusty wagon.
His broken fingers are the twisted harvests
That never seemed to measure out, and his face
The grass burning up and beyond all aid of rain.

The land is a leech charting each day's bloody stint,
Watering and feeding its bottomless gullies from his heart;
The land is a serpent always holding forth an apple
In such a way the sun conceals the rioting worms.

But still:
With a stub pencil he scrawls portentous figures.
Always the figures. . .Now, next year with good luck
He'll make a killing, sure as hell. And then
He'll square the merchants and the banks, and buy Martha
That bunch of curtains whose spangled promises
Have fought the chills of long winters past.

As viewed by the traveler on the highway, a field of
growing tobacco is only a burst of remote greenery, a sea of
emerald weeds, although the cigarette in his mouth may be a
fragrant, sensuous alter-ego.

The farmer in the field, among the big green leaves, sees
tobacco as a wily antagonist, a capricious pawn of the
demigods of sun, wind, drought, and rain. Yet the cultivation
of tobacco, for this man, is a direct means of existence, the
only known route to the pursuit of personal happiness. Year
in and season in or out, tobacco is a growing physical fact
with diverse and devious ramifications. But tobacco is never

referred to as "her" as a car or boat may be called, nor as "it," as a calling or a game may be termed.

Tobacco is "THE CROP" and no matter how the word is spelled, misspelled, or pronounced, it is always in capital letters. Yet I am no expert. I have lived among tobacco farmers all of my life. I have studied them from the compulsions of compassion alone. Also, I have been confronted and annoyed by their myopic adamance to expanding horizons. I have tried to get inside them as a math professor might tackle a problem whose answer seems obvious but remains tantalizingly elusive. My failures do not affront me. No one really understands a tobacco farmer save another tobacco farmer.

From the way these men talk about a crop, a stranger would assume the health of a cherished relative is being discussed. The sun, the moon, and the stars always have to wait for the current crop. This crop always has the personality of a human being. The image this crop projects puts all other human emotions into total eclipse. It bites into every facet of rural society with the vibrance of honeysuckle, and the grower's almanac is never kept by the dates of wars nor by the follies and triumphs of other men.

When a memorable occasion in current history is alluded to, the farmer resurrects automatically, in all of its rewarding gladness or in all of its monstrous cruelty, the crop he made that particular season. Time beats out in suns and winds, in wilts and worms, in oceans of lugs, leaves, and smokers.

The farmer understands that fabulous realms are said to lie above and beyond the fields, but the aromatic sweet-madness of one curing barn dispels these other realms and vanquishes even morbid curiosity about them.

In this era of intricate specializations, the tobacco farmer, be he high or low, is the one man who knows all there is to know about his trade. From birth he is swaddled in "THE CROP," but even when he exhausts all knowledge his desire is

242

yet unrequited. For his heart is grounded in "THE CROP" as his purposes and hopes are anchored there. And when he gets to heaven, if the angels on his street don't want to talk about growing a crop of tobacco, there will be a celestial congress to rout the fervor of the original Farmers' Alliance.

ENTRIES FROM OXFORD

Oxford, June 10, 1971:

The population of Oxford is just above 7000. I am told that forty percent of the population is composed of adults. I am reasonably sure this ratio is high relative to the national ratio of adults and youngsters, but we have an unusually large number of old people in Oxford.

Anyway if there are 2800 adults, there must be close to 2500 memberships in a wide assortment of social, civic, fraternal, patriotic, religious, and cultural organizations. Indeed, most of the 2500 belong to several such organizations.

There is a chapter of every civic club of which I have ever heard, but most of our local ones are relatively new, certainly in relationship to the long history of the town.

To my own knowledge, there are at least twenty-seven women's literary clubs that meet regularly. But if there is a single literary organization for males, I am unaware of its existence. There used to be one, "Sans-Souci," or "the History Club," as it was commonly designated.

"Sans-Souci" faded many years ago, when I was a boy. Its dissolution was simply a tragic matter of the attrition of death. The membership died off, and no suitable replacements seemed to be available.

However, I think the demise of "Sans-Souci" related more to changing mores, especially to the incessant flood of new entertainments. Again, "Sans-Souci" was not an eating club, primarily. It held no "Ladies' Nights," and it bucked for no industries. It was not even remotely geared to civic improvement, not in the current sense, certainly. . . .

For many years new members were taken in save when an

old member died. It was said that the president of our bank waited his turn for two decades. He was never tapped, although he spent a long, abortive apprenticeship boning up on Sidney Lanier so he would be ready when the great hour came.

I don't know the real extent of the President's special study of Sidney Lanier, but I know it to be a fact that he owned — had acquired in some fashion — one of the collected editions of Lanier's poems, *Poems of Sidney Lanier*, which the poet's widow got out in 1884. The President also had copies of such posthumous works of Lanier's as *The English Novel, Music and Poetry, Letters of Sidney Lanier,* and *Shakspere and His Forerunners.* (Shakespeare is spelled "Shakspere.")

The President owned the biography of Lanier written by Professor Edwin Mims, in 1905. (Mims, who taught Papa at Trinity College, went on to Vanderbilt and lived through and saw through the unrealistic hogwash of the celebrated "Fugitive Movement.") The President's "piece de resistance" was his copy of *Tiger Lilies*, published in 1867, during Lanier's lifetime.

For many years the President had an annual display of his Lanier collection on February 3, the poet's birthday.

The President displayed his fabulous collection under glass. We kids could look at, but never touch, sacred immortality.

The President love to quote the passage from "Song of the Chattahoochie" that tells how:

> The white quartz shone and the smooth brook-stone
> Did bar me passage with friendly brawl,
> And many a luminous jewel lone
> — Crystals clear or a-cloud with mist,
> Ruby, garnett, and amethyst —

The President's eyes glittered as brightly as the show-window at Mr. I. Ferguson's jewelry store, and his mouth watered the way I imagined Silas Marner's mouth watered with ecstasy when he counted his gold.

Papa always came back by quoting the opening of Lanier's long poem, "The Symphony":

O Trade! O Trade! would thou wert dead!
The time needs heart — 'tis tired of head:
'We're all for love, the violins said.
'Of what avail the rigorous tale
Of bill for coin and box for bale'?

This was pretty shifty of Papa. It upset the President as much as Mr. Matson's malicious innuendoes about bank examiners.

I am sure vanity had much to do with the unchanging composition of "Sans-Souci." Papa used to smile, indulgently, and quote Mencken: "The essence of a self-reliant and autonomous culture is an unshakable egoism." Papa was alluding to the difficulty of gaining membership.

Getting in "Sans-Souci" reminded me of something "Brer" Thompson told Mrs. Piano Hutchins, who weighed a ton. Mrs. Hutchins asked how she could inherit eternal life.

"Eat less," "Brer" Thompson replied, "The gate to heaven is exceedingly narrow."

Whatever "Sans-Souci" was, it was the fruitful antithesis of Carlyle's "Such is SOCIETY, the vital articulation of many individuals into a new collective individual."

I was allowed to sit in a corner, in total silence, each time Papa was the host for "Sans-Souci," when it met at our house. Many years later I remembered a paper "Governor Poly" read on Johnson Jones Hooper's marvelously out-rageous book, *The Adventures of Captain Simon Suggs.* The "Guv" said the Duke in *Huckleberry Finn,* was the literary reincarnation of Captain Simon Suggs, that ingratiating devil. I mentioned this in an English class at Duke, some years later, and I seemed to have impressed my professor.

The "Sans-Souci" was founded in 1872, in the back room of the Eagle Tavern and Bar, by George Worley, a Confederate colonel, scion of a long-line of local gentry, and a lawyer.

The membership was limited to eight. One story says Colonel Worley limited the "Sans-Souci" to eight because nine or more made an awkward poker game. Another account says that eight was hit upon because there are 16 ounces of whiskey in a pint. Thus, eight men could get two ounces each, or what was called "a small eye-opener," or "enough for a hollow tooth."

Colonel Worley, rendered completely destitute by the Civil War, made a precarious living, barely an existence, from 1865 to 1870, by tutoring a few children in Greek and Latin and by investing his small stipend at the poker table in the back room of the Eagle.

One day in 1872 he found a Sunday school lesson on the floor of the bar-room, one dropped, evidently, by some thirsty farmer. Worley read the lesson and pronounced it, "The poorest damned attempt I ever read."

The bar-keeper dared him to do better. "By, God, I will," Colonel Worley said, picking up the gauntlet. So, acquiring Bible, tracts, paper and ink he proceeded to write some sample lessons.

Shortly, he was commissioned to write the International Sunday School Lesson. Papa said his father told him it was generally understood that Colonel Worley was paid the munificent sum of $50.00 a month for his contributions.

For four years the Biblical scribe led a life of affluence and luxury, all the while using the back room of the Eagle for his study.

Then in 1876 the editor of the magazine that published the International Sunday School Lesson came to Philadelphia to attend some British-American brotherhood assembly. Since he was only a few hundred miles from Oxford, the British divine decided he must come to Oxford to pay his personal respects to "the Reverend Dr. Worley," his lucid and consecrated scribe.

In his zeal to pay deference to Oxford's Gamaliel, the British divine seems to have neglected to announce his intention. At any event he alighted from the stage coach, at the old stand in front of the courthouse. (The railroad did not come to Oxford until 1881.)

He asked someone where he could find "the Reverend Dr. Worley" and his informant merely pointed to the Eagle. Perhaps, the English gentleman was so aflame with rapt expectancy he was not aware of his surroundings. Nay more, he may have been totally unfamiliar with the interior of American saloons.

Attaining the Eagle he asked the bar-keeper the location of the good Reverend's study, and the publican pointed, wordlessly, to the back room. Still abysmally ignorant of imminent disaster, the pilgrim strode on to the back room. He knocked and when he was admitted, there sat "the Reverend Doctor Worley" holding a heart flush. His Bible, tracts, and writing materials were stacked by his chair. A bottle was at his right hand, and a "tarnished thrush," a painted saloon-woman, was leaning over his left shoulder.

Colonel Worley was fired by an unintelligible shriek of incredulity and righteous indignation, and by the steady retreat of two horrified feet.

To this very hour, a heart flush is sometimes called "an Indian massacre" in Oxford. It amuses me whenever I hear the phrase because the speaker has never heard of the hand in relationship to Colonel Worley's literary demise. Indeed, the modern poker player has never heard of the Colonel, much less of his writing the International Sunday School Lesson.

Beyond peradventure, "an Indian massacre" predates "Dead Man's Hand" in conjunction to the two pairs, aces and

248

eights, Wild Bill Hickok held when he was shot and killed.

Colonel Worley's first associate in the "Sans-Souci" was Benjamin Thorpe, another impoverished scion, who was twenty-five in 1872. "Squire Ben," as he came to be called, lived until 1915. Although he died before I was born, I have always felt that I knew "Squire Ben" in the flesh, and intimately.

At Gettysbury, as a sixteen-year-old sharpshooter in the 26th North Carolina Infantry, Ben Thorpe was stationed, on the first day of the battle, in the region of the McPherson farm, on the east. Young Thorpe was placed atop of one of McPherson's cherry trees, and he was armed with one of the few telescopic rifles in the Confederate army. Ben's lieutenant, who had positioned him atop the cherry tree, stood near by to observe the enemy through binoculars.

From his perch Ben saw a group of Union officers halt on a knoll several hundred yards away. The lieutenant surveyed the group through his field glasses. (For the following dialogue I am indebted to my friend, Glenn Tucker and his *Lee and Longstreet at Gettysburg*, published by Bobbs Merrill.)

"Ben," he shouted up, "do you see that tall, straight man in the center of the group? He is evidently an officer of some high rank and is directing operations. Sight your gun at 700 yards and see if you can reach him."

These were the precise words, as Tucker records and as "Squire Ben" remembered them, in a conversation with Papa.

The first shot fell short.

"That was a little short, Ben," said the lieutenant. "Sight her at 900 yards this time and hold steady, for we must have him."

Ben sighted carefully, resting his long-barreled rifle on a limb of the cherry tree. He held his aim and squeezed the trigger. "I knew before the report died away that the shot had been a good one."

Later Ben learned that he had killed General John Reynolds, ("the great and good Reynolds" as "Squire Ben" told it to Papa,) who was in command of the Union Army the first day at Gettysburg, in the temporary absence of General George Meade.

"I've been sorry ever since," he said whenever he recalled the incident.

General Reynolds was reburied in his home town, Lancaster, Pa., and it is an irrefutable fact that "Squire Ben" arranged for flowers to be placed on the grave, on several occasions. He had some correspondence with Reynold's widow.

I understand Mrs. Reynolds was bitter when "Squire Ben" began his correspondence, but, in time, she accepted his sincere regret, his active sense of personal sorrow and guilt.

Papa, who acceded to the "Sans-Souci" upon "Squire Ben's" death in 1915, always referred to the old gentleman as one of the Civil War's most tragic casualties. Apparently, there was never a day for fifty-two years, from 1863 to his death in 1915, in which Reynolds did not occupy a portion of "Squire Ben's" thoughts.

While he was not a religious man in the orthodox sense, he went to Old St. Mark's church almost every day for an interlude of meditation or lamentation. He rode a horse, to the end of his days, and he was always followed by several hounds, even when he came to town to buy something or to attend the meetings of "Sans-Souci."

Apparently, he never used the word "bitch." No, female hounds were "little ladies."

His hounds went to Old St. Mark's whenever he went. The church was built on the Thorpe ancestral plantation, about 1820. It had six short pews on either side of a narrow aisle, and there was a small slave balcony. The wood for the building, for the pews, for all of the church furniture, and for the communion cups came from trees grown on "Old

Goshen," the Thorpe plantation.

Towards the last of "Squire Ben's" life he was the only communicant left at Old St. Mark's. There was no rector, of course, but the rector in Oxford would drive out three or four times a year to give communion to "Squire Ben."

I remember a conversation when Papa and "Brer" Thompson were talking about old "Squire Ben," about how it was that he lived with guilt as intimately as other men live with love, as intimately as flowers live with sunshine and rain.

"Brer" Thompson said there should be a literal heaven just so old "Squire Ben" could speak his piece with General Reynolds, make his peace and find his peace. Each tried to project the scene. Each tried to conjure the words old "Squire Ben" would say to the man he had killed.

Finally, Papa and "Brer" Thompson agreed that the meeting would be along the lines of one of Lord Byron's stanzas:

If I should meet thee
After long years,
How should I greet thee? —
With silence and tears.

I spoke of the difficulty of getting into "Sans-Souci," of the President's lengthy, empty vigil. One of the most ingenious devices at ingratiation was done by Mr. Gus Tulgin, father of Jo-Jo. Mr. Tulgin, who made, installed, and repaired house gutters, and had a handsome collection of arrowheads and sundry Indian relics.

He invited the membership of "Sans-Souci," solely as individuals, mind you, to a barbecue and to an exhibition of his Indian artifacts.

At noon, on the big day, Mr. Tulgin filled two huge wooden buckets two-thirds full with well water. He placed the buckets on a shelf on his back porch. He gave Jo-Jo a quarter. Jo-Jo was to ride his bicycle to the ice plant at five o'clock and bring back two bits worth of ice. That would be about as large a piece as one could put into the basket of a bicycle. Jo-Jo was to chop the ice into chunks and fill the two buckets with the pieces of ice.

Thus, the water would be good and cold for the juleps when Mr. Tulgin came home from his gutter shop. But Jo-Jo spent the two bits. As I recall, Jo-Jo went to the movie matinee. When he came home, about five o'clock, he filled both buckets with lumps of coal, from Mr. Tulgin's back yard coal pile.

Mr. Tulgin shook both buckets when he got home. It was about dark by then. The "ice" sloshed around nicely in the buckets. When he tasted the water to test it, it was lukewarm. He figured the ice hadn't been in long enough to cool the water.

When he made a second test, about thirty minutes later, the water tasted even hotter. He wondered what was wrong with the ice. He explained his vexation to his wife. She told him ice didn't make water hotter, that he was so filled with whiskey everything tasted hot to him.

The next time he drank he got coal dust and dirt all over his face. Mrs. Tulgin screamed. She said Mr. Tulgin had "the black foot in the mouth," or some kind of new and pernicious "hoof and mouth disease."

He looked at himself in the mirror, and he really went off his rocker. Mrs. Tulgin called Dr. Henley, and the doctor gave Mr. Tulgin something to calm his nerves.

In the meantime Jo-Jo, seeing the havoc he had caused, "borrowed" 35 cents of his mother's egg money, went to the ice-plant, and half-filled both buckets with real ice.

By then Dr. Henley's medicine, or shot, had quieted Mr. Tulgin. He wanted to show Dr. Henley he really wasn't crazy. He led the doctor to the back porch. "Now, see for yourself, Doc. That ice water is hot enough to shave with."

Both men sipped, and when the icy cold water hit Mr. Tulgin's mouth he really "broke bad." This time Dr. Henley had to give him a big shot of morphine to get him under control.

It was several years before Jo-Jo found the courage, or gall, to explain to his father what had really happened. The event quickly became a vibrant foot-maker, a book-marker, a time-marker, in local history. Until fairly recently, many events were equated, with time, "To the night when Gus Tulgin tried to make time with the history club and went crazy doing it."

FOR A GIRL ON A BICYCLE

Sometimes I think you are a poem a good poet made up
To give October swift motion and music of lyric tires.
But you are an exciting fact of skin and bones when the wind
Takes your flashing thighs for a 'cello. And I know
It isn't always an illusion, or my naivete,
That you fly the pavement unobserved (save by me),
Swallowed up eternally in my vision by crimson puddles
Of splashing autumn leaves. But loving is as various
As those gray cloud-shawls October wears against the eventide,
And you are likely to be a lollypop on rubber wheels, or
A glass of wine when the wind comes sliding snidely
With pinking shears up his sleeves. Often
You are a blanket stitched with dawning's last dreams,
Or that last golden apple left quivering on the tree
To slake a lifetime of hungers. Even the postman
Would agree you are some sort of Highland Mary
With exquisite taste and a generous charge account.
. . . . .But time runs so crazily, back and forth,
  Around many mulberry bushes and prickly pears,
  I think it, time, must be a bird at the window-sill
  When the whole house is being let. . . . .
So, I leave you on your bicycle,
A poem in motion for yesterday and tomorrow,
A song that never had any words,
A whistled tune, a catch in the throat,
A lamentation and an exaltation.
I leave you to your solitar musings,
To leaves, as laurels, in your hair,
To the wind upon your bosom's heavings.
So, ride, then, ride,

Down to all the Zions,
Publishing glad tidings soundlessly,
Sensing, but never acknowledging,
You are my poem on bicycle wheels,
The secret unclaimed in my heart,
The desire always unsated in my loins,
My picture against the vacant sky,
The sun warm upon my face,
The vine leaves in my hands, and
Ride, ride, ride.

Many people are curious about what a writer had in mind when he wrote a specific item, and several folks have asked me about the inspiration for this poem. I don't know that I am capable of inspiration, as these folks ask the question, but I was thinking of my wife. And I have neither had any reason to alter the "inspiration."

My most savage disappointment wasn't the unfrocking of Santa Claus or learning that God is not a Methodist. It was locking myself in the upstairs bathroom, when I was a school boy of sweet sixteen, but sans some of the lyrics, to read Rupert Brooke's poem, "The Great Lover." Surely, I thought, rolling the title over the licentious acres of my mind, our teacher had lost her mind. This opinion was intensified because half our class was composed of girls — nay, more, ones of such rarefied virtue that had they been frying-size chickens not even the most inveterate glutton would dare to touch a feather.

I obtained the book with the poem as if it were a "fix" in hard covers, and I locked myself in to scamper across rolling fields of scantily attired beauties who had never once spoken the word "No." I was still an unbounded, lascivious comet when I hit the fourth line and the gut-smirking phrase, "Desire illimitable." But as I read on to see Poet Brooke list his great loves I thought of our maiden teacher more as a purveyor of wooden nutmegs than as a victim of momentary aberration.

Brooke said, right out in the poem, that he loved plates, cups, and something called faery dust (I wondered how many plates his mamma had ever made him dry, especially just before picture show time on Saturday); the rough male kiss of blankets (that was a jarring punch from Dempsey); the smell of last year's ferns and the smell of friendly fingers (nobody in Oxford saved old ferns, and the friendliest and best-smelling fingers had erratic habits of thumping small noggings); holes in the ground, washen stones, and the cold graveness of iron (I thought Poet Brooke had confused that hole in the ground with something else. "Washen" was a knocked-down hurdle, but my first actual poetic attempt was rewriting the last great love to read, "The iron graveness of cold.")

My pal, Russ, and I pondered this demoralizing fiasco.

"Don't you reckon Mr. Brooke ever heard of. . ." I broke in: "England isn't Granville County, boy. Maybe that's why the old folks came over here, because, well, good God, some of them were bound to figure out there's something besides last year's ferns and that damn faery dust stuff."

We walked on, as if we had been cheated by a carnival man. Russ drew a circle and spat in the center. He seized my arm with both hands: "I betchu one damn thing, I betchu. If Mr. Brooke ever went to one Sad-dy night dance at Banner Warehouse he wouldn't give it back for all of Big England with Whales thrown in for good measure."

Today, I take a brighter view of Brooke's poem, but my vote is for a pretty girl on a bicycle. And if any worthy portion of me, of any man, rides with her, she says to the wind: "Of course he loves me. Do you think he was born with that quizzically stupid face?"

When one considers the incurable virus produced by acquiring physical possessions, one reverses the majesty, exhilaration, and awe of watching a pretty girl ride her bicycle, and I'm talking about grown girls and men, all right enough.

The view makes a man do all the dances from the Virginia reel through the Watusi, although he never moves a muscle and stands as still as a city-slicking Buddha who conceals his watery mouth and his ravenous eyes. It is a reverse type of sky-diving that needs no plane or launching pad.

COUSIN HATTIE'S AUTOBIOGRAPHY

When I was very young I sowed my heart with apple-seeds,
Not to be called a female John Chapman, or to deter a doctor,
But to harvest one ever-lasting, ecstatic love.

Across many green and scented seasons my heart
Was an orchard so heavy with fruit I thought
The bending boughs would make earth-tremors, surely.

Some fruit was pickled by migrants,
And ebullient rascals shook the limbs, now and then,
For anything, ripe or green, that might fall their way.

Naturally, some crops were marred by storms and droughts.
By worms, insects, birds, and despite my ardor
Some fruit was sapped by killing frosts.

But I had a plan, you know. I saved the best bin, —
Winesaps, lovely, whole, sound, and untouched, —
For one exclusive, eternal, red-rich October Fair.

It, that, he never happened to me. Hence for a season
I gave my luscious fruit away, and for a season I sold it,
Assuaging much hunger, and finding joy, both ways.

ENTRIES FROM OXFORD

Oxford, N.C., November 18, 1965:

The old-timey whorehouse such as we had in Oxford must have gone to Texas or to hell without a hack. I have not read any authoritative treatise on the demise of the small-town sporting-house, and to my knowledge there is no palpable point of embarkation such as the late Jerome Kern used in his old tune, "The Place Where the Good Songs Go." But anyone with the realism of a sober jaybird knows it was pitiless amateur competition that put the kibosh of the madam and her girls and dispatched them without so much as a testimonial fish-fry from the alumni.

I don't know what happened to the high-steppers who clicked their heels so lasciviously on the sidewalk and twirled their parasols so hypnotically under lamp-posts when these were known as iron lillies. Some of the preempted soiled doves may be in Florida drawing social security, playing shuffleboard, and contemplating their memoirs. Some may be in cities giving on-the-job lectures to soiled doves who long to fly as she-eagles. I suspect some are financial counselors to snazzy call-girls who get more money in a night than all of Miss Opal's girls took in during a month. But assembling these superannuated whores in a deluxe reunion has obvious perils, to say nothing of the fact that when someone attempted to hold a reunion of the late Thomas Wolfe's University of North Carolina room-mates, the hotel in Chapel Hill couldn't hold the throng.

Perhaps, Jim Bishop, who has found death more lucrative than many undertakers, will write another deathless opus, *The Day the Small-Town Whorehouse Died*. Then we shall know what God and Bishop have known all along.

Today, there's a drive-in bank where Miss Opal's place

stretched in the sun and cowered in the icy wind. By now, our corporate limits run wildly as a big-headed creek in flooding time, and this drive-in bank is within our corporate limits. But when I was a bug-eyed boy smitten with an insatiable type of glandular fever peculiar to growing boys, Miss Opal's place was about twenty yards beyond the corporate limits.

And location was vital. The whorehouse was beyond the ordinary jurisdiction of Oxford's police force, both of our cops. Actually, the city police had a legal right to make arrests in extreme cases one mile beyond the city limits, but Luther Baggs, our chief, had impeccable respect for the niceties of the minutiae of the law. As he explained it, "Unless it's a mergency, I don't intercourse with the sheriff's jurisdiction and he don't intercourse with mine." (Mr. Baggs always was a stickler for declarative chasteness. Once the town board gave him a slight salary raise when he was expecting a reduction. He beamed to Papa: "Candyally, I was suspectin' to be shat upon.")

Our night policeman, Mr. Arnie Tatum, had the job ten years before his wife knew about it. He was always at home in bed with her by ten o'clock, at the very latest. He sold chill tonic during the day, probably for less money than the $75.00 he received as night policeman, but his wife was supposed to be from an aristocratic Virginia family, and I assume she would have thought Mr. Tatum's being a police-man wasn't couth or refined.

Miss Opal's place was too close in for our sheriff, Matt Venable, to take the trouble to start his Ford and drive such a short distance, and, besides, in pretty weather he walked down there almost every night. Miss Opal's house was painted gray, what was known as "Wabash blue," like the celebrated "Wabash Cannonball." When one of Miss Opal's girls walked up town, on the rare occasions when they left the house, some of the parlor-lizzards who hung out in front of the drug stores whistled "Little Gray Home In the West" and every other tune they could muster that had gray in it. Everytime Papa and "Brer" Thompson heard this whistling they asked Doc Henley if he couldn't slip something into their cokes to give them lockjaw?

If the house was gray it took a spy-glass to tell just what color it was. The hedge in front and on both sides of Miss Opal's home was so high I used to image it goosed low-flying clouds with long, green fingers. This privet, as high as the top of the whorehouse, was never pruned or clipped when I was a boy, and it conformed to my notion of a vast South American jungle when I read W.H. Hudson's *The Green Mansions*, as a high school student.

At one time, before I was born, the whorehouse had been the local Manse, and the old Presbyterian Church had been next door. The church burned down, about 1890, and a new church building and Manse were built up town. Miss Opal bought the deserted Manse about 1918, and Papa said the deacons thought they had hornswoggled Miss Opal. She paid them $2000.00 for the place, and they had tried to get rid of it for $800.00. Later on the deacons swore that they thought Miss Opal was a seamstress, and sometimes they said they thought Miss Opal was coming to town to give music or elocution lessons.

Miss Opal told Papa the deacons thought she was such a sucker, were so anxious to close the deal, that only one even took time to comment on the dry weather we were having. Later when one irascible Presbyterian mogul branded Miss Opal as a whore, Papa said, "The whore's beauties are the dread/Of peevish virtue and the chilly bed." I never found out who said it.

By my time, when Miss Opal was "not active in the profession," but merely a "supervisor," as Papa put it, the old issue about the desecration of the Manse was almost forgotten. Albeit, occasionally some old-timer said something about "gathering moss from the old Manse." About once a month Just Plain Snake Imboden, soused on his own stuff, would stumble down the path toward Miss Opal's place. He always sang "Bringing In the Sheaves," and he emitted little apostrophes, to trees and birds, about "Susanah and the Elders."

But Miss Opal never let Just Plain Snake Imboden in the front door. He entered through the back. And Miss Opal made him pay the spot cash (I think it was $2.00) everytime he came to pleasure himself. Miss Opal never let Just Plain Snake Imboden carry a bill over until the early fall, when the tobacco market opened, the way she did with Hughie and Hector Scott, identical twins, who farmed and kept batch out in Sassafras Fork, ten miles from town.

As I understand it, there had always been whores in Oxford, but our ladies stayed at home in the old days. They weren't in political activities and social reformations. Indeed, the solid old phrase, "Up in Mabel's Room," indicates the continuity of soiled doves. Too, Judge Robert W. Winston, in his book of memoirs, *It's a Far Cry* (Henry Holt and Co., 1937) says, in the 1870's, that there were more churches in Oxford, according to population, than in any town in the state, that there were twice as many saloons as churches and twice as many bordellos as saloons.

In my time Miss Opal's place was the whole shooting match. Of course, whores were about as rootless and homeless as poker chips. But at the time I am writing about there were the three girls whom I called by name, Jessie Lee, Sula Mae, and Maude Rose. It is my honest opinion that these three are accurate examples of the type found in Oxford, in that era, or in almost any small, sleepy Southern town.

I knew them pretty well, if never intimately, if never physically. Miss Opal used to order candy, magazines, and other oddments from the "Ivanhoe," and Mr. Hasbrook and Mr. Matson let me deliver the packages. I always backtracked, through Mr. Ed Settle's lovely woods. When I brought the package to the back door, Miss Opal always inquired about Papa, and she always gave me some refreshments.

Each girl had a separate tale, or history. I heard these stories many times, as I sat on the back porch, eating a piece of gingerbread or sipping a big dipper of root beer. Miss Opal usually had a barrel of pickled pigs' feet and a barrel of salted herring on the back porch. I loved them and she handed the pigs' feet and the salted herring to me with both of her fat hands.

Later on, if someone said he smelled "whorehouse" on me, where I wiped my hands on my britches, he wasn't referring to any "inside the whorehouse" odors, whatever they were.

I almost forgot that Miss Opal subscribed to *Grit* and to the *Southern Planter*. I delivered these, to the front door, from the "Ivanhoe," because I delivered all the other *Grits* and *Southern Planters* to the front doors in town.

I suppose I was "King of the Mountain" in the curious eyes of my friends. They asked me a lot of questions, especially if any man was inside the place "a-doing-of it" with one of the gals. Actually, I never saw or heard anything. When I delivered *Grit* and the *Southern Planter*, Miss Opal always met me at the front door.

She was cordial and she asked about the news downtown, but she never asked me to come in and take a chair, or anything like that.

If Papa knew about my errands — and surely he must have known — he never said a word, not to me. However, a few years later, I'm sure it happened after Miss Opal passed away, Papa saw me coming from the pool room: "I'd rather see you walking from a whorehouse than a stinking pool room," he told me. "So would I," I answered him, "but on my allowance I can't afford it."

He must have laughed later on, even if I was a smart-aleck, because I knew that "Brer" Thompson and Dr. Henley knew about our exchange.

Alas, my mother found out about my errands. From the way Mother carried on one might have thought I owned a harem. I am sure she thought I had gonorrhea, or "the gonorrhea," as we called it (an article was placed before virtually every malady, "the pneumonia," "the typhoid fever") just from knocking on Miss Opal's front door.

If she had known about the gingerbread there is no question a stomach pump would have been applied to my belly, but by "Brer" Thompson rather than by Dr. Henley.

The important thing, to me, though, was I got to know all about the "din of sin."

Jessie Lee couldn't have been much more than twenty. She was the youngest of the three girls. When I saw her on the back porch, when she didn't have on all of her having dating paints and that perfume I could smell thirty yards away, she looked like a farm girl who was waiting to milk the cow or gather the eggs.

She was friendly but sort of withdrawn, and she reminded me a lot of the farm girl, Maude Muller, in Whittier's poem. Several times when I delivered stuff from the "Ivanhoe," she was sitting in the back yard drying her hair.

Her hair was yellow and it fell all the way to her shoulders. It reminded me of a yellow daisy-chain. I guess she washed it a lot. When it was dry and she started combing and brushing it, I thought of small yellow rosebuds on a trellis. I know she was just another whore. But I remember a verse Ramsay Davis used to say about every yellow-haired girl he knew, from Jessie Lee to P.A. Duncan. Ramsay Davis said he wrote the verse. If so, the muse struck but once:
"St. Paul swore, and St. Peter said,
And all the saints alive or dead,
Vowed she had the sweetest head
Of yellow, yellow hair."

The other girls evidently resented the verse. I heard Sula

264

Mae and Maude Rose sing the song about "Mary Ann," substituting "Jessie Lee," somewhat evenly:
"Pull your shades down, Jessie Lee,
  Last night in the pale moonlight,
  I saw her, I saw her,
  She was combing her golden hair,
  It was on a rocking-chair."

Jessie Lee'd give her hair a yank to let me know it wasn't a wig.

I didn't know much about bosoms except some were big and some weren't. If the word "falsie" wasn't used back then, the two others accused Jessie Lee of wearing "gay deceivers."

Of course, I had sense enough to know how she made her living but when she sat there in the back yard, her face free of everything but a few freckles, I wouldn't have been surprised to hear her mother call her in to learn her piano piece for the recital.

Dr. Henley said she was a "little light for the traffic," but "Struttin' Bud" Davenport said Rabbit Maranville, the shortstop, didn't weigh more than 125 pounds, wringing wet. Just Plain Snake Imboden said when she drank a little cherry smash she looked like a thermometer.

Maybe, that was why I heard grown men say that Jessie Lee wouldn't sell Just Plain Snake a glass of lemonade in the bad place.

Jessie Lee said she came from "up the country." The place never was specific. However, some men said they knew her folks. Sometimes her folks lived on a farm two counties away. Again, the place was seventy miles from Oxford.

She went into this business solely to help her family out of a financial jam. The wilt got the tobacco crop, or the boll weevil got the cotton. (This varied.) But Jessie Lee's folks were straightforward, all right from the ground up. They had voted three times for Bryan. They were such good Christians they wouldn't allow an Ingersoll watch on the place. But the bank failed, or the "time" store got the whole crop, or her Papa had "the T and the B's" in both lungs, and the landlord ran them off the farm.

Jessie Lee was doing her family duty. That was all. In fact, some people thought she was the girl Old Man Rufe was protecting with his stick each night, the girl in the city, with the brother named Jack.

Frankly, I never thought she came from any farm. I say this because one day, in the back yard, we were talking about Hughie and Hector Scott. She liked both of them, and she couldn't tell one from the other. Anyway, she said they'd be in to see her as soon as they "kilt theer hogs and skint 'em."

I never heard of anyone's skinning a hog, except in one of John Ehle's novels.

I suppose a psychologist would say that in exonerating Jessie Lee the local sportsters exonerated themselves. What they did with Jessie Lee was the same as playing a crooked faro wheel at a church benefit. The money went for a fine cause.

After she left our community, the alumni told Horatio Alger stories about Jessie Lee. She moved to a big city, to some place like Danville or Norfolk. It was better to have the state-line drawn in the mind. She had bailed out her family. She had saved enough for a business course. She learned to write on a typewriting machine. She got a job working for a brilliant young lawyer. Now, Jessie Lee and the lawyer had two fine sons. It was reported that her husband would go to Congress soon.

So, all of the local blades felt the same pride men feel today when they contribute to some educational foundation that really pays off tangibly in human dividends.

Sula Mae said she was from a big city, but she never did say precisely which one. She talked a lot about riding the trolley. The big city might have been Richmond, Baltimore, or St. Louis. It must not have been New York since she never

266

mentioned the subway.

She, too, was a victim of circumstances, a creature of life's hard storms. She had been seduced, under promise of marriage, by this rich sport who took her to elegant cafes where the meals cost as much as $1.50, without counting the champagne, or "com-pag-na," as Sula Mae called the wine.

Her beau really loved her, but his parents tricked him off to France or Europe. The hateful parents wouldn't give Sula Mae a street car token back up town when she told them she was with their son's child. Then she was thrown out, always on an inclement day, by her own stern, Christian parents. She asked for shelter, and they shouted back the commandment about adultery. ("Brer" Thompson told Papa he had in mind a sermon, "Let Him Without Stones Throw the First Sin," but I don't know if "Brer" Thompson knew Sula Mae's story.)

The baby, now a little girl, as bright as sunshine and as smart as Frances Perkins, was in an orphanage. Sula Mae was hustling just to keep her child in the orphanage. She had to send money to the orphanage once a month. Hughie and Hector Scott said they had contributed so much to the child's education they were going to be sure to attend her graduation.

However, Sula Mae's real objective was to save enough, at Miss Opal's, to take the little girl out of the orphanage. Then the two would go out west, as far as Memphis, maybe, and get a fresh start together.

If Sula Mae never made positive identification of the mythical swell who supposedly got her pregnant, her eyes and facial expressions cast innuendoes everytime she looked at the rotogravure section of the Baltimore *Sunday American*. (Ramsay Davis said Sula Mae used her eyes and facial twitches the way those characters in James Fenimore Cooper's Indian novels dropped bits of clothing in the forests for trail-blazers.)

She would see a picture of some polo player or yachtsman

and she would jerk the rotogravure section tightly to her bosom. Then she would run from the room, biting her lip hard. Whenever this happened Jessie Lee and Maude Rose figured, or they figured that Sula Mae figured that they figured, that Sula Mae was looking straight at the picture of the alleged father of her alleged child.

In the reflective days after the departure of the whore-house, the news came to Oxford occasionally that this child was a nurse who worked twenty-four hours a day among the sick in some big city's slum.

Again, it was reported that this nebulous child had become a movie star. Some of the alumni assumed that Sula Mae was living in "Hollywoods" with her daughter-star. For a fact, someone said he saw Sula Mae in a newsreel picture of a swanky Hollywood swimming pool party. Once Ramsay Davis said he had heard that the daughter-star was a good friend of the silent screen queen, Mary Miles Minter, whom many local people confused with a brand of chewing gum.

There was in town a sign-painter named Baldy Moore. Actually, he was named for Major Archibald Harris, popularly called "Major Baldy." But, Baldy Moore's folks didn't mess with "Archibald." Everyone called him "Baldy Mo." Once or twice each year he got tired of Oxford, and he'd hobo around the country painting signs, barns, street numbers, or doing odd jobs for spending money. It was Baldy who said he saw Sula Mae in Hollywood.

Some folks didn't believe Baldy because he said Sula Mae's daughter had some orange trees in her back yard, and he'd pull an orange, straight from the tree, and eat one whenever it pleased him.

Somebody said, most casually: "When was this, Baldy?"

"Why it wuz lass spring, it wuz."

People nudged each other. They knew it was a damned lie because, as they said, who in the hell ever saw an orange except at Christmastime?

268

When people in town wanted Baldy Moore, they yelled out: "Baldy Mo. Where is Baldy Mo?"

He'd come running. "My name ain't no damn town. My name is 'Baldy Mo,' dammit, not any 'Baldy Mo'."

Sula Mae must have been about twenty-five. I am sure she was younger than Maude Rose and older than Jessie Lee. She wasn't bad looking at all. She would never let out that she knew a man, if she saw him in public. She didn't get maudlin drunk more than two or three times a year. But she did chew Blackjack Gum. I delivered many packages of it from the "Ivanhoe."

Ramsay Davis said he just couldn't imagine a lady's chewing gum, especially in somebody's damned ear. But again, as the Scott twins pointed out, and I reckon they knew, Sula Mae never ate any parched peanuts when she was pleasuring a man, not the way that Maude Rose did.

At the time, I considered Maude Rose quite mercenary. I contrasted her to Jessie Lee and Sula Mae as I contrasted the Hessians to the legions of Nathanael Greene.

If her family had been victimized by economics, she said nothing about it. Nor did she mention anything about being violated by a rich, blue-blood. Indeed, from the way I got it, if she said anything about being mistreated it was about some sailor who roughed her up in Norfolk, or how some hick cop "taken it" away from her in a cell, how he gave her "boudacious" laughter in lieu of currency of the realm.

However, she did introduce the town to the X-ray, to what Dr. Henley called the "Roentgen machine." As I said, she was the one who did the strolling, and some of the gentlemen said Maude Rose could tell a buck from a five dollar bill on a moonless night, under the depot platform.

She may have been dull if all work and no lollygagging makes one dull. As Ramsay Davis said: "Maude Rose is short on social amenities. You have to show her spot-cash before she even says 'howdy'." The way I got it, Maude Rose worked with the bloodless efficiency of one of the new adding machines. Ramsay Davis said: "Her mind is a cash-drawer."

I always heard that even when she got tree-top drunk she wouldn't give you a dab of chocolate if she owned the Hershey factory. But liquor loosened her tongue, if not her favors. To hear Maude Rose tell it, she knew all the fighters from Willard to Sharkey. She had a picture of the late Kid McCoy, and she claimed to be one of his innumerable wives. She had lain on silken pillows with the cattle barons in the west and she had been on the special Pullman palaces of some of the big railroad tycoons.

I saw her eat, a few times, on the back porch, in hot weather, and she held her fork as if she were milking a cow. And Miss Opal was always calling her down for saying "barnyard" words. Just the same she had been intimate with plushy sports all the way from Saratoga to Palm Beach.

I guess her trouble was she had traveled too far. She had known too many intimacies. Anyway, Hector Scott said he and Hughie figured out that Maude Rose would have to be at least three hundred to have done half of the things she said she had done.

Maude Rose was about thirty, I suppose. I think "blowsy" is the word for her. Some years later when I read Somerset Maugham's short story, "Miss Thompson," and then saw the movie version, called *Rain*, I really wondered if Somerset Maugham had run across Maude Rose somewhere in his travels?

When she left Oxford, she was hardly ever mentioned. Occasionally, someone might say: "What was the name of that big-mouthed whore that was here towards Miss Opal's last days?"

When I was big enough to know Miss Opal, eye-ball to eye-ball, she must have been around sixty. She reminded me of one of those fat, kind looking old ladies that Copley painted.

270

She never came down town unless the trip was necessary. But when she came down town to go to the bank or to see Papa on some legal business, she dressed up, fit to kill, but she didn't rouge her face. She wore large picture hats, blue and red ones. She carried a gold-headed cane, really more of a staff than a walking-stick. It had no handle. It was the same kind that I saw in pictures when a British bailiff, or whatever he was, led the procession to announce that court had opened or that Parliament had convened.

She carried a lorgnette downtown. She could thread a needle without any sort of spectacles. Papa said the lorgnette was to stare down any pious sisters who gave her uppity looks.

Insofar as public recognition was concerned, Papa and Dr. Henley and the other gentlemen were total strangers, if she met them on the street. She always came down town in the public hack, or the taxi, operated by Lee Fuller. (Lee was a wall-paperer, too, and both sides of the hack — first a surry, and then the taxi — were hung with samples of various kinds of wall-paper, the big sheets that came in large rolls.)

Lee would park around the corner from wherever it was Miss Opal had business. When her business was done, she came back around the corner and left for her place.

I never heard of but one unseemly confrontation. That was the day Just Plain Snake Imboden was "dillified" and slapped Miss Opal on the back, in front of the courthouse, where she had been to list her taxes. Just Plain Snake slapped her behind and said, in a loud voice, "Howz bidness, Mist Opal, old gal?"

Sheriff Venable ran out from the courthouse. He threw Just Plain Snake in the old cement horse-trough that used to be in front of the courthouse, and then he locked him up until the next day.

As I said, the front and the sides of the house were virtually obscured by the enormously tall growth of the privets. The screened-in front porch was almost obliterated by clematis and nandina. This grew as a jungle in summer. Of course, the clematis played out in winter, but no one sat on the porch in cold weather. And, the nandina, with its jolly, red berries, was a Christmas scene straight from Dickens, who, Papa said, was really responsible for rescuing the secular joy of the Yuletide from old Cromwell and our Puritans.

The front porch was not for any "hoe-hoppers." It was reserved exclusively by Miss Opal for a type of foregathering that was surreptitious but not clandestine. (If I seem to split hairs, I still think the distinction is valid.)

A few gentlemen of our town met regularly, but still spasmodically, never by rote, to pass the compliments of a star-struck evening with Miss Opal and with one another.

It was a sort of club, a home away from home, I guess it was a place for men who didn't get enough attention at home or who got too much attention.

Men such as Papa, Dr. Henley and Sheriff Venable sat there on the cool, shrouded porch, with no lights save the stars and moon. They sat and told their favorite stories. They didn't have their stories interrupted by wives, who always seemed to think they could tell the stories better, and they didn't have to edit anything or do any pantomime for the benefit of the children.

As they talked, or as they sat in cool quiet, with silence doing the talking, they drank juleps made from local corn, well water, mint and powdered sugar.

The gentlemen and Miss Opal never kicked up any racket anyone on the dirt sidewalk could hear. Still the place was a kind of open-secret in town. People didn't talk about the porch club for the same reason they didn't talk about their demented relatives. Everyone in town had some kind of open-secret, I guess.

None of the whores was ever allowed on the front porch while Miss Opal's male contemporaries were there. She never called one to bring a pitcher of lemonade, even. No, she got whatever was needed, herself.

Of course, there was usually some implied threat to the continuation of the porch club. But this related to the whorehouse, to "Sodom and Gomorrah," itself.

The Ladies' Society, abetted by the missionary circles, said Miss Opal's place was an affront to all decent people. Usually, the desire to purge Miss Opal came when there was a serious drought or when a terrific hailstorm had damaged the tobacco crop. I remember two public meetings in the courthouse. One was during a summer when wilt almost wrecked the tobacco crop. The other one came in the middle of a local epidemic of dysentery, which some ascribed to bad drinking water.

Albeit, the "Ladies" were seriously handicapped. They talked behind their fans, pretty much, because the subject matter was so shocking. And even without a fan, none had the temerity to say the word "whorehouse" loudly and clearly. (Everyone in town knew that no one abided more closely to the exact letter of the Sunday blue-laws than Miss Opal. As Old Man Rufe said: "There are no bed-springs a-creakin' on the Sabbath at Miss Opal's and who else can say the same?")

On both occasions, Sheriff Venable said it wouldn't do at all to give Oxford a black-eye all over the state by really blowing up the issue about Miss Opal. He didn't say so, but the women got the drift that the names of some of the patrons might slip out. There might be some surprises.

"This has to be handled with delicacy," the Sheriff said at both public meetings. He went on to say that although he was bowed down with innumerable pressing matters, he's just step down to the place in question and have a word with the party concerned.

But, ere long, Miss Opal's menancing shadow was purged by a badly needed rain, or attention was diverted by some newer sin. Nonetheless, Miss Opal endured as Oxford's emotional ace-in-the-hole, even during the times where her den of sin was not an overt issue. The self-righteous used her for a community scapegoat, if not precisely the same way Aaron used one in the Book of Leviticus.

Several times Papa quoted a ballad from W.S. Gilbert's "Gentle Alice Brown" in relationship to the attitude of the righteous to Miss Opal. I learned this ballad by heart from Papa's maliciously delicious quotings of it:
" 'I have helped Mama to steal a little kiddy from its dad,
    I've assisted dear papa in cutting up a little lad;
    I've planned a little burglary and forged a little check,
    And slain a little baby for the coral on its neck.'
    The worthy pastor heaved a sigh, and dropped a silent tear —
    And said 'You mustn't judge yourself too heavily, my dear —
    It's wrong to murder babies, little corals for to fleece;
    But sins like these are expatiated at half-a-crown apiece'."

In my greasy-bread days Miss Opal was an old whore for whom time was running up the white flag. She ran the whorehouse the same way a big league star might take a job managing a bush league team when his active playing days ended.

While I've never been sure, I think the Sheriff knew Miss Opal when she was active in the trade, in some city. He and Papa referred to her occasionally, and always privately, as a "former lobbyist-at-large for the best interests of the people."

Apparently, Miss Opal had been pressed into service, in her active days, when it was important that some legislator had to be persuaded to vote for a certain important bill. Again, she prevented negative votes against important legislation by entertaining some recalcitrant solon so lavishly he missed the roll-call.

The regular coterie visited the front porch during warm weather, but Dr. Henley came by the year round. He always brought his bag. Actually, he treated Miss Opal and the girls when they were sick, and he examined the girls regularly for venereal disease.

274

Sometimes Papa brought the circuit judge or an out-of-town lawyer to the porch for a cool drink and a long conversation. The Sheriff brought special guests, too. One of these was a United State Marshal. The Marshal was a tremendous man. The Sheriff said he was too big to be human and not quite big enough to be a horse. Papa said the Marshal used a whole julep to chase a whopping drink of straight whiskey.

I talked with the Marshal several times, but not at Miss Opal's. I was astonished to learn that Bat Masterson, the celebrated western law man, whom I would encounter later on in a TV series, spent most of his life as a reporter. Masterson was a reporter for the Washington *Evening Star* when he died in 1924. He died at his typewriter, and the last words he wrote were these: "There is an equal distribution in nature. Take ice. In summer the rich get all they want and in winter the poor get more than they want."

The other gentlemen sauntered along and sort of slipped up on the blind side of the place. Dr. Henley, who had the first "machine" in town, always parked his Oldsmobile right in front. Generally, during the spring and summer, he came by when his nightly rounds were done. His car was there, in plain view, if someone needed his services. He came by so he could drink a whole mint julep without having to let the ice melt while he went out on call. He dropped in so he could smoke a whole cigar without having it go out forty times. He visited Miss Opal for the same surcease that his present equivalent finds at the country club or in watching the big board at the stock exchange.

People said Dr. Henley was "stout," or he "carried some flesh." He was fat. At Miss Opal's he took off his collar, put a handkerchief around his neck, let his suspenders drop until his belly hung down like a boulder over a cliff, and he kicked off his shoes and rubbed one aching foot against the other one.

Many times, late at night, after his rounds, he and Miss

Opal sat alone. (Invariably, Dr. Henley sat in an overstuffed chair, the very same kind tht Scattergood Baines sat in, in the short stories by Clarence Buddington Kelland.) No one else ever sat in his chair. Miss Opal called it "the Doctor's place."

He had a lot to tell her and she had a lot to tell him. Most of the by-play was inside stuff. During the day Dr. Henley had been everywhere. He had seen it all.

Miss Opal was a combination gossip columnist, sports editor and society writer. The back-chat between the two was a good deal similar to the Huntley-Brinkley reports. But there was never any of this insufferable Rotary Club "David" and "Chet," or "Joe" and "Opal" business.

I remember old Dr. Henley as being as outgoing as the receding tide. I always see him as a chunky Samaritan toting a black satchel.

Papa was there, with his feet on the railing. He tended books and poems the way other men tended growing plants. I think, and I thought, of him as the laureate of Miss Opal's front porch. He recited poems, without having to answer the telephone or to stop and hand something to Mother.

And I knew something the others may not have known: Papa was always writing down his thoughts. Frequently, these thoughts came out as bits of verse, as poems. When he quoted one of his poems on the porch he said it was something he had read in some paper or magazine. He couldn't remember just which paper or magazine it was.

Papa loved the night. The sky was an old post road. The moon was a coach rumbling across it. Here and there a star was a lantern at an inn.

He wrote a poem in which he compared thunder to barrels rolling across an old wooden bridge. Another one had the wind playing power lines for a 'cello. There was another poem about hot weather. I remember the conclusion to the one about hot weather, even it I didn't get the analogy at that time:

"From the nimble way the sparrow pirouettes
On one toe, you'd think he's a ballet dancer,
If you didn't know his antipathy for Tschaikovsky."

The Sheriff was a bachelor. He was said to be a real hand with the ladies, but he didn't run around in Oxford. People said he had lady-friends in the cities, whom he visited, when he needed to visit a lady. He never fooled with any local women, to my knowledge, but his presence there on the porch had a wholesome influence on the activities inside.

The Sheriff must have been at least fifty, but he was trim. You could see the muscles rippling through his sleeves, and against his pants in the calves of his legs. He was red-headed. There was all over him an almost incredible redness.

His hair was naturally curly. It seemed to be on fire with crackling flames. But no one ever called him "Red." Ordinary people had too much respect for the Sheriff to use a nickname. Too, red was still a hoo-do color at this time.

The image of complete, cruel neglect was "a red-headed stepchild," and if someone was "red-headed" he could be arrogant or he could have been sandbagged, caught for a cedar-bird, in some card game or business deal.

"Brer" Thompson said red was a jinx because the earliest sins were scarlet. He said the artists usually gave Cain and Judas red heads. However, I don't think I saw any paintings of the two.

Dr. Henley said physicians at one time had tried to diagnose illness by a patient's color, and a red complexion was considered a symptom of terrible humor and sick blood.

Papa said the superstitions about red hair had historic roots. He came to a boil when I accused him of making a pun. He said the British were terrified of their red-headed Danish enemies, that the symbol for terror remained after the Danes went into pastry business.

I don't know how generally these legends were known around home, but no one ever called the Sheriff "Red."

He was the political "boss," if we had one at home. He did favors for people, got them jobs and small loans, and they voted for him. Just the same, Papa said the Sheriff's honesty was impeccable.

Papa and Dr. Henley and "Brer" Thompson kidded him a little, on the side, when no one else was around. They referred to him as the "generalissimo." They called him the "Kingfish," long before anyone ever heard of Huey Long. Papa called him "Mr. Murphy," after Charles F. Murphey, the head sachem at Tammany Hall.

Sometimes on the porch, but never anywhere else, the coterie sang "Tammany," Gus Edwards' old song.

"Tammany, Tam-ma-ny,
Big Chief sits in his te-pee
Cheering braves to vic-to-ry."

"Struttin' Bud" Davenport came by infrequently. He was a nice fellow. He didn't get in just because of his wealth. While his main contribution was pitching, he could do the multiplication table up to 24 times 24. (That may seem something today. It's really a trick, though.) He knew, by heart, the time-tables of virtually every railroad in the nation.

Papa and the other hard-working gentlemen hardly ever had any real vacations, not in their whole lives, except the ones they took on "Struttin' Bud's" high-balling trains. He knew where to change and which trains had deluxe dinners and how many tunnels there were through any big mountain in the country.

They would sit on the porch, sip their juleps, and take leisurely train trips. While "Struttin' Bud" didn't love engineers as much as he loved ball players, he knew a lot of them. In fact he was the only man in town who called Casey Jones "John Luther" Jones, his proper name. He said, too, that "Casey" was a mess-up. It was really "Cayce," from the Illinois town in which John Luther Jones lived until he got himself killed, driving the "Cannonball," at Vaughan,

Mississippi, in April, 1906.

"Struttin' Bud" was in a hurry, all of the time, it seemed to me, and he might drop by the porch just to pay the compliments of the evening and to pitch, for both teams, the post-season game between the Giants and Cubs that decided the National League pennant in 1908.

If he got too upset about "Bonehead" Merkle's failure to run on to second base, Dr. Henley would switch him off to Young Babe Adams, winning three games in the 1909 series.

There was a pianola in what the coterie called the "physical enthusiasm" portion of Miss Opal's place. When the gentlemen weren't on the porch, the music was a little louder.

A couple of pals and I used to lie on the edge of Mr. Ed Settle's beautiful woods and listen. The pianola didn't play "The Joyous Farmer," "March Militaire," or "I'll Sing Thee Songs of Araby."

The music was low-down as a wiggling snake yet it was saturated with comet's hair. Instead of "The Rosary," it played "Bill Bailey," "Salty Dog," and "O, You Beautiful Doll," and "I Wish That I Could Shimmy Like My Sister Kate."

I would lie there in the sharp sweetness of pine litter while the music took off with the wild magic of Santa Claus' sleigh. As I lay there I imagined that the piano keys were horses shod with lyrical lightning.

The titillating music, and the proximity of the whorehouse, perhaps, induced a flood of sensual speculations. I was aflame with an itch that defied all scratchings. Of course, I didn't believe in the stork but that sensuous music stripped the world of all winged creatures, for an interlude, and it not only routed the cabbage patch but vanquished the world of horticulture.

In common with most small-town boys of our section and generation, I was invested, certainly obliquely, with grandiose notions about the purity of Southern womanhood. I had many recurring day-dreams wherein I, at deadly peril, saved the purity of some noblewoman, albeit, the immaculate, high-born lady was always as lovely and as fetching as P.A. Duncan and Dovey Simpson.

But the music and the knowledge of what occurred in the backrooms at Miss Opal's took the edge off the blade which I inherited for the protection of imperiled purity. As I lay there in the pine litter my long, long thoughts were ones that Mother would certainly label as carnal.

And I had some practical speculations also. In that era before the pill, before sexual liberation, I wondered if whores ever became pregnant? I never heard of any whore's becoming pregnant. I wondered if whores had some special protective powers, some sort of sacrosanct goober-dust, perhaps?

Then one day at the "Ivanhoe" I put all of my brass and guts in my throat and asked Mr. Matson if whores ever had babies.

He was sweeping the rental library with the featherduster. Without looking my way or without pausing for deliberation, the old Indian scout thundered: "Hell, yeah, boy. Where do you think all the cot ding bill collectors and bank presidents come from, anyhow?"

As I wondered about sex I wondered equally as much about growing up and getting good sense and taking my place on the porch. If sex was one of the privileges of maturity, liberation from the niggling world of school report cards, of eating at the second or the third table at big family dinners was just as rapturous to contemplate.

I was curious, not curious yellow, but green, if curiosity has to have a color. What I call curiosity is a desire to know, to know why and how. Surely, this is a lust of mind, a perseverance of delight in the indefatigable pursuit of knowledge. This sort of curiosity may be sensual or even lascivious, but it exceeds in scope and intensity the brief vehemence of anything that Mother would have called carnal pleasure.

280

Well, all that was another world, and one world at a time is more than enough. Yet I go back sometimes when the wind whistles old ragtime tunes in the tree-tops, when the moon is a fat, happy man, like Mr. Ed Settle, overlooking his bountiful sacred domain.

On fall nights I am likely to be seized by a sort of inverted wanderlust, inexplicably, and I walk out where the whore-house used to be. I tell my folks I want to stretch my legs. Perhaps, I am trying to stretch my heart, a formidable chore.

On these wine-heady, perfumed fall nights I don't see the drive-in bank or the shopping center that flares its neon sign where Mr. Ed Settle's lovely woods used to dance in the moonlight. I never see the new housing development because I always see those marvelous fire horses, Bertha and Matt.

Miss Opal's yonder in the old cemetery. Papa was her executor, and I think he and the Sheriff put up the stone that says:

> "Here lies Miss Opal Galehouse
> A Friend to Mankind and To Men"

I never knew she had a last name until I saw the stone.

But on these exquisite fall nights the whorehouse is back behind the scented jungle, and Papa, Dr. Henley, Miss Opal and the others are on the porch. A phantom pianola is knocking out "O, You Beautiful Doll" and "I Wish That I Could Shimmy Like My Sister Kate."

When the phantom music stops, I almost agree with Henry Miller that chaos is the score upon which reality is written. For, there's no Kate in town anymore. Nor a Katie, either. Her name is "Kathryn" today, and the society reporter for the local newspaper better make damned sure it is spelled that way.

FIRST WARM DAYS

When the first few warm days are golden-haired girls preempting the town for a game of hop-scotch, everyone goes outside to take some kind of personal inventory. From the incredulous way people gaze, you'd think they expected all the walls, fences and gates to be held for ransom by winter's fury. Some people look at their flower beds and garden plots as if they had assumed winter's marlinspikes had driven those things below Chile.

Others peek at public squares, little malls and spacious lawns as if these places have been off-limits, under strict quarantine, since last October. People seem to want to touch the earth to be certain it is not some illusion, some Indian gift, conjured by these unexpected suns that swarm excitedly as yellow bees. And in every little place there is one dear, elderly lady who hasn't been expected to survive a winter for the past twenty-five years. Each year, when December gets out of hand, everyone in town says: "Well, old Miss Lucy can't last out another winter. This one will get her surely, poor, dear lady."

But when the sun defies March and starts turning cartwheels, there's Miss Lucy puttering around her beds and borders, her old black shawl fluttering with the sure grace of a flag of defiance, her eyes sharp as winter's bluest pools, and her gnarled fingers reaching far into the future for the sweet tasting joys of May mornings and June nights.

FARE THEE WELL, OLD BEAUTIES

"Stone walls do not a prison make," but these stone walls are benign and solid custodians of the best of our traditions. Every place has some stone walls and the hand-wrought art of the early masons has brought the past into our daily lives with the graphic poetry of durable rook lines bound with concrete jackets.

A single expanse of obdurate stone wall, taking its ease in the sun or setting its teeth against the ravages of sleet, denotes the former presence of human laughter and tears as clearly as if these outpourings had been bottled for all time. But now many of these stone walls are being bulldozerized into dust and rubble. The rubble is supposed to be a wind-tossed footnote to future progress. The walls, everywhere, seem to be a path someone wants to travel. And the idea everywhere is: "Full steam ahead, and damn the stone walls." Although the engineers and various blueprint artists must know best, none seems ever to have attended a school that taught anything about "going round."

So, if the stone wall (old tree, well, or tiny, Colonial brick office) is in the way of where we think we want to go, it must come down, not like a flag being furled reverently to be unfurled in another place, but as the walls of Jericho came toppling down. Maybe nothing can be done. Maybe, the bulldozer is our exalted national symbol. Maybe, we must roll with its mightly punches or stay clear of its devastating surge. But since every hamlet has an official group that plans for the future, as an experiment, each place might have some patriotic citizens to start planning how to keep its local traditions. For, every unborn little green apple knows that "the bulldozer'll git you, ef you don' watch out."

LEAF REPORT

The first leaves cower stolidly on the limb as if they are green birds too timorous to try their baby wings. But when sun and wind come along to toss out spices and health potions, these leaves are boys in green overalls playing "Follow the Leader."

Then when sun and wind strum the tree as if it is a harp, these leaves are tumblers and acrobats. They race towards the air's naked infinity as if they are to illustrate perpetual motion in green leap-frogging and somersaulting. They get into such an excited pile of whirls, the wind has to take his fingers and put them back into proper place, the same way a barber does the wild, unruly hair of a growing boy.

Yet, these leaves are impervious to ordinary discipline. They get so big for their green britches, it's a miracle the limb doesn't crack beneath them like a dry stick. One day they're in a kindergarten for maple leaves and the next day they're brash and saucy as school boys reveling in the initial thrills of finding the secret sweets of a season. The only way to gauge their growth is to take a string and make them brace against the wall and mark the spot clearly to contrast with the morrow's tabulation. But they'd never stand for this. They'd never hold still long enough. That is, they wouldn't stand still even if you asked them to, and you never do, since you've always been to another school.

SOMETHING CALLED GRASS

Grass is a growing, physical fact, but its countless intangible facets and implications are as great as the fact, itself. The unending fascination is difficult to summarize because, perhaps, it has almost as many vibrant evocations as it has beholders.

The dictionary calls it "green herbage," but Walt Whitman called it "the handkerchief of the Lord." Other poets, notably John Gould Fletcher, have seen grass as an endless green symphony. Perhaps, the lawn is the violin section when green leaves and sunbeams and shadows are woodwinds and percussion instruments. Sandburg saw it as a sort of divine leveler that obscures mankind's follies and furies. With others it is a type of suit of armor for the soul, or a tossing sea whose breakers bring fragrance, remembrance, and sustenance to the troubled mind and heart.

Happily, though, most of us are captivated and delighted without the vexations of trying to describe flowering grass, or to define its origins and immortal designs. We see and love it from the vantage of grass-cutters and spectators. When the morning sun is happy and free, the grass may be a green river swamping rapids and swirls. Later on it may be a mossy pool leased to the sun to swim his goldfish in and around. And even when your back is turned the earthy perfumes rub against the body with the easy affection of a puppy, and the most unemotional among us go to their work or play anointed with a legacy that had to be planted and harbored, but one which no one has to deserve, define, or account for.

THE TENDER ESPIONAGE

It is amazing how many brides and bridegrooms of many long years of tender sharings say the same things about their mates behind their backs.

The wife will take her middle-aged son aside and whisper: "Your papa is getting so absent-minded I have to keep my eyes on him every second." A few minutes later the father says the same words about his wife: "Your mother is a wonderful woman and her health is good but if I didn't watch her she'd go to church without her shoes."

This really isn't tattling or snitching or telling tales out of school. It is a poetic type of espionage, a selfless spy system, an awareness so gentle and considerate it never slumbers, even when its eyelids are heavy with fatigue. It is the classic example of true interdependence, of mutual admiration without any vainglorious gimmicks or any fawning or fake chivalry. It is love when the act of loving awareness is the supreme accolade and the most profound joy, too.

This blessed sort of counter-espionage keeps both alive and hale, mentally alert, and as physically keen as the toll of the years allows. Although they no longer use a drugstore booth as an exalted trysting place, they are still sipping soda through the same straw, as they did in the rousing days of youth. Each one is the strop to the other's razor, alternately the bow and the fiddle.

Each one has to stay alive and vital to sustain the other in a process, simultaneously intricate and simple, that transcends logic.

THE LOST ORACLE

There used to be one man in every little town whose eyes were above the clouds while his green thumbs were magic trowels taking the pulse beats of the earth. He predicted local weather so accurately people asked his advice when planning picnics and outings. But his skill transcended mere weather predictions.

He could look at the sky in February and know what clothing would be appropriate Easter and he could look again on Easter and tell if local gardens would be wet or dry in July. He was consulted regularly about what to plant, how deep to plant it, and when to plant. But he wasn't just a pedant giving wholesale tips. He was his own best testimonial. His corn was always the sweetest, his butter beans the juiciest, and his tomatoes big as melons and red as rubies.

He smelled eternally of the warm, rich soil and the long lessons and poems of suns, rains, and winds were written upon his face and hands. He seemed to have nature's ear constantly and they communed in an unearthly language known but to them. And yet he wasn't a farmer or gardener except by blessed avocation. Nature had a thousand secret doors and in some miraculous, mysterious manner he had all the keys, big and little.

He was given the deference accorded all oracles, tribal leaders and elders. Today he's gone and there is a gap upon the local streets. Of course, we have thousands of books, pamphlets, and lectures on planting and on the weather. But old-timers feel the weather is likely to get out of hand any time, since no one is left in town with a direct line to the clouds and a high personalized radar to the soil. No one in town seems to be responsible for the weather today nor in charge of it, for that matter.

MOONLIGHT AND FOUR ROSES

Dancing is as indigenous to North Carolina as buttered biscuits and pears ripening on a back porch shelf. It is as much a part of our environment as green fields and white orchards. Dancing prances in and around our mores with the timelessness of rail fences and with the drama of the twelve o'clock whistle.

We have been dancing ever since the first gangplank was lowered at Roanoke Island. Actually, we find the spell of music so entrancing that a lot of us are able to dance while we sit in chairs, and some even master the art, with one foot, while taking siestas on gliders or in hammocks.

And although thousands and thousands of Tarheels still dance as eagerly as if wealth and status were to be attained solely with one leg in the air, the formats and mores have changed immeasurably. The "local" dances, compared to those of two decades ago, are similar to comparing a trained, self-effacing goldfish with a whale suffering acutely from seven years' itch.

The mammoth "town dance" reached its gallivanting apogee at the beginning of World War II. Until that time, each place had its seasonal snollygosters, embracing and compelling people for counties around. There were seasonal dances, harvest balls and hops, Germans, and huge "town dances" in most of the tobacco towns. Indeed, one could pussyfoot or jitterbug or Big Apple all the way from Oxford, down through Rocky Mount on to the coast without missing a hop or a skip.

Even if today's youngsters can't swallow it, there were as many as ten thousand people at some of these small town musical riots. It took all the homes, rooms, cots, sofas, beds, daybeds, and trundle beds in town to accommodate the visiting girls. And it was a common sight to see boys (males from eighteen to forty) sleeping on blankets on courthouse lawns, in malls and parks, or even on the town benches. They used all the hotel hallways, closets, and rest rooms for dressing places, but scores and scores dressed in cornfields, back alleys, automobiles, and on depot platforms. And since no one ever entered the dancing arena until 10:30 p.m., at the earliest, it was not singular to see boys shaving in filling station rest rooms and in the local fire house and police station, nor was it rare to see a local resident toting a pitcher of hot shaving water to a group of out-of-town blades huddled on the depot platform, around a flashlight.

Every town was wide open, even if this width suggests little that is luminous to today's sport. But as widely ajar as the welcome signs waved, there were many local inadequacies; however, these inadequacies seemed to add zest and merriment. "Make-do" was the operating procedure everywhere. For instance, no one in his right mind expected the local cafes to have food or tables to accommodate the throngs, and no one saw anything incongruous in the spectacle of boys in tuxedos eating canned peaches, potted meat or fig newtons in a grocery store.

Sidewalk caterers helped considerably but such wares were ineffectual. The church sisters, agreeing, evidently, with John Wesley that it isn't fair to let the devil use all the best tunes, peddled eats from street corner stands, and itinerant hucksters filled store doorways with all sorts of fruits and melons.

As .a rule, the seasonal "town dance" was at least two dances. The night before the count-down for leg-shaking in outer space, there was a dance at which some college orchestra or some good local or state band played. This was a glittering preliminary for the main event. Admission was charged, and the affair was sponsored by some local patriotic, civic, or fraternal organization, but it was a sort of bargain night tune-up for the following night's cannon crackers and Roman candles.

And, many towns had smaller dances embroidering the preliminary and the championship match. Most of these satellites were called "tea" dances. They were held by friends, for local and visiting guests, in big basements, or the local woman's club, Legion or lodge hall. You could get anything to drink except a glass or cup of tea. Some had four- or five-piece bands and some had victrola records played through amplifiers.

There were home parties before and after these smaller shindigs. Each town, through individuals, had its "dance breakfasts," luncheons and gypsy teas. Each town was overwhelmed with a spirited contagion. Even those who denounced dancing were caught up in the emotional riptides. Homes and gardens were "opened." The town had on its Sunday clothes and party manners. Times might be tight, but everyone saved up for the rollicking splash. There was a corny saying that still epitomizes the infection of those freewheeling times.

"Aw right. It's time fur uvabody to get on bode and those who caint get uh bode can get a plank." Somehow or other, uvabody managed to get on bode, despite the exigencies of parlous times and space limitations.

The big dance was in a tobacco warehouse because that was the only place big enough to hold the crowd. A name band came down from the north, and a tremendous door prize, usually a new car, was given the lucky ticket. The most popular bands in North Carolina were Guy Lombardo, Hal Kemp, Glenn Gray, the Dorsey boys and Henry Bussee. Each band played here, for several straight seasons. Some appeared in the same town as many as four times. For reasons that always eluded me, Guy Lombardo was called "Guy-Lumbago" by half our people, and Henry Bussee was "Harry Boss."

These dances were held when the weather was hot enough

to make an eel sweat. The warehouse, its tin roof mercilessly exposed to the pitiless sun, had the devil wondering if he shouldn't relocate his establishment. Large electric fans blew through hundred-pound blocks of ice, but usually the only tangible by-products were huge puddles on the floor and a democratic dissemination of the essences of the unending rows of fertilizer and nitrate of soda.

It was generally conceded, sartorial finery notwithstanding, that Tarheel dancers, like baseball pitchers, worked better when saturated with moisture. However, attempts were made to placate the wrath of the demonic heat. A common device was to have local firemen play hose on the roof of the warehouse. This gave the tenuous illusion of cool air even if it didn't lessen the moisture content under the collar.

No matter how long the dance lasted, it always lasted at least an hour longer. Someone always got up money to pay the orchestra to play an extra hour. This was called "mason-jar-rich" and not just because money might be collected in half gallon containers.

Since the evening was well-nigh interminable, there were usually three intermissions: One was for eating, another for the presentation of celebrities, and the other was stunts or skits, and all three were for copious gargling.

For instance, I attended one dance at which the daughters of all, and I do mean all, the ambassadors from Latin, Central and South America were presented at the second intermission. They floated down a runway that led from the bandstand to the warehouse office. The runway was paved with that green material undertakers use around graves, and there was a wire fence on either side. The fence was decorated with local flowers and with flags, made of bunting, of the countries represented by the ambassadors' daughters. The fence, after ten minutes, had gaps and gapes, and it looked as if a snaggled-tooth May queen were posing for a denture ad, before she got the plates.

As each girl came down the runway, the band was supposed to play her national anthem, but it was a bit thick to expect even such an indefatigable musical researcher as Guy-Lumbago to know the national tunes of such places as Puerto Rica, Bolivia, and Chile. The band usually had to compromise with "You're a Sweetheart" or "Ain't She Sweet." One smart leader, really helping FDR's "Good Neighbor" policy, hit upon the delightful expedient of alternating "You're the Cream In My Coffee" and "Drinking Rum and Co-ca-Cola-ah." These two tunes seemed catholically pertinent and encompassing.

No one thought it strange for these girls in lovely evening gowns, sweet with mystic perfumes, to walk along imperially under the signs that exclaimed the succulence of "Brown's Mule" chewing tobacco or "Railroad Mills" snuff. And if you couldn't hear the sacks of fertilizer saying anything for the ruckus of the firehoses on the roof, you could never be fully impervious to their presence in the crystal ballroom.

Although local candidates for office were never permitted to yap, yammer, and yack up a second intermission, candidates for governor or big office spoke regularly — naturally and obviously — there being a crowd, an amplifier, and no cut throats.

(If younger readers and those generally uninitiated think I am just whistling "Dixie," building something to proportions it never attained, I now point out that the big newsreel companies, Fox-Movietone, Pathe, etc., came to North Carolina annually for several years so that the gigantic dances could be seen by movie audiences the nation over.)

The reasons for the decline and termination are varied. World War II scattered local populations and homecomings were unable to build up the steam essential for such undertakings. Too, statutes were passed making the giving of cars, various big door prizes, unlawful acts. The Music Corporation of America charged about $2500.00 a night, in the currency of the late 1930's, for one night of Guy-Lumbago. Towns had to have brisk advance sales to get up this formidable kitty.

Making all the arrangements, decorating the town and the warehouse, doing all the advertising, and hustling tickets for miles around required infinite time, labor, and patience. After World War II, surplus energy seemed to be usurped more and more by conjuring new industries, making cow pastures into snazzy suburban developments, and by the many athletic and social facets of the new country clubs that seemed to pop up in every alfalfa patch.

But, Tarheels still dance. We'd like to have the name of the town that doesn't have regular dance instructions. Indeed, these new schools, skittering off from Arthur Murray, have more applicants in most towns than instructors and space can accommodate. You can learn to do any dance extant, even if the alumni can't seem to shake the habit of dancing to the numbers, whether doing the polka, the Twist, or the three-fifths' waltz. This includes the alumni who graduate magna summa cum laude, too.

These irrepressible dancing schools result directly in endless coteries and cliques. Actually, the same people who are neighbors or have common interests in certain things take dancing lessons together. The extension is more of the same. Thus, even in small towns there are dances at the country club, or whatever, rather than a Country Club Dance. The small soiree has our towns fast as hot molasses on very porous battercake.

But it doesn't matter at all. Everyone seems just as happy as a man who wears dentures is at a debate on fluoridation. It isn't what an old prom-trotter thinks of as ebullience. Rather it is astute and sedate, even when done to the latest, "Huh-one-huh-two-Hah, Hah-Three-Hah." It is friendly and neighborly even if you know a cow isn't going to jump over the moon. People today are better educated, perhaps, more sophisticated. They wear expensive dinner jackets and do, by the number, the new dances, but most of these Astaires don't know a sack of "Red Dog" from a bale of "Tuberose" snuff.

But there is sterling improvement in morals and manners, and, maybe, in health and hygiene. At a current dance one sees highball glasses, flasks, cocktail shakers, and all sorts of pint and fifth bottles of bourbon, scotch, gin and vodka, but nary a fruit jar. Today, few if any, permanent indentations are made in noses from the almost perpetual juxtaposition of fruit jars, with their huge, round, open ends. Indeed, Tarheels of endless ages and stations drink all sorts of fancy booze right out in the open, with far more boldness and savoir-faire than women of the late 1930's smoked in public.

All this high-society guzzling looks as elegant as one of the old *Life* photo-stories of an exclusive New York City bash, and it may be as exhilarating as it looks. But it will always be inadequate for those men who were brought up believing that liquor wouldn't flow downhill into the gullet unless one emulated the baseball catcher and squatted on his haunches behind an automobile or a bush. Back in the great dancing days, liquor and inside-the-house had the same inherent animosity of the McCoys and the Hatfields.

Some of us superannuates go through the gurgles of sipping booze right out in public at the country club ring-around, but if war simply hasn't been war since 1945, whiskey hasn't been ambrosia since we squatted behind a bush, passed the mason-jar, shook, gagged, went blind temporarily and declared fervently, "Boys, th, this is the b-b-best d-d-damned c-cawn l-liquor I e-ever t-tasted," without cracking more than three teeth during the testimonial.

And even today it is difficult for some of us to smell fertilizer and not hear, simultaneously, the duclet voice of Skinny Ennis singing "Got a Date With an Angel."

JUST AS EASY AS

The cliche probably has the same usefulness to the language that the mortgage folks have to housing developments. We probably couldn't last, verbally, to 10 a.m. without the cliche, but some ought to go. Some were hoary before Social Security started and some are directly misleading.

For instance, every hour someone says doing something is "easy as taking candy from a baby." The confirmed bachelor who first spoke this sheer idiocy knew little of candy and he was a total stranger to all children. It isn't easy to take anything from a child, even if you don't mind bitten fingers, broken eyeglasses, barked shins, and hair pulled out by the roots. Taking candy from a child's clutched hand is about as rudimentary as disarming a cornered hood, even if you don't mind chocolate all over your shirt and face and saliva and dirt from your forehead to your knees. But if the child has candy in its mouth, it is much simpler, and about as inexpensive, to send for a throat specialist and have the tonsils removed along with the candy.

DOWNGRADING ROBIN HOOD

This new attempt by British legal and historical investigators to downgrade Robin Hood will be about as effective as denouncing school holidays, free circus tickets, and bubble gum. If the infamous Sheriff of Nottingham couldn't ensnare Robin Hood, despite many snide, illegal, and dastardly ruses, no modern investigator will get the woodland sprite and his merrie men into any post-mortem detention.

Whether or not Robin was an actual person, he is in the eyes and hearts of children as ageless Peter Pan firing arrows that can dot an "i" at two hundred paces. And Sherwood Forest is not a place but a proposition, a dream, and a home-free pasture for wistfulness to run and to romp. It is the magic carpet of childhood. It is Camelot without the impediments of iron clothing and portentous moral dictums. It is a never-never land where the boys are as fleet as the deer, where the water is as racy as wine, and where stars can be plucked to adorn rustic caps, even when rain is falling.

Robin Hood remains as a joy and a challenge because he is the spirit of the virgin forests in the nuclear age. Those who play his role must have the imagination to go back a thousand years or to go beyond all space in the twinkling of an eye. And Maid Marian, despite the slander of the British investigators, is always as pure as the first dew-drop because she is played by little girls who are purer than anything else in sight today. Besides that, every good game needs at least one little girl in the cast, if only for contrast.

If the British investigators really try, they may convict Robin Hood, Friar Tuck and Little John of heinous crimes. If the statute of limitations doesn't run, Robin and his men may be put in moral jeopardy for Sabbath-breaking. Peter Pan may be convicted of violating the Lindbergh law, and the Good Fairy may be sent up for stealing teeth to make illegal dentures. But Robin will be safe in the hearts of children because he isn't a man who gets sick and dies. Robin Hood is a morning in May, a bowl of strawberries, a boy on a stick horse, the scent of muscadines, and the sun after a storm.

HIGH-BALLING TO HEAVEN

The harsh news of the dismantling of so many of the nation's train stations puts a ruthless cinder in the throats of all of us who once took a lunch to eat on the train as we journeyed on a pink, magic cloud from Babylon to Bagdad, from Xanadu to the Road to Mandalay.

And who gives a fig if terse reality insists that the fabulous journey was on a grubby day coach that jerked, jolted, and wheezed thirty convoluted miles of incessant but death-defying stops on a dinky branch line from inertia to apathy.

The younger reader of this hour, weaned on jets and given blueprints of outer space along with his pablum, cannot be expected to understand the royal romance of old-time rail-roading any quicker than a man born totally deaf can under-stand how nature rewards him when he is forced to attend a rock session.

But yesterday, a town without a train was comparable to a banjo virtuoso with two broken hands. The train was an imperial charger that waved black flags of roaring, brawling triumph in form of smoky poetry. It carried people and it hauled freight, but it was a time-marker, a weather-vane, a rustic almanac, and a gritty watch fob to be rubbed by a whole community. It was radio, TV, and hi-fi on driving, piling, slashing wheels before these entertainments were known, or perfected.

It threw out its sooty hands to grab the whole countryside by the neck and pull its urgencies down to the dee-po. For, as much as we may laugh now and call ourselves gauche or naive, all of us went to the dee-po to see the train come and go with that same spirit of rapt expectancy we now watch the astronaut make creation as small and simple as the Camptown Race Track.

A few people saw the trains in and out on week days. These, the real devotees, made their working or loafing habits compatible with the somewhat erratic schedules of our desultory trains. If one of the coterie wasn't at the station his compatriots removed their hats because they knew he was dead. These unofficial but highly dedicated town greeters began meandering towards the dee-po a minute or two before the train was scheduled to arrive.

Actually, the morning train that was posted for 11:05 was called the "elleben somep'n" train by the inner sanctum. In other words, when the "elleben somep'n" started blowing, blowing the way Stonewall Jackson made war, about a mile from town, people who ate dinner at twelve noon knew it was about time to close the shop and head for home. Albeit, those who tended the train, as David tended sheep, always went a minute or two before the scheduled time because there was always an infinitesimal chance the frothing old charger might be on time, and to be late on such an earth-shaking occasion would be as bad as having only a dime when a front seat in heaven costs a quarter.

Those who went on week days had a proprietary interest in the train. They had a charge to keep. They had to go back up town and tell who got off the train and who got on. And back then a mere picayune was as filled with dramatic intensity as a play by Paul Green, when it was translated and editorialized on by the cult. The people who got off the train might be a lamp chimney salesman from Danville, Va., a piano tuner from such an exotic place as Loris, S.C., and the great aunt of a local family who was "paying a short visit." (This was before Social Security and old-age benefits and the poor, dear lady was coming to town for her allotted stay with those who had to keep her because she didn't have anywhere else to go. Numerous relatives back then, who had committed no sin save aging, were farmed out as ball players are now.)

But the eyes of the tenders were bright as the lights on

Times Square. Virtually anyone who alighted from the train was a world traveler. People who had been as far as Atlanta were almost qualified to teach world geography, and, was it anything but right, those who had been all the way to Atlantic City were perfectly capable of settling the argument about whether we sprang from Adam and Eve or monkeys.

Often a little boy got off the train. It might be a little girl, from an increasingly modern home, but little girls didn't usually travel alone on such dangerous missions. However, intrepid boys could travel alone to visit their grandparents. The grandparents would be down at the dee-po to meet the "elleben somep'n" train at "ten somep'n'." The grandparents walked farther, and almost as fast, in and around the station, than the train ran that day. The grandfather took his pocket watch out so often he wore the case slick. He shook it and held it to his ear repeatedly, and the grandmother twisted her handkerchief until it was a limp rag.

But, ultimately and miraculously, the choo-choo screeched in, a one-eyed owl flying, flailing, and hooting in a shower of mist, steam, and cinders. And when the little boy jumped from the steps, the grandparents acted as if he had slain Goliath with his boy scout knife.

As ludicrous as it seems to this sophisticated generation, meeting people at the station and seeing them off was a ritual that ran over with all the heady elements of Confederate Memorial Day, a Sunday school picnic, and a Mack Sennett comedy. When Cousin Mabel came visiting, the whole family went to the dee-po. Papa shaved, put on a fresh collar, and his other good coat, the one he didn't wear on Sundays and to funerals. Mama put up her billowing hair the way a load of hay was stacked on a wagon. She wore her big hat with the enormous pin that was as lethal as a switchblade. She carried her parasol as if it were General Lee's sword, and she wore the locket her own dear Papa gave her when she was sweet sixteen and pure as a cherub.

It took two hours and a half the well and a cord of wood to wash the children, but everyone was scrubbed until a stranger might have assumed the family was getting ready to receive St. Peter as a house guest.

The immediate family was joined by innumerable "distant" and "kissing" and "claiming" cousins and friends. When Cousin Mabel came down the steps of the coach the throng of greeters went into the same voluble paroxyms that permeate a covey of quail flushing before gun fire. Everyone ran to kiss her, and there was more bussing, smooching, and slurping around the old depot than there is in a big city night club at twelve on New Year's Eve. And in order to obviate the ultimate transgression, to fail to kiss Cousin Mabel, everyone kissed everyone else, and during the wholesale melee that ensued, the lamp-chimney salesman from Danville, the piano-tuner from Loris, and the station-master got smooched several times each. Indeed, many of the remote cousins of high school age got behind baggage trucks and almost made-out.

Actually, a few resolute, or, perhaps, desperate, kids, used Cousin Mabel's advent the same way some people used to put on mourning bands and visit the homes of the just-dead folks whom they really didn't know. They did this because there was always a succulent, bountiful spread when someone died, and the chance to cadge a free banquet was more than a hungry person could withstand.

So Lochinvar and Fair Helen scooted to the depot, and when Cousin Mabel detrained they let fly at each other. (For the sake of the uninitiated, this ruse was necessary in the days when virtually all courting was chaperoned rigorously.)

Once Cousin Mabel had rested and changed her "traveling attire," the family held an "at home" so that she could regale local people with the thrilling tidbits of the journey and the recondite thrills of the vast world beyond. Refreshments had been collected copiously and meticulously well in advance of the great visit. The food and drinks at this "at home" were as scrumptious as those served at a corn-shucking or a barn-raising, and you didn't have to work for your food.

Usually, Cousin Mabel spoke for about thirty minutes, with informal gaiety but with sustaining interest. Then she answered questions for about thirty minutes. However, if Cousin Mabel had been to Baltimore the question and answer period might run beyond an hour. In insular society, Baltimore was the West Berlin for people who beat the sheriff to the county line, for local inventors and hustlers who were impeded by the stagnation of the local tempo, and for all local people who were supposed to be "missing."

From the local perspective, Baltimore was a cross between Casablanca and the Malamute Saloon in Alaska. All local vagrants or transients, regardless of the reason for absence from home, were said to turn up in Baltimore ultimately. It was, naturally, thought to be a city of infinite charm and debonaire rakishness. It was an exciting cake frosted over with delicious wickedness in the form of metropolitan singularity. Of course, if Cousin Mabel knew Baltimore, she had many personal questions to answer, and, quite often, she scheduled private interviews after the big "at home."

If meeting the weekday trains was a series of uninterrputed one-act dramas, the Sunday trains brought the entire country-side together in the very first symphonic play or festival, and this was many years before *The Lost Colony*. A lot of people went from church directly down to the dee-po to see the "elleben somep'n" come in. Church was out at twelve and that was about the time the 11:05 spewed in with the snorting fury of a black bull with a cow-catcher for horns.

However, the high noon visit was a "restricted showing," more or less. It was for local "first nighters" and those adroit enough to ensnare furtive thrills on the fly. It was also probably the first local status symbol. The ones who balled-the-jack to the dee-po, right after church, were akin to people who had already seen the circus, or said they had, before it

302

came to town.

Everyone came down to the station in cars, buggies, or on foot, for the command performance of the "three somep'n" train. Everyone came the way we now attend college football games or go to New York to see the newest musical comedies. Since this train came in about four, everyone had a chance to eat, rest, hang up his Sunday clothing, shake it out, and put it back on again for the trip to the station. Those who had slipped down right after church went from buggy to buggy or from Model T to Overland telling the juicy tidbits emanating from the morning show. Some of these floating drama critics were a bit of a nuisance at times, but, then again, everyone listened because there was no sense in taking a chance on missing some delectable item.

As the afternoon crowd waited, people visited back and forth, and a lot of Monday's business was done in advance. It was considered most unsporting and in poor taste to dun someone for an overdue bill on Sunday, but much actual business was accomplished amid the incessant talk of weather, dogs, politics, deaths, illnesses, and the undercurrent of speculation about whether or not someone could afford a new Overland or a buggy.

Semi-official vendors were always present to hawk fresh fruit and berries, during the season, or hot oysters in a pie plate, or sandwiches made of boneless chicken breasts or country ham. In summer the whole area around the station was flooded with the juice from watermelons. There were freezers of all kinds of homemade ice cream, wagon loads of cantaloupes, strawberries and blackberries. Usually, a missionary society set up a booth, with the blessings of the minister, to fight sin in China or in the Congo (wherever and whatever that was and however the people sinned.) About everything that ever flew, swarmed, crowed, laid, grunted, brayed, or grew on vine, tree, stalk, or under the earth made the supreme sacrifice to smite sin on its hungry jowl. In fact, a lot of us were grown and away from home before we ever knew there was any antidote or anodyne for sin save man's glorious and innate gluttony.

Each town usually had a Silver Comet Band, and frequently the crowd at the station was serenaded as it waited for the train. Of course, the drums were likely to be sporadic thunderstorms, and the silver cornets had a way of going on, rooty-tooty-ta-toot, when the clarinets and trombones were through and were resting for the next number. Someone always got knocked in the eye with a parasol that was too gay musically, and right in the middle of "El Captain" the local policeman had to get on a baggage truck to announce that someone's cow was raising hell in someone's garden.

Devilish boys dropped alum in the lemonade, and puckered the Lord's missionary work, and the "Poet and Peasant" had to march in and out and around a lot of hay fever sufferers. The cornet solo of the "Rosary" had more bubbles than a TV soap commercial, but everyone cheered as loudly as if Bryan were serving a third or fourth term as President.

The depot, itself, if not a thing of beauty, was close to a joy forever. It was a hub, a magnet, a focal point. It was a poor man's country club, a forum, a debating society, and all of this was put to the eerie arabesques of the telegraph key that had a million flying fingers and a million singing tongues. The operator was a man of mystery and awe. His thumping instrument was a bottomless geyser of fact and wisdom. Into his cunning ears poured the history the land made each hour and the fabulous news from the far marts of creation. In election and World Series times people jammed the country dee-pos as the man of mystery plastered his window with notices that were signal triumphs or pitiless tragedies. When this man walked on Main Street, folks gave him plenty of deferential elbow room. He was the custodian of a million riddles, an all-wise Buddha who kept certified knowledge in his brain as another might guard a vault of teeming treasures.

304

Some of the city stations were Grecian Temples, almost. They were glittering expanses of tile, marble, and majestic columns, especially by existing standards. There were "red caps" resplendent in livery, and dining rooms with menus on printed cards. There were news stands and booths that sold candies and novelties unknown in small places. And the whole was permeated with implications of frenetic activities.

Mankind was perpetually on the go. The dispatcher called out such resounding names as Louisville, Cincinnati, St. Louis, and Philadelphia with the resonant and elegant nonchalance the local postaman would give directions to a house-to-house agent.

Every boy who visited such a gleaming terminal (and virtually every man, too) had to put hamstrings on himself to keep from using the tile floors as skating rinks, and there was the vast and almost overpowering compulsion to yell some exultant cry of animal heartiness so that the far-flung corridors and the high arches and the great columns and the mighty domes would send back echoes in the form of bread cast on magic waters. But despite its dazzlements, the "city" terminal was big business. Everyone in it seemed to be on urgent business.

As overwhelming as its grandeur was, it lacked the offhand infection of the local dee-po. It wasn't somewhere one dropped in just to see what trumps were at a given hour nor who was taking in the tricks. The local dee-po might smell as if wet saddle blankets were drying, or if some scientists were doing experiments on mildew, dry rot, and fungus growths. The walls might be snaggled-toothed and have jaundiced eyes. The floors might have the mumps, and they might look as if all the walnuts in creation had been dumped and hulled there.

Still, the station was a place of enchantment because the candidates for high state office debated on the platform of the freight depot; because the local fire and military companies held drills in the big street in front of the depot, and because they left for their summer encampments and tournaments through the portals of the depot and returned the same way; and because the spontaneous shows, the dog and pony shows, the trick bicycle riders, and the one-man-bands all used the street in front of the depot for a stage or show ground.

But above and beyond all this, the grubby, stinking station was enshrined in the hearts and wistfulness of all boys. Many a boy whose wealth was limited to a cane fishing pole, a few marbles, a bottle of ticks, and a knife with one blade, traveled the length of the nation without ever leaving the safe security of the crusty platform. This enchanted journey was vicarious, but it was supercharged with all the glamour and the poetry of musical wanderlust.

The train was the mystery and awe of the outside world. It was the dramatic lightning and the magic thunder of a world beyond. Time and space were laid bare and reduced to workable proportions. Some eternal portion of the boy's yearning and ardor chewed up the rails and the countryside of the nation. The boy was a royal hobo, the child of October, the gold-haired scion of all the harvests. All the oceans, lakes, and rivers forejoined in one stream, and this stream rushed from the boy's toes to his brain and back and forth as if his innermost secrets and joys were put upon a singing shuttle. The mountains and plains melted into the palm of his hand, and the wheeling amalgam of the shining wonder of the whole of it was a yellow top spinning and making whirlwinds of little symphonies whenever he whipped the string.

He was the personal recipient of the supreme accolade when a brakeman, using the narrow catwalk atop a car for a dazzling, perilous tightrope, waved him a merry greeting. This was a pass, in fee simple, to ride the headwinds of all adventure. Again, bindlestiff would wave to him from his precarious perch on the rods, or from the dark edges of an empty boxcar. This greeting was a joke on the owners of the railroad, an open-handed invitation to the bluff confraternity of the knights of the long road and the vast sky. For a few days, after these rousing experiences, the boy was a disembodied vagrant, homeless even in his mother's sight and protective vision. His heart, for a few days, sailed with the wild geese. His real home was in the red caboose, with the brakeman, or in the "jungle'. by the railroad track with his hobo friend. He was free from walls and ceilings and the safe comforts of the back yard.

And when a dinner passed, he made a vow that one day he would see the world through the big windows of the hurtling eating palace on wheels. He would merge his spirit and his substance with the unbounded merriment and high-hog eating he imagined he saw in his glimpse of the diner, of its smiling waiters, its patrons, apparently so redolent with aplomb and verve, of a roaring, green world carried always alongside the big windows of the diner.

That same boy will laugh today, chuckle at his tempestuous dreams, as he looks docilely from the window of the jet passenger plane. But even so, those once addicted to trains, in the pink days of personal and national innocence, will never erase from their ears, brains, and hearts the galli-vanting challenges of train whistles in the night, the blue-moans that relate irrevocably to a boy's will. The whistles, when heard today or imagined, still grab him and fling him from bed when the vapor of morning is blasted by the old tin rooster with gravel and smoke in its throat. As it was then, some whistles are cornets with bees swarming inside and some are hounds red hot on the trail of exciting new adventure.

Each small town inn or boarding house had "arrange-ments" with the hack drivers who met the local trains. These drivers had enough imagination to transform the staple fare of the "Johnson House" into a feast so sumptuous Diamond Jim Brady would stand in line to buy a ticket.

The beds were so soft they were used for clouds on

Sunday afternoons. There hadn't been a bug in town since the Opera House burned in 1882. Indeed, each inn had one room that had not been slept in since Zeb Vance came to town to debate with Settle. This royal "sue-tee" was never rented, in deference to Vance's memory, but it just happened to be available to this particular drummer who shook off a miniature blizzard of cinders as he alighted from the day coach.

All the hacks were immaculate because they just returned from a funeral. (It was strongly implied that the deceased had been a patron of a rival inn.) In addition to extolling the virtues of his own sponsor, a hack driver, in spirit of fair play, would admit that the coffee at the other inn was the best medicine in town for cuts, bruises, and mosquitoes, even if it wasn't fit to be drunk. His inn's biscuits were made by angels for a Sunday school picnic, but those at the rival house, though inedible, were excellent to chunk at mad dogs.

But ridiculously enough, the most zealous apostle was likely to be a human cadaver who drove a whopping horse, and inevitably, some smart-alecky traveling salesman would say: "Just take me where your horse eats, and then maybe I'll be lucky enough to get locked up for the night in the county jail and be sure of comfortable lodging."

THE MAN IN THE MOON

Young folks of all former generations have thought of the man in the moon as a gentle guardian and a benign master. The man in the moon has been as close to human ectasy and agony as the kisses of the lovers. He has heard ten billion petitions, and if he has not granted all of them immediately, he has not yet uttered a single harsh demurrer.

Although the man in the moon has been gentle as a yellow lamb and sweet as an orange lollipop in recent generations, he was once thought of as a person banished for punishment, and it may be that our yearnings have made a singing shepherd boy of an incorrigible or a miscreant. In one old version, the man was sent to the moon for picking up wood on Sunday. (This seems to relate, in some fashion, to Numbers 15:32: "And while the children of Israel were in the wilderness, they found a man that gathered sticks on the sabbath day.")

It was told, also that the spots on the moon were children who were forced to carry water in buckets, as some undefined punishment, and another account had it that the man in the moon was really a woman put there alone for churning on a holy day. Again, the man in the moon was exiled because he had put briars on the path to the church to keep people from attending mass. In the *Tempest*, Shakespeare refers to the man in the moon as a "most poor credulous monster," without revealing the cause of the condition. But the folklore of old Oxfordshire has left words and music to carry a graphic picture:

"The man in the moon was caught in a trap
For stealing the thorns out of another man's gap.
If he had gone and let the thorns lie,
He'd never been a man in the moon so high."

Maybe, we'll find out shortly, or maybe the transients from earth will make him flee before we get a close look at his real nature.

WHITE STALLION, BLACK MARE

The fall morning comes to town on a leisurely gait, as if a strolling troubadour in a Sherwood Forest suit is making up bits of songs about scarlet leaves, red apples, or golden shocks of corn and using a field for a tandem bicycle. But the winter morning comes to town in the guise of a great, tossing, pitching, white stallion.

The mighty heaving of the white stallion's nostrils frosts over the bare ribs and hip bones of creation made gaunt by harvests and storms. The nervous neighing of the white horse assails the rooftops in the form of tumblers and acrobats who have heavy hands and feet, and each resounding thud leaves echoes in the shape of question marks for sleepy-headed folks hugging the covers as if the way to salvation lies in a little precious pre-breakfast warmth.

Outside, the white charger has ice on his mane, and the mane strikes the denuded tree limbs to give the shrill reverberations of cymbals inexpertly but passionately bonged. But by the time the coffee pots inside the house are spewing brown geysers of courage to meet the outer challenge, the sun is a freckle-faced jockey in a yellow suit and cap. He digs his heels into the flanks of the great, white stallion, and horse and rider pass into the forests to splash the creeks alive from meditative lethargy. The white stallion remains to riot and toss and heave in the waste places until eventide, that ancient alchemist, turns the stallion into a black mare and sends her back to take the icy residue of the spent day to a safe harbor across the hills, to the place where the yellow moon is a guardian angel and a shepherd boy keeping watch over the day's dreams and lavish trinkets.

WINTER RAIN

When late spring is a pretty girl with a rose in her hair, the gentle raindrops are nimble dancers using silver-toed magic to turn lawns and fields into ballet stages. At other times the spring rain is a group of girls having a tea party on the greensward, and the air is quick with laughter and jokes and the day is washed down with the myrrh of lilacs and violets.

But the winter rain is a troop of heavy-footed tumblers. They get up before daylight when the whole sky is a mired-up gray field, and all the skyland highways run together in the manner of indiscriminate pig paths. This rain comes to town in an old slouch hat, with its coat collar turned up and its hat brim turned down. It is bereft of the gifts of singing and dancing, and it stands in one place marking time in icy puddles as if it were waiting for the weatherman to tell it where to go and what to do.

The morning has beady eyes and a nose colder than a half-frozen puppy, but the clumsy rain, for all its want of poetry and grace, is an old magician endowed with vast powers of hypnotism. Its bony fingers tap the roof as if soaking kittens were scratching there with icy needles to inoculate the world with sleep. And the bare limbs and gnarled vines that press the windows are hypnotic telegraph instruments tapping messages in which every word is a lullaby.

Daylight finally beats his challenge but his lance is rent and his sword bends with the elements. But light, like mercy begging, stakes out small circles of proprietary rights, and the morning proceeds to its appointed rounds, even if the first men and women out feel as if they are black bears preempted from the downy bliss of hibernation by the cruel tricks of some sadistic magician.

MIDWINTER NOCTURNE

In January old fields are books handled roughly and care-
lessly by so many generations of wintry hands the few
remaining pages are dog-eared and blurred. The face of the
day is rheumy and watery-eyed where wind-lashed pine trees
are sullen scarecrows morbidly keeping watch over a slice of
earth that is, for all the world, a rent banner.

An old dog huddles in an alley between two buildings,
dreaming of the indolent suns of the summers of puppyhood.
He turns his back against the wind's claw hammers as if this
gesture will make the frigid panorama fade away. The streets
and lawns of the town are smudged, smoky nocturnes painted
with the blunt ends of burnt cork, and shrubs and bushes are
gray cats made restively fractious by the wind's tantalizations,
but still too glutted with gloom to scratch or to strike.

But the wind is really the big dog in the meat house. The
world in midwinter is his private toy. He uses the creeks and
brooks as if they were modeling clay. One minute he uses a
whole forest as if it were a tennis racket, but the next minute
he's rummaging in vacant lots and gutters, seeking lost
coppers for his grandchildren, perhaps, and gathering up old
newspapers and shopping lists as industriously as a civic
clubber on a waste-paper drive.

The sun is as game as Jeb Stuart at Yellow Tavern, but the
fiery lance he brandished in summer is splintered and chipped.
The season for overpowering frontal attacks is gone, but the
sun snipes at the edges of the pack, galloping in and out the
flanks. Primarily, though, the sun is a cavalry troop guarding
the high passes in the sky's unguarded mountains.

At times, though, the sun might as well be a golden knob
on the door to nothing. The men below are too busy kneeling

to the wind and trying to dodge the infighting of the old barroom brawler even to turn their heads to the sun. At such times the sun languishes for attention and gives in to doleful introspections and to self-pity. When man's inattention becomes painful, he drops a handful of beams in the form of yellow fish hooks or golden apples bobbing on a string. Again these sunbeams stand in a golden puddle to warm the aching back of the day as best they can with sparks from slow-firing flint.

The wind comes back to run a race. The sky is a ghostly race track and the wind runs a race against himself, using the time to think up minor pestiferations and major affronts for man and nature. When the wind blunders off to seek new mischief, he leaves an icy silence behind him in the form of a hollow echo. Human beings feel this silence but they do not always understand this force for what it really is. Small animals and plants know that the wind is death and that silence is a grim requiem. They know that this force is even more stealthy than the men who come rampaging with guns and dogs. The little creatures know the very second winter begins to exercise his supreme lordship. All the birds are beggars that seem to listen for food rather than to look for food. It is easy to imagine that these birds are listening for some hidden worm to move clumsily below the barren soil. As the birds listen for sounds that may be livelihood, their startled and haunted eyes do a poor job at guarding and hiding their fears. For, this silence is a positive, a wanton force. It isn't at all the silence that follows a mighty din. It creeps into all bones with cold, impersonal questions.

But nature tries valiantly to emulate the soldiers who used to dig foxholes. She tries to take her vulnerable armor under the ground for a spell. She tries to bury her fragile jewels, the ones the wind would steal and smash just for the sake of lust.

There are hours when it seems that creation has just been made but not thawed, or that the Big Bomb has come and gone and left maddening footnotes and annotations in the form of icy wastelands. When the earth is frozen over in January, creation looks as if rigor mortis is setting in rapidly. The face of creation is pinched and drawn the way a drum can be stretched until it has a gray, ghostly transparence. All the open land is a boneyard. For, freezing weather lays bare the cheek bones and ribs of fields that are gripped by the long sleep. True, some fields are smeared with stiff, sporadic stubble, but this stuff is merely the beard of an old man who played out in October and has been forgotten ever since. Here and there, in the waste places, whole skeletons seem to lie in tight, frigid groups. The wind comes by counting the bones as if he is checking up on the accuracy of an anatomy lesson he took long ago.

Even the creek can become a sullen, clay pigeon. Its voice becomes cracked and goslined. All the frogs of summer seem to be stuck in its throat, and the sound it gives off lies somewhere between outrageous agony and a moan of dejected resignation.

From the edge of the creek bank a rabbit bounces suddenly from nowhere, as if a terrified genie has catapulted from a bottle hidden deeply within the crusty innards of the earth. The rabbit leaps high and bounces, rather more than it runs, and it is as if a dab of grayish brown, with frightened eyes and with ears trimmed down to wicks, is pity flying as a homeless indigent.

But the rabbit will have to use all the cunning of the most adroit genie if he finds a place to hide his head and to warm his body. The morning is as lean as a bony man inadvertently put on a milk toast diet. The field is an old woman, a penniless widow, abandoned by her brood, and left to tend a pitiful fire, a supplicant trying to use a tenuous veil of mist to hide her from the great white wolves the wind sends to prowl.

Save for the furtive bouncing of the rabbit, the earth is as still as an ax iced over during the night, and if the sky lowered her tongue to kiss the ax her lips would stick to the blade. When the sky's lips finally tore and ripped away from the ax, there would be such an earth-shaking repercussion the tip end of Florida might wind up in the north end of Maine.

Again, the sky is a hungry hawk using space for a perch. If the earth, the land below, so much as wiggles a frozen ear, the hawk will swoop down and bite it off.

For earth and sky seem to be two separate realisms, two warring unions, and just as mankind is about to mark it from the calendar as a frozen void, the sun rakes his coals into a pile and pours on enough wood to start a light blaze. The sullen earth starts to thaw, almost imperceptibly, and shakes and stamps his bloodless feet and pitches a fit on his bloodless haunches.

The trees, shorn of their leafy finery, are hung on winter's line with the pitiless nakedness of poor turkeys plucked for a "starvation" dinner. The wind comes back to sit in a corner of the forest, smacking his jaws and licking his fingers. Some of the trees cower before the wind's bristling gluttony. They cast shadows that run out as if misshapen, listless animals were morosely sniffing. Others are hatless soldiers walking guard over the fallen wreckage of summer's grandeur. These are soldiers left to walk a dreary line, expendables left behind in a foredoomed delaying action when the remainder of the army has gone to safety. They point wet, empty guns in the direction of the ravenous wind and flex their humped shoulders for the little bit of warmth they get.

Some of the leaves were burned when November was making cider and whistling to and from the cider mill. They were burned as out-of-date books might be burned, and some were carted off to the dark anonymity of a waste place, and others were returned to the soil to brighten upcoming April with a portion of September's exultant paeans to death. And a few, like mistakes that can never be obscured, fly, spin, crash, and fly ineptly again, as if they are decrepit relatives searching for the brothers and sisters who abandoned them and forgot to come back and take them in out of the weather.

And the wind is the big exalted yard master. He barks without remembering the immediate object of his fury. He's a great white wolf on the prowl. He's a ghost with his pockets filled with brass knucks. He's Huck Finn and he's John L. Sullivan. He's the Boston Strong Boy taking on all comers. He's the big dog in the meat house, and he barks without remembering the objects of his prodigious scorn.

Then as the sun piles his breakfast fire higher, and his coffee pot begins perking and his strips of side meat start to sizzle, the earth stretches and yawns and stamps its feet and waves its arms in a greeting, a desultory greeting, to be sure, but with a sort of go-to-hell hello that is really a gesture to survival.

Lights come on in breakfast nooks and black smoke streams from chimneys as animated talismans. Finally, the doors open and school children plummet out as if a red-faced apple orchard has taken human forms and is bent on education.

The school boy patrol in its white boots, coats, and hats dots street corners in such a perky way you think a crate of penguins has fallen from a passing airplane.

And everywhere there is the grinding of gears and the spluttering and chugging of balky motors. Some cars wheeze in the crisp air as if asthma sufferers and one racking whoop from the cemetery. Others bray so one thinks of these cars as mules that are impervious to all of man's mechanical arts and forms of psychological flattery and persuasion. You almost expect some volatile and exasperated man to get out and build a fire under one of these mule-cars to get it into motion. But some purr as if huge cats have had a nine course fish breakfast and are making contented music to show their gratitude. But always two or three cars in every neighborhood

317

seem to be afire with pungent, noxious fumes. You don't know whether they are trying to destroy the world by fire and smoke, per se, or whether they are out to asphyxiate an entire end of town.

But by 9 a.m. the day is running on about four cylinders, and by mid-morning the chaos of dawning has been transformed until it has something of the power and grace of a fawn running on three legs, running on three legs and using the fourth as a spare as it tries to kick some steam and fire into it.

But by late afternoon the weather has gone from the frigid and inert "A's" through the valiant and warmer "J's" and "K's" and is back at the scissors and blackjacks of the windtorn "Z's" and is starting at the "A's" once again.

The late afternoon is a man-hating bulldog biting down savagely and trying to draw blood with its teeth. It is also that grim and resolute turtle biting and holding on until thunder booms across the sky. People hurry home as if they are trying to win a footrace with the few, remaining tatters of light. The parlor lights are a kind of compulsive Cherokee Strip and any laggards will have to remain homeless for the night. And the wind is once more the prowling wolf, keeping the whole town and the countryside under monstrous surveillance. Along the chilled shank of the afternoon, the wind has the town and the countryside in the same sort of "protective custody" that the Chicago gangsters once used as lethal bribes, and you know that if you so much as bat your eye the wrong way, the vandal will come to reap his tribute.

The chief offenders, and those likely to bring retribution, are boys going home from skating and from trying to make the wolf a docile pony to ride or to lead by the head. Boys stake off the frozen world of the afternoon. Adults forfeit, but boys claim the glories of squatters' rights. The harvest of curious may be woefully short, but the harvesters are dead game for all the outer and inner weathers. They have to see

318

whether the creek survived the night and the morning, and if the gypsies stole the ice pond. And, all things considered, a boy can't get to be a real man until he has been intimate with nature's roughest, bluffest personality.

Of course, he may attain his normal height and growth, but there will be a vacuum if he doesn't know how it is to walk and stumble and run when his feet are wooden blocks and his face is cut by the wind that raps with the quick mischief of a whetted knife.

But dusk routs all moving beings as it sweeps over the land with the crisp rustle and the slight swish of a horde of bats just out of deep-freeze. Then darkness settles firmly as crepe glued down. Darkness is serenaded by floods of kitchen lights, with the rattling of pots and pans, and with the masculine pungence of baking bread and frying meat.

Outside the wind is the wolf huffing and puffing and trying to blow the house down. Yet, if home is ever sanctuary it is a haven of simple opulence when the winter night is a vampire just beyond the door. The cold stars are so bright and so close you know you can dip them with a bucket, but aside from such poetic conjectures man wants no business that takes him beyond the window. Half drunk with the downy contentment of warmth and food he thinks of the night beyond as a poor and profitless trinket left to the wind's mauling, and to the frightened investigations of the tormented little creatures.

There isn't even a memorial tablet to mark the anomalous spot the sun occupied, and no songs of gratitude are lifted, amid such household comforts, to the memory of that deposed monarch who waged such an intrepid fight for so many precarious hours against such long odds. However, the smeared and ragged grass that was a dirty beard by day is now streaked with silver, and snaggled-toothed fences and arthritic gates are now bedecked with diamonds. The pallor of the enfeebled fields is flushed with a yellow fever, and the hard-hearted stones of walkways glitter as if they are being tapped for some august honor or society.

During the rough-handed, alley-cat day, the unevenness and unbalance of plucked, frayed, and picked nature are so many swollen jaws, eyeless sockets, runny noses, and twisted bodies. But on the winter night, unevenness is smoothed to flawless precision. The most bedraggled field is a lake of lilies when the cold stars are so bright and so near you can grab one for a stick-pen for your tie. If you use both hands and all your poetic impulses, you can grab enough to make a jeweled crown for your wife or for your sweetheart and show, truly, the truth of letting treasures and hearts lie together.

ON MEDICINES

A lot of today's medicine is cracked up to be plumb succulent. From the mouth-watering commercials, you wonder why some of this medicine isn't on the dessert menus. It is hard not to understand why a completely healthy person doesn't buy a sack full, just for the exquisite taste. Certainly, a bellyache is a small price to pay for the delicious medicine you get to take.

But when we were kids, almost any kind of medicine made Satanic faces and had a horrible taste, even before you tasted it. The very mention of castor oil was sufficient to sour a bucket of fresh, cold milk and pucker its face as badly as that of a frost-wizened crab apple. But all this kind of medicine was bound to be magnificently beneficial. It had such a terrible and rank taste it had to be good for you. And anything you took for an upset condition or the summer complaint brought such pains and discomforts, of itself, you always felt you had somehow miraculously escaped a ghastly death.

Of course, most mothers "mixed" castor oil, and such other horrendous potions, in lemonade or some syrup to try to camouflage the presence of the vile medication. But this was as impossible as trying to make a docile house cat of a Bengal tiger by putting a ribbon around the tiger's neck. You could drop an ounce of such medicine off Hatteras and taste it in the water around Liverpool. True, there were some pills and capsules, for ubiquitous liver troubles, that wouldn't pucker your mouth more than a green persimmon, but once down inside, you knew how it was to swallow a live hand grenade. Today's kids, raised on needles, magic drugs, and chocolate eclair medicines, may live on the moon forever, but they will never know that some potions were liquid corporal punishment that enabled former generations to develop the hardihood to withstand wars, depressions, and the P.T.A.

FIDDLERS' CONVENTIONS

The old fiddler's convention probably never will reach hurricane proportions again, but it is coming back with the lyrical furies of lean hounds and starry nights and salty winds.

And although the local and sectional champions will not get the attention given to local golfers or high school football players, the men who can make fiddles walk and talk and sing and cry are part and parcel of a fine tradition that is magnetically indigenous. Our old-time fiddlers made more than peacock-strutting music. They were lively focal points around which a whole community rallied in times of bad roads, slow travel, and tight-cash insularities. They were the closest to strolling minstrels we ever came.

They not only banished care and fret, they put local history to all kinds of tunes. The whopping events and the minutiae of localities were given secular posterity in sprightly tunes or doleful ditties. Hopes, sorrows, anecdotes, legends, oddments, and straight history were taken from one part of the country to another part by the men with the fiddles. Indeed, these fiddlers were local anthologists before the word was ever used. From the murky mysteries of the swamplands to the smoky edges of the mountainous horizons the tales and tunes were unfolded. When a champion fiddler retired, he didn't give merely his violin and bow to his successor. He gave the new champion a flaming charge to keep and to carry.

Today, books carry the noble burdens of tales once told by fiddles, but the secret heart of a people is still revealed when the fiddles call down the stars and the storms, when they send for the men who carried squirrel rifles and axes, when they call up the ghosts of raw courage, pitted against the nameless fears and joys beyond the hills. So, now as then, "bile 'em cabbage down, turn 'em hoe-cakes round," and dance and sing until the last rooster crows.

FROM TOM SAWYER TO ANY JUNE

Despite the enormous increase of private and public swimming pools, many boys still seek the secluded bend of a creek or a small river when June starts whistling like a peanut roaster. Water may be water in a pool or in a creek, but boys have a desperate need of something man didn't build and doesn't run.

And although all bathing suits are scanty enough, some boys seem to feel summer can't be celebrated properly unless they dive in, as naked as their companions, the jaybirds and tadpoles. This impulse may be a subconscious revolt against the rules and restrictions of nine months of school. A boy may even think he has been some kind of public ward and that jumping into the water naked will foil the establishment. But beyond any specious psychology, boys swim a while and play-act a while. The big rock is not just a diving board. It is a launching pad, a missile base, a lectern, and a concert stage.

Naked orators and entertainers take the stage by turns to speak their joys, vexations, and compulsions without the fears of censorship and editing. What they say may come out as outrageous banter. For a naked boy doesn't expose everything. Yet, between the ridiculous dictums and the literary conceits there is a ring of sheer truth that mows down the underbrush of subterfuge.

Betimes, they chase the flying squirrel and hunt for the arrowheads, berries, and exotic herbs that are supposed to abound here. They buck and snort along the dusty wagon paths and pop the heads from milkweed and create the startling illusion of a snowstorm in June. And having given superimposed reality a fling, to satisfy the persistent demands of the test-tube world uptown, they become small brigands and stalk the decks of ghostly pirate ships.

Captain Kidd is burying treasure on tropical islands that have sprung up where lily pads flourish, and over on the other bank Lieutenant Maynard is doing Blackbeard in with a sword pulled from a sweet-gum tree. Then young David Balfour and Allan Breck-Stuart are holding off the heinous kidnapers and making ready for new adventures through grassy lanes that are now thick and heavy with heather and with Highland mists. Bold Jean LaFitte, with a pair of shorts tied around his head, races from the murky haven of the swampland to stand at New Orleans with Andy Jackson. And, naturally, old Long John Silver thumps the creek bed so hard the reverberations must upset the tea glasses at the bridge parties in the far end of town.

A thousand games and tunes are put to their own devices and time-tables. And when the boy walks home the world of streets and houses and cars is make-believe and the only world of reality is the one he created at the water's edge. At supper, the father asks his son how he spent his afternoon. The boy says he went swimming, and he changes the subject quickly.

How can he explain about sailing under the ocean with Captain Nemo or of crossing the Atlantic in the balloon Edgar Allan Poe inflated with the poetic hot air of profound wistfulness? How can he explain that he has been back as far as time goes and ahead as far as space and infinity go? So, he says he went swimming the same way that President Ford might disarm a nervous innocent by saying he sort of works for the government.

A TEAR FOR THE DEAD LIAR

The official town liar, the radiant old pro, is dead, and all the squawks of TV never can fill the awkward vacuum. The professional town liar had the effortless imagination of forty-four children playing King Arthur's Knights. From his flying tongue sailed the music of the mocking bird and ten billion strutting frauds in the form of sparkling stories. No one ever believed a word he spoke, but the town raced to make a gay circle about him. He was always the magic riddle in the middle of the community's eagerness for exploration.

He had always been hunting with Bill Cody, to the Pole with Perry (or Byrd), had caught Christy Matthewson, fought in the Foreign Legion, and helped Edison with a couple of inventions. Everyone knew his only real adventure was an excursion to Raleigh to the State Fair, but no matter what revolutionary news the papers proclaimed, the liar-oracle had done the same thing twenty years before, and much better.

The beautiful part of it all was the utter absence of malice or predatoriness in these Gargantuan fantasies. Had he come a few centuries sooner, surely, he would have been a respected elder of the tribe or a strolling minstrel. As it was he was mint and sugar in the town's julep, nutmeg and cinnamon in our milkshake.

But the people who were uptight about financial success, — and it does seem now that all the lovely, sparking things were cheap while all the ignoble things were enormously costly, — said he could have amounted to something if he hadn't wasted his time and substance spinning outrageous yarns. But it must be, as Shakespeare put it in *Othello*: "He that is robb'd, not wanting what is stolen,/Let him not know 't, and he's not robbed at all." And if one can't lose what he's never had, one certainly can't lose what he has never wanted.

It wasn't until the old stemwinder died, when society became as uniform as the green peas at a civic club luncheon, that many came to realize the tremendous local importance of the dead liar. He left holes in daily life as big as the Grand Canyon, but even if he could come back from the other side his audience would be too ensnared with money, status, and doing alike to listen to his marvelous yarns. But one supposes that it is inevitable in a society that has conned itself into thinking it will attain the millennium when it comes to resemble a whole crate of empty bottles, neatly and gleamingly arrayed.

OTHER BOOKS BY MOORE

THE CURIOUS WINE, Mena Webb, $4.95 LC 79-77149
THE BALLAD OF TOM DULA, John Foster West, $6.95
APPALACHIAN DAWN, John Foster West, 46.95, LC 73-77500
CAROLINA COUNTRY READER, Jim Chaney, $5.95 LC 73-86780
TIDE'S RISE, June Sellars Strader, $5.95, LC 73-86776
SKETCHBOOK FROM HELL, Edward Garner, $5.95, LC 73-86778
SENATOR SAM ERVIN'S BEST STORIES, Thad Stem, Jr. & Alan Butler, $5.95
        LC 73-86470
BOTTOMS UP WITH A REAR ADMIRAL, E. Aubrey Cox, M.D., $4.95
THE CLOCKWATCHER'S COOKBOOK, Bette Elliott, $5.95
THE HAND-ME-DOWN COOKBOOK, Cherry Parker & Frances Bradsher, $5.95
        LC 70-99140
DANGERS TO CHILDREN AND YOUTH, Jay Arena, M.D., $14.50 LC 79-99141
LIVING WITH TODAY'S TEENAGERS, Samuel Fudge, $6.95
SCHOLARS BEFORE SCHOOL, Joseph C. Johnson, II, Ph.D., $7.95, LC 74-140951
MY HELENKA, Mary Lee McMillan & Ruth Dorval Jones, $6.95, LC 72-90714
METRIC 16, Meredith L. Butterton, $9.95, LC 72-90711
INVENTING: HOW THE MASTERS DID IT, Byron M. Vanderbilt, $8.95, LC 74-14959
DIVIDED WE STAND (History of Baptists in American Life), Bynum Shaw, $8.95,
        LC 73-86777